Infants' Sense of People

Infants' Sense of People focuses on infants during their first year of life, exploring how they begin to think about other people, their feelings, emotions, and intentions, and how they become aware of these aspects of their own development. Drawing on a broad range of research and developmental theory, Maria Legerstee takes the view that infants have an innate sense of people at birth, which is activated through sympathetic emotions. She questions the idea that infants use physical parameters such as contingencies or motion to distinguish people from objects, and rejects the assumption that infants are mechanical creatures before they become psychological ones. She argues persuasively that before infants learn to speak, interactions with others are possible because infants have a primitive pre-linguistic "Theory of Mind." This accessible book provides a valuable synthesis of current thinking on early social and cognitive development and the origins of Theory of Mind.

MARIA LEGERSTEE is Professor of Psychology at York University, Toronto, where she established the Centre for Infancy Studies in 1991. She has published in journals of developmental psychology and child development.

Infants' Sense of People:

Precursors to a Theory of Mind

Maria Legerstee

York University, Toronto

CAMBRIDGE UNIVERSITY PRESS
Cambridge, New York, Melbourne, Madrid, Cape Town, Singapore, São Paulo

CAMBRIDGE UNIVERSITY PRESS
The Edinburgh Building, Cambridge CB2 2RU, UK

Published in the United States of America by Cambridge University Press,
New York

www.cambridge.org
Information on this title: www.cambridge.org/9780521521697

First published 2005

Printed in the United Kingdom at the University Press, Cambridge

A catalogue record for this book is available from the British Library

ISBN-13 978-0-521-81848-3 hardback
ISBN-10 0-521-81848-6 hardback
ISBN-13 978-0-521-52169-7 paperback
ISBN-10 0-521-52169-6 paperback

Contents

Preface

A few years ago I received a call from Sarah Caro, senior editor with Cambridge University Press, who asked me to write a monograph about my research on infants' understanding of people. The timing was opportune as I had concluded various published studies and had several others in progress. I felt it was time to think about how to fit them into a developmental story. I decided to accept Sarah's generous offer.

My work belongs to a somewhat specialized view that (1) proposes that infants have an innate sense of people at birth, which is activated through sympathetic emotions, (2) questions the idea that infants use physical parameters such as contingency or motion to distinguish people from things, and (3) does not accept the assumption that infants are mechanical creatures before they become psychological ones.

This book is the product of twenty years of academic development and family life. Many people have contributed to the way I think about infants and their development. My first (undergraduate) mentor Jean Koepke, with whom I conducted my Honors thesis on neonatal imitation, proposed that it was more rewarding if, in addition to having children, one knew how their mental lives developed. My second mentor and friend, the late Helga Feider, with whom I examined pronoun development and prelinguistic mother–infant interactions, demonstrated how an understanding of mental lives of even very young infants could be examined through communication.

I continued my graduate work on infants' sense of people in the Skinnerian laboratory of Andree Pomerleau and Gerard Malcuit, and with their full support developed a constraint constructivist stance regarding the process of development, combining nativism (innate representations) and active constructivism (redescription of the representations through social interactions). My daughter Johanna and infant son Tor provided, in part, the impetus and case histories for this conviction. The year was 1985.

Since then I have been inspired by the work of various colleagues. In particular, Alan Fogel, Jerome Bruner, Elisabeth Spelke, Andrew

Meltzoff, Tiffany Field, Colwyn Trevarthen, Daniel Stern, Edward Tronick, Henry Wellman, and John Flavell. They have guided my work as reviewers, commentators, editors, and friends. I hope I have interpreted their theories accurately and borrowed from their ideas appropriately and respectfully.

The most recent influential colleagues are those who have read and critically reviewed parts, or all, of the book: Alan Fogel, whose work has inspired me since my undergraduate studies, Colwyn Trevarthen, and Kurt Fisher. I accept their support and criticism with sincere gratitude but I will be responsible for errors and omissions that remain.

While writing the book, portions of it were also read by students in my Graduate Seminar "Development of Affect, Consciousness, and Social Cognition." Gabriela Markova, Chang Su, Jean Varghese, Tamara Fisher, Edwin Romero, Raluca Barac, Rachel Horton, Jessica Mariano, and Heidi Marsh provided insight through their questions and comments (and also performed some editorial work!). I especially thank Gabriela for reading all the chapters and providing elaborations and examples that helped further clarify what I thought, but did not say.

The studies described in chapters 6, 7, 8, 9, and 10 were developed under my grant "The influence of mothering on social and cognitive competence" (410–2001–0971) from the Social Sciences and Humanities Research Council, Canada. I filmed the infants during a research leave I spent in the Infancy Laboratory of the Junior Scientists at the Max Planck Institute for Evolutionary Anthropology in Leipzig, Germany. All the data was then coded and analyzed in my laboratory at York University by various students, in particular Tamara Fisher and Gabriela Markova, except for the study in chapter 9, which was analyzed by staff at the MPI.

I am grateful for the major source of continued financial support from the Social Sciences and Humanities Research Council (Canada). The SSHRC has been invaluable in sustaining my research efforts as a doctoral and post-doctoral student, Canada research fellow, and as Director of the Centre for Infancy Studies at York University.

The year is 2005. My research has continued to support and deepen a constraint constructivist stance; that developmental trajectories that create new and original beings and thinkers are the result of nativism and constructivism. Johanna and Tor continue to confirm this position.

1   Definitions, theories, and plan of the book

> If infant members of a mind-reading species give us the strong feeling
> that they are doing some kind of mind reading, they probably are.
>
> (Flavell, 1999, p. 32)

In a recent chapter, Meltzoff and Brooks (2001) introduced the magical
Canadian ice hockey player Wayne Gretzky as the prototype or exemplary human mind reader because he is able to predict accurately where the
puck will end up and hence he is already skating toward it before the puck
is shot. My golden Labrador retriever Aquarius shows similar traits,
however. When I play fetch with him he predicts accurately where an
object will land, and hence is running toward the spot as soon as I lift up
my arm into a certain direction in an attempt to throw it. Although both
Wayne and Aquarius, when in the right situation, can predict accurately
what the other will do, their predictions are based on different abilities.
Whereas Wayne makes his predictions on where he thinks a teammate
might direct the ball (based on mind-reading abilities, a knowledge of the
rules of the game, and certain inherited skills from his expert hockey
playing father), Aquarius does not make his predictions on mind-reading
abilities. Aquarius has an innate ability to catch and retrieve things, and
consequently will run toward the spot to which I direct my hand, arm, and
ball, or where the ball may land or has landed before. Thus Aquarius
relies on my actions, my observable behavior. Aquarius does not read
minds. He never predicts that I may deceive him and throw the ball in a
different direction. He does not understand that I can change my mind,
or that I can make mistakes. No matter how often I play with him, he
always responds to a predictable pattern of play and never understands
my intentions in the absence of behavioral indices.

Although the young infant is neither a good skater nor a good fetcher,
she is born with some specific abilities to predict what people can do. She
quickly learns that people can change their minds and may make mistakes. These capacities are the result of some innate foundations or
predispositions infants have, that facilitate their interactions with people.

For instance, infant understanding at birth that people are similar to self (e.g. like me) and different from inanimate objects prepares infants to interact socially with people and to identify with them. Such identification is not based on perceptual features only (e.g. size, shape, color, face, hands etc.) but instead is based on more complex properties that are unique to people. That is, there is evidence that from very early on, infants apply specific psychological principles to people. They have particular expectations of what people can and cannot do (Legerstee, Barna, and DiAdamo, 2000). Thus it seems that puppy dogs and babies are equipped with some rudimentary innate abilities; for Labrador retrievers it is to fetch sticks, but for the human infant it is the social cognitive ability to read minds.

In this book I will provide a general framework for thinking about infant social-cognitive development. In particular, I will be describing the *foundational abilities*, such as protoforms of Theory of Mind knowledge, including an awareness of emotions, intentionality and goal directed behavior in people, during the first year of life.

Defining a Theory of Mind

By about 4 years of age, children produce a variety of internal state terms when describing people's actions, such as believing, thinking, and feeling (Bretherton and Beeghly, 1982; Bartsch and Wellman, 1995). It has been suggested that the use of these terms implies that children hold complex mental states that allow them to attribute internal representations to people (e.g. "John believes that the apple is in the cupboard," Bartsch and Wellman, 1995). Three-year-olds do not readily understand or talk about beliefs; instead, they focus on the person's desire (e.g. John wants an apple). Even 2-year-olds understand that people want or desire things, and that therefore they will act to get these things (Wellman, 1990). Consequently, Wellman (1990, p. 16) has argued that "before becoming belief-desire psychologists, young children are simple desire psychologists." Because these developmental changes – from primitive to complex understandings of emotions, desires, and beliefs – seem like actual theory changes, this phenomenon is called the infant's developing Theory of Mind (ToM) (Gopnik and Wellman, 1992). For instance, when watching people directing their attention and emotion toward objects in the environment, infants with a primitive understanding of mental states are aware that these cues may signal the person's *intention* to act on the object, but they do not understand that people may have mental representations about the object (e.g. that the person *thinks* that the apple is sweet). Although much work has been done to investigate the child's understanding of beliefs and desires (Bartsch and Wellman, 1995; Flavell, Green, and Flavell, 1986; Flavell, Flavell, Green, and Moses, 1990; Lillard and Flavell, 1990; Schultz and Wellman, 1997; Wimmer and Perner, 1983), little is known about the relationship between Theory of Mind and intentionality and how an awareness of intentions in others develops in infants.

Defining intentions

Socio-cognitive view

Tomasello (1995) makes an analogy between the development of the various levels of Theory of Mind and the various levels of understanding of intentionality through which infants develop. He argues that during the first two years of life, infants progress from understanding other persons as intentional agents, to understanding that others have intentions that may differ from their own, and finally to an understanding that not all observable acts are intentional (accidental versus purposeful acts etc.). By the third and fourth year, infants' developing Theory of Mind goes through similar hierarchical levels: from understanding that other people have thoughts and beliefs, to understanding that these thoughts and beliefs may differ from their own, to an awareness that people may have beliefs that do not match reality. The difference in social cognition of the first two years versus that of the third and the fourth year of life is that during the first two years infants do not understand that people have thoughts (can represent things); they only understand that people are driven by concrete goals and purposes (have simple mental states).

Traditionally, philosophers and socio-cognitive psychologists have defined intentionality as actions or behaviors that are about things, e.g. that are directed toward a goal (e.g. Brentano, 1874; Merleau-Ponty, 1942; Searle, 1983). Some theorists propose that actions that are directed toward things are driven by mental states (e.g. the infant has a plan in its head before it is behaviorally executed); whereas others put forth a purely behavioral or perceptual explanation (e.g. the infant's behavior is a response to a particular stimulus).

Descartes proposed that an awareness of our mind through introspection is a basic, direct, and probably prewired ability of our mind, and so knowledge of the self as a mental agent is an innately given rather than a developing or constructed capacity, whereas classical cognitivists would propose it develops late, from nothing to something. This makes Descartes a continuous theorist in my book, because he views the development of mental states in infants as beginning at birth.

The Cartesian doctrine is an accepted view among many psychologists interested in "intersubjectivity" (Gergely, 2002). In terms of ontology (study of being) Descartes proposed the most influential division of reality: *res extensa* (extended substance) versus *res cogitans* (thinking substance, soul). The extended substance can be studied with the methods of physics while the soul needs a different treatment. However, Descartes (Cartesius is his Latin name) was also an interactionist, believing that there is a mutual influence of *res extensa* and *res cogitans* (mutual influence of mind and body). In contrast, monists believe that, for example, everything is physical or the soul does not really exist (behaviorists), or that the soul/mind is a result of the physical.[1] These theorists are the materialists; their philosophical position I call discontinuous.

Most cognitive developmental psychologists do not argue about whether the infant's behavior is driven by mental states. If they did, there would be no reason to study their existence. Instead, the debate surrounds the age of onset of an awareness of mental states. If it is true, that an awareness of people as intentional beings implies an awareness that their behavior is about things, then such an awareness begins early. Bruner (1999; see also Reddy, 2003) has argued that from birth infants are aware that they are the object of people's attention and that some months later they become aware that a third object (in addition to the infant) becomes the focus of attention of their communicative partner. Thus, from very early on in life, infants reveal that they are related to objects and that they perceive others to be related to objects. During the dyadic period infants interpret people's attention as an intention to communicate; if they don't, infants get upset. During the triadic period, infants interpret people's attention as an awareness of the external world, and may point to share interesting aspects of this world.

Thus, these authors argue that infants have simple mental states from birth that allow them to perceive people's behavior to be "about" things. If so, then the development of mental states is a continuous process and an understanding of more complex mental states is constructed with experience. These authors also argue that intentions are precursors to the development of a Theory of Mind later on.

There are others who argue that the behaviors I listed above do not reveal anything about the mental state of infants. That is because they believe that an awareness of intentions in others occurs toward the end of the first year when infants begin to use several means to achieve a goal

---

[1] Tomas Theo, personal communication, January, 2004.

(Piagetian stage 4). Becoming intentional themselves leads infants to perceive intentions in others as a result of biological abilities to perceive others "like me" (Tomasello, 1995).

Other discontinuous theorists differentiate between behaving intentionally and understanding intentions in others. More classically cognitive (Piaget, 1952; Perner, 1991) and prepared learning theorists (Barresi and Moore, 1996) propose that an understanding of the self as an intentional agent only lays *the foundation* for an understanding that the other is an intentional agent who has internal experiences, such as emotions, beliefs, and desires. These theorists argue that the infants' socio-cognitive development is the result of innate biological processes (e.g. assimilation, accommodation, and interiorization) that prepares the infant to act intentionally around 8–10 months and to perceive others as intentional agents around 18–24 months. These discontinuous theorists propose that infants develop from a stage where they are viewed as little behaviorists whose behavior is elicited by environmental stimuli. This materialistic stage is followed by a mentalistic stage (often toward the end of the sensorimotor period, Piaget, 1954; Barresi and Moore, 1996; Corkum and Moore, 1998; Perner, 1991) when infants become little psychologists whose actions are driven by ideas in the mind.

The strength of the discontinuous positions is that intentionality is definitely present by 1 or 2 years of age. The three weaknesses are that (1) there is no discussion of the mechanisms that bring about developmental changes in behavior (e.g. how does the infant proceed from being a behaviorist to becoming a psychologist during the first year of life), (2) there is no explanation or description on what the *origin* of mental state awareness is (e.g. it is suddenly there), and (3) the role social interaction in the development of an awareness of mental states plays (Zeedyk, 1996; Legerstee, 2001a, b). Thus, discontinuous theorists adopt the stance that infants progress from being a behavioral organism during the first year of life, to a psychological organism thereafter, and are therefore void of any mental activity during the behavioral period.

Social view

Whereas the cognitive and prepared learning views, whether of the continuous or discontinuous stance, emphasize the infant's own cognitive processes in the development of intentions and Theory of Mind thinking, social-interactionists argue that through interacting with people infants build representations that are important for Theory of Mind reasoning. Vygotsky (1962) for instance proposes that before infants are able to represent knowledge (intramental knowledge), this knowledge is represented between the infant and the adult (intermental knowledge). That is, infants are particularly sensitive to species specific interaction patterns that facilitate this sharing of knowledge between two minds. The aspects of the interaction infants are sensitive to are mutual gazes and sharing of emotions during the dyadic stage, and communication about, and sharing attention to, objects during the triadic period (Adamson and Bakeman, 1982; Legerstee, Pomerleau, Malacuit, and Feider, 1987).

Innate inter-subjectivity theorists The social-interactionists can be divided into more nativist oriented theorists who argue that infants are born with an innate awareness of intentionality; 'as if' social interactionists who focus on parental interpretations of infant behavior 'as if' it were intentional; and dynamic systems theorists, who focus on how the system of the infant (endogenous and exogenous factors) combine to achieve a certain goal.

Those with a nativist orientation believe that infants have an innate capacity to perceive simple mental states in others. With experience and as a result of social interactions this awareness becomes more complex. Consequently, there is no shift in the awareness of mental states (e.g. from absence to presence of such mental states).

There is a large body of evidence indicating that infants from the beginning of life show a special sensitivity to communication and engage in bi-directional affective interactions with their caregivers that are characterized by a turn-taking structure during which both infants and caregiver participate in emotional sharing (Brazelton, Koslowsky, and Main, 1974; Tronick, 2003; Stern, 1985; Trevarthen, 1979). For instance, Legerstee et al. (1987) showed in a longitudinal study (from 3 to 53 weeks) that, already by 5 weeks, infants had specific expectations about the communicative behavior of their partners. Infants were presented with conditions where communicative people and interactive dolls responded contingently to the eye movements of the infants, but also with conditions where the person remained 'passive' and the doll remained immobile. Already by 5 weeks, infants expected people to communicate with them when in face to face situations. If they didn't infants became upset and began to cry. No such behaviors were exhibited in front of the immobile inanimate object (the doll). It has been argued that the infants' negative responses reveal a violation of an expectation that people in face to face situations communicate (Murray and Trevarthen, 1985; Stern, 1995; Tronick, 2003; Reddy, 1991; Hobson, 1990). This period in communicative development is referred to as revealing primary inter-subjectivity (Trevarthen, 1979; Tronick, 2003; Reddy, 1991; Hobson, 1990).

By about 6 months infants begin to look where others are looking and start to integrate object-focused attention into their play. Adamson and Bakeman (1982, p. 219) call this period in communication development of the infant the nonverbal *referencing* phase, when "gaze patterns, vocalizations, and gestures increasingly serve the referential function of introducing a new topic for discussion, a new message that the thing over there is what I want to communicate about, to comment on." This period where infants begin to communicate about objects and events in the environment has been called secondary inter-subjectivity (Trevarthen and Hubley, 1978; Stern, 1985).

Thus infants progress in communicative development from expressing their intentions in dyadic interactions early in development (either with people *or* objects) to expressing their intentions involving objects during triadic interactions during the second half of the first year (Bakeman and Adamson, 1984; Fogel, 1993). Toward the end of the first year, infants use points and vocalizations to direct people's attention to interesting sights (Legerstee and Barillas, 2003), and use others as social reference points (Baldwin and Moses, 1994; Baron-Cohen, 1991; Carpenter, Nagell, and Tomasello, 1998).

As-if theorists Although all social interactionists agree that social interaction plays an important role in the development of knowledge, not all perceive simple communicative intentions as originating at birth. Many social interactionists argue that infant behaviors acquire meaning, because parents act "as if" infants have minds. They attribute intentions to the smiles, vocalizations, and actions of their infants (e.g. Gergely and Watson, 1996; Schaffer, Collins, and Parsons, 1977; Snow, 1977; Vedeler, 1994), and interact in contingent ways to the various responses infants emit. Thus infant intentionality is a property of adult perception rather than of the infant's behavior.

Dynamic systems theorists Rather than focusing uniquely on the innateness of intentionality or how subjectivity is created by parents who treat infants "as if" they have intentions, dynamic systems theorists define behavior as mental, but also visual, muscular, neural, and contextual. These theorists argue that cognition does not always happen prior to action. Instead, they propose that in order to explain behavior, an examination of the changes that occur within each of these components (e.g. cognition and actions) is important. According to Fogel (1993) intentions are created within a communicative framework between parent and child. Infant development is not fixed to a genetic or maturational timetable (it is not linear), nor is it entirely predictable from adult guidance or infant learning; rather new abilities emerge through the dynamic indeterminacy (behavior cannot be predicted from known laws) of self-organization (maintenance and development of the system arises from the mutual transactions and feedback processes between the components of the system), rather than being imposed on the system by some pre-existing plan (see Fogel, 1993; Fogel, 2001, pp. 55–59). Because development is seen as a nonlinear, dynamical, self-organizing process, infant intentionality can only be understood in the process of solving problems.

Some of the recent work of dynamic systems theorists support the idea of the close link between mind and body (see Lewis and Granic, 2000). For instance, emotions are said to be self-organizing products of mental and bodily processes that arise and develop in interpersonal interactions. This is evident in the ontogeny of communication where rituals develop between mother and infant during dyadic interactions through reciprocal coordination of actions, vocalizations, and emotional expressions and gestures (Fogel, 1993; Fogel and Thelen, 1987; Hsu and Fogel, 2003).

Thus rather than focusing on purely cognitive conceptions of the mind, ideas of nonlinearity and emergence are being explored when evaluating the intentions of infants.

Integrative view

In summary, there are various definitions of intentionality. Zeedyk (1996) proposes that theorists should opt for an integrated account of the development of intentionality. This would require an integrated definition of intentionality of course. This integrated approach needs to encompass both cognitive and social behaviors as well as personal and interpersonal behaviors. Zeedyk feels that the lack of an integrated approach has been counterproductive, and in order to advance in the field a more coherent account needs to be achieved.

Intentions as precursors to Theory of Mind

Regardless of the controversy among theorists about the definition of intentions, the majority of them agree that an understanding of intentions in others is a precursor to the development of a Theory of Mind. A Theory of Mind is one of the most fundamental aspects of human development. In order to participate in social interactions, to understand early nonverbal behavior and emotional expressions, to predict goal-directed behavior of others, humans need to understand that they and other people have mental states, that both possess information (in their minds) that can be predicted to some extend and also shared, and that the information two people have about a particular event may differ.

Until recently, little attention was paid to the infants' understanding of the social world. Consequently little was known about infants' fascination for how people think, feel, and emote. Before that, the focus was primarily on the child's understanding of the physical world. This research showed that infants as young as 3 months were aware that objects move as a whole and do not come apart; thus these infants understand the principle of cohesion. Somewhat later, between 3 and 6 months, infants begin to recognize that objects move on nonintersecting paths (principle of continuity) and that they cannot occupy the same space at the same time (principle of solidity). Infants younger than 6 months also realize that objects can make other objects move if and only if they touch; thus at that age infants are also aware of the principle of contact (see Spelke, Phillips, and Woodward, 1995 for a review).

The focus has now shifted from a predominant concern with the physical to the social cognitive development of infants in order to investigate infants' sense of people. Although an understanding of physical principles may facilitate an understanding of some aspects of people, such as an awareness of the occlusion and collision of their bodies (Poulin-Dubois, 1999), physical principles will not help in understanding people as psychological entities. When infants start to see others as psychological entities, they begin to understand that people are motivated by mental states.

As discussed earlier, whereas many social cognitive theorists are very clear that infants develop an awareness of simple mental states (intentions), they are not clear about the age of onset (e.g. at birth; around 9–12; or at 18–24 months of life). More importantly, they are less clear on what happens prior to the onset of intentions in infants. When questioning Tomasello (January, 2003 – personal communication) about the type of mental states infants had prior to 12 months, he stated that "For now, I have just simple-mindedly talked about understanding goals and intentions at one year as one thing and understanding thoughts and beliefs at four years as another. The latter are clearly 'mental states'. Whether or not the former are depends on your definition of 'mental state'. I don't think anything important rides on this definition." Although this may seem a glib answer, as I discussed in the beginning of this chapter "intentionality" is defined in various ways by various authors, depending much on their theoretical orientation, namely whether they emphasize biological (innate) versus cultural/environmental factors, or an interaction between the two in the development of an understanding of intentionality in infants (Zeedyk, 1996).

It would, however, seem essential that developmental psychologists provide a detailed account of how *the baby becomes linked up with the environment.* That is, do babies have a set of reflexes that make them react to external stimulation, or do they have innate structures or predispositions that allow them to recognize people as special categories in the world? In the following paragraphs I will discuss how some influential theoretical orientations deal with these questions. It has been argued that "intentionality" like other hypothetical constructs cannot be measured (Harding, 1982). This argument brings us back again to the way intentionality is defined. Regardless of whether one proposes a continuous or discontinuous view of the development of mental states in infants, if something called "development" exists, it should be fully described, whether this description entails going from simple structures to more complex structures or from the absence of mentalism to its presence.

Thus in this book I will investigate one of the most interesting and hotly debated questions about the development of social cognitive capacities in children, namely whether infants perceive people as sentient beings with emotions, goals, and intentions. Because I believe that the development of a Theory of Mind is a continuous process (rather than discontinuous), I propose that there are *precursors* to a Theory of Mind. The aim of the present book is to focus on these precursors; in particular, it seeks to determine when human children first become aware that people have minds and what the mechanisms are that promote such awareness. There is converging evidence from developmental and cognitive psychology to indicate that the precursors to a Theory of Mind can be found in infancy as a result of cognitive processes that are within the child but that social interaction is an important factor supporting Theory of Mind development.

Theoretical speculations: onset of mental state awareness

Piaget's view

According to Piaget (1952) the newborn baby does not have an awareness of the mental states of other people. Rather, Piaget designed a baby with reflexes that only reacts to incoming stimulation for the first months of life. After much reflexive action on the world (e.g. sucking on a blanket or the breast) and with the help of biological mechanisms of assimilation and accommodation, infants learn to discriminate between the two classes. It is at that moment that reflexes turn into action schemas and that cognitive structures develop which direct infants for the first time to act on (rather than being acted upon) the environment. Although for the next 18 months the cognitive structures allow for more enriched and refined experiences, they never enable the infant a glimpse into the mind of the other. People are known behaviorally but never psychologically. It is not until the end of the sensori-motor period that action schemas turn into symbols and that children become aware of other minds (see also Barresi and Moore, 1996; Perner, 1991).

Skinner's view

Behavioral theorists propose that the infant (and also the adult) identify people by their behaviors, by what they see, never by what they may infer. Thus, there is no investigation into the precursors to a Theory of Mind in this theory. Both Piaget and Skinner agree on the initial beginnings of the infant; namely an absence of mentalism, and the presence of a full set of reflexes to link the infant with the environment. According to Skinner, infants are born with powerful abilities for contingency analysis. Subsequent development of behavior is through operant conditioning of existing behaviors and the shaping of new behaviors (see chapter 3 for a rebuttal of this position).

Premack's view

Many nativists or modular theorists argue that an understanding of other people and their intentions (simple mental states) is hard wired into infants: "When a self-propelled object changes its motion without assistance from another object, the infant's principal hard-wired perception is intention" (Premack, 1990). However, Premack made a distinction between infantile and adult's common sense understanding of intentions. Whereas infants may identify self-propelledness as a goal directed entity, "common sense understanding is an inferred state of mind based on evidence for desire, belief, and planning" (p. 12). Thus, in the beginning infants interpret anything that appears self-moving as an intentional object. Such interpretation does not rely on an awareness of mental states of the object, and in fact, infants may attribute "intentions" to physical objects that appear to move by themselves. Although this is an interesting proposition, there is a considerable amount of evidence that argues against it. This evidence shows that soon after birth infants have different responses to people and objects when movements and other physical attributes of the stimuli are controlled for (Bruner, 1973; Gelman and Spelke, 1981; Legerstee et al., 1987; Legerstee, 1992; 2000). I will deal with this evidence in detail in chapter 4, and undoubtedly throughout the book.

Baron-Cohen's view

Another interesting modular theory has been developed by Baron-Cohen (1991). The author argues that infants are born with an eye detection module to perceive intentions. Infants use the direction of eyes to detect what people are attending to and what their subsequent actions might be. Thus infants use gaze direction to infer simple mental states in others during the first 9 months of life.

The maturation and expression of modular abilities are not much influenced by the social environment. This is a problem, because as discussed earlier, in order to understand what people feel and think it is imperative that infants participate in social interaction, so that they can be exposed to human thinking and emotions.

We know from studies assessing the effects of maternal scaffolding and sensitivity that the social milieu is an important factor in the infant's developing understanding of people and the way they think. As discussed earlier, social interactionists (Fogel, 1993; Hobson, 1990, Reddy, 1991; Vygotsky, 1978; Trevarthen, 1991; Tronick, 2003) propose that an understanding of what people mean comes primarily through interacting with them. One group of authors argues that it is primarily through *these* interactions that young infants' understanding of persons as intentional agents develops; others however posit that an understanding of intentional behavior is present at birth and that interactions with people gives rise to more complex forms of understanding of intentions in infants.

Meltzoff's view

For Meltzoff and his colleagues (see Meltzoff and Gopnik, 1993; Meltzoff and Moore, 1997) the social partner is an essential component in the infant's awareness of mental states. Meltzoff proposes innate mechanisms to perceive intentions in others, such as the biological mechanism to perceive others "like me" at birth, and the innate ability to imitate social actions of people which generates corresponding subjective emotions of their partners in the self through "active intermodal mapping." It is through these activities that infants become aware of their own and others' mental states. Although I will discuss this important foundational model in later chapters of the book, suffice it to say, this "starting state nativism" model implies that learning about the social world in the first few weeks is unidirectional, relying mostly on the child's own inferential capabilities. Social interactionists do not support such reasoning. They argue that all psychological experience depends on relationships with the social and nonsocial environment (Fogel, 2001).

In particular, the quality of the interpersonal relationship infants have with their primary caretaker seems to play an important role for infants' appreciation of their social world.

Karmiloff-Smith's view

Although Karmiloff-Smith argues that many of the computations of Theory of Mind develop by themselves initially, she credits the social milieu as playing an important role in further development. Empirical evidence suggests that infants may indeed have innate predispositions that allow for a richer innate state than the discontinuous theorists (Piagetians and the "as-if" social interactionists) might predict. According to Piaget, the development of knowledge proceeds in a domain-general manner (there are no specific predispositions that give the infants a leg up). Knowledge of the mind develops like other knowledge, from a focus on the person's behavior or actions during the first 2 years of life to a focus on the person's intentions and mental states thereafter. In contrast, the nativist account views the infant as possessing innate pre-specified modules that determine what and how the infant interprets incoming stimuli. Although at first glance the two theories seem quite divergent, Karmiloff-Smith takes a position between the two and makes an effort to blend them together. This blending depends on two conditions: (1) that Piagetian theory incorporate innate, domain-specific biases; (2) the initial state of the infant (the innate component) has less pre-specificity and involves more progressive modularization processes than nativists allow for. Thus Karmiloff-Smith reconciles nativism and Piaget's constructivism.

It should be noted that domain-general and domain-specific theorists have different meanings for the word "constraint." In the former, "constraint" is viewed in a negative light and refers to factors that dampen an individual's development. In the latter theory, "constraint" is seen in a positive way, as fostering learning by limiting and organizing input which makes for a more manageable knowledge system. Thus, constraint constructivists perceive constraints as an organization of knowledge that facilitate learning in the child.

Legerstee's view

In my account of constraint constructivism, I postulate that there are three types of predispositions that give the infants a leg up in their acquisition of a Theory of Mind: (1) self-inferential processes that allow infants an awareness of their mental states through the perception of their own emotions. Thus when infants are in an emotional state they have certain mental experiences (Fogel, 1993; Hobson, 2002; Reddy, 2003). Hence, the earliest simple mental states are associated with feelings and emotions, (2) interpersonal awareness that allows infants to recognize emotions of others, and *innate sense of emotional attunement* (see also Meltzoff and Brooks, 2001). That is, when infants engage with others who reflect the infants' emotions back to them, infants attribute the same mental experience they have to others. These three predispositions work together from birth and allow infants to perceive others as similar to self, and communicate with them pre-verbally until language sets in.

Various theorists have proposed that infants pick up concrete knowledge and have intuitive expectations about concepts during their cognitive development (Flavell, 1999; Fodor, 1992; Gelman, Durgin, and Kaufman, 1995; Harris, 1992; Gelman and Spelke, 1981; Wellman, 1993). These processes allow infants to interpret people's actions in ways that are precursory and continuous with more mature conceptual understandings of people. Indeed, it would be difficult to understand how infants could learn to make inferential attributions later, if totally incapable of something similar to inferential thought earlier (Flavell, 1999). The mechanisms that allow infants to develop an understanding of conspecifics as intentional beings like themselves whose interests, desires, and attention to outside entities may be followed, directed, shared, and understood is rooted in these initial mental structures (Karmiloff-Smith, 1992). "The present argument, then, is that if infant members of a mind-reading species give us the strong feeling that they are doing some kind of mind reading, they probably are" (Flavell, 1999, p. 32).

Thus, my brand of constraint constructivism argues that evolution has provided humans with predispositions to recognize people as similar to self and to interact with them. This recognition, which I argue is first on an emotional level, rather than a purely cognitive one, provides an understanding of the equivalences between self and other. This recognition and the ensuing social interactions open the road to the beginning of social cognitive abilities.

Dynamic systems

My kind of reasoning, albeit different in many respects, can be consolidated with other theorists who stress the importance of affective exchanges during early interactions, such as dynamic systems theorists (Bruner, 1990; Fogel, 1993). DS theorists argue that there are preferential pathways and receptivities in the newborn (what I call innate) which form the core of later development. These authors suggest that the sense of "like me" which clearly is there for the newborn may be a particular felt resonance and attraction that emerges when certain conditions are met, rather than being the result of a hardwired cognitive module. According to Fogel (1993) psychological experience develops during relationships. Mother–infant face-to-face interactions at birth are dynamic systems composed of multiple constituents (Fogel and Thelen, 1987). Through the process of co-regulation the dyad dynamically alter their actions (Fogel, 1993). All developmental outcomes can thus be explained as the spontaneous emergence of coherent, higher-order forms through recursive interactions among simpler components. This process is called self-organization. Accumulating history of interactions over time provide the dynamic context for dyad interactions (Lollis and Kuczynski, 1997). Thus each interaction is influenced by past interactions and each new reorganization of the system is constrained by the previous pattern (Lewis, 1997). In sum, development is propelled by interactions that begin at birth. Subsequent development is the result of a shared, co-constructed history which shapes the dynamics of moment to moment interactions.

The importance of social interaction with caregivers for the development of cognitive processes in infants finds support in the writings of Hobson (2002). Hobson argued that an understanding of the mind/mental states derives out of the infants' interaction with adults well before the first birthday. He proposes that the 3-month-old infant, in perceiving a smile, perceives something of the mental state of the adult (e.g. emotions, à la Hobson, 2002).

A study by Legerstee and Varghese (2001) provides support for the idea that infants when interacting with their mothers perceive more than just facial expressions (e.g. physical movements). We showed that they expect and thrive on a particular *quality* of social interaction of their mothers which is defined as (1) warm sensitivity, (2) reciprocity, and (3) maintaining infant focus of attention. Mothers who ranked high on these behaviors had infants who ranked high on socio-cognitive competence and were more effective in the way they interacted with their social and cognitive environment than infants whose mothers ranked low. Thus, when certain conditions are met between the dyad which allows for optimal reciprocal coordination of communicative gestures, vocalizations, and emotional expressions, new capabilities arise in infants (Fogel, 1993).

In another study with young infants of similar intelligence, aged 3, 5, 7, and 10 months (filmed at the Infancy laboratory of the Max Planck

Institute-Leipzig),[2] it was found that maternal interactive strategies that contained high levels of sensitivity and scaffolding of socio-cognitive abilities influenced infants' gaze monitoring at 3 months, and the infants' subsequent ability to coordinate attention (CA) between object and person at 5, 7, and 10 months, because these infants had a higher level of responding of gazing and coordinated attention than infants of less sensitive mothers. It was further found that maternal interactive skills had an enduring effect on the communicative capacities of infants rather than being a result of temporary 'on-line' effect, because infants of low sensitive mothers maintained lower frequencies of gaze monitoring and CA during interactions with highly attuned strangers than infants of highly sensitive mothers (Legerstee, Fisher, and Markova, 2005) (see chapter 8).

Although maternal behavior can accelerate some cognitive capacities in infants, most children should acquire the ability to perceive intentions and Theory of Mind abilities. However, the above studies reveal that maternal affect attunement may stimulate the acquisition of certain developmental milestones in children, which must have a generalizing effect on learning of other social and cognitive abilities. Maternal sensitivity makes the learning process more agreeable and improves not only infants' social/cognitive competence, but also their mental state awareness. I will come back to the importance of maternal scaffolding for mentalism in chapters 7, 8, and 9.

Infants are born with an innate capacity to identify with conspecifics

To conclude, I propose that infants are born with an innate capacity to identify with conspecifics. Whether progress in the development of ToM is a result of primarily endogenous changes (internal) or a function of exogenous (environmental) factors is still an empirical question, and may depend on the particular aspect of Theory of Mind reasoning. The available evidence is strongly in favor of the idea that infants are able to perceive simple mental states in people at birth as evidenced during mutual sharing of emotions in dyadic interactions. This awareness undergoes developmental changes through the infants' interactions with the social milieu (see also Fogel, 1993). By the middle of the first year, the dyadic interactions (infants playing with people, *or* objects) expand to include objects; in a sense that they involve the referential triangle of infant, adult, and another object to which they share attention. An

---

[2] Laboratory of the Cultural Ontogeny Group.

awareness of people's purposes and goals, particularly pertaining to objects outside of the dyad, becomes evident now. This development suggests an inferential process in infants that begins at birth but that develops into hierarchically more complex inferential processes toward the end of the first year. Finally, although the developmental process outlined above occurs in a similar sequence in all normal infants, and thus is a universal phenomenon, they may not have a similar developmental timetable. As discussed earlier, infants who engage in optimal social interactions with caretakers progress sooner and develop a more enriched and deeper understanding of the mental states of others than infants who receive less nurturing and scaffolding in these domains. On the extreme end, infants who through some genetic defect fail to connect with people, and therefore are unable to learn from their interactions with them, such as children with autism, do not develop an awareness of the emotions and intentions of others and subsequently fail to develop a Theory of Mind (see Baron-Cohen, 1991; Camaioni, Perucchini, Muratori, and Milone, 1997).

Plan of the book

In chapter 2, I will examine in more detail the endogenous (innate) and exogenous (environmental) factors that interact in the ontogeny of a Theory of Mind. I will discus empirical support for the proposition that infants are born with an ability to recognize others to be similar to the self, e.g. to be "like me." Simultaneous to an awareness that they are like others is the ability to perceive emotions in self and others and to share these emotions with others (Fogel, 1993; Hobson, 1990; Reddy, 2003; Trevarthen, 1979). Tronick (2003) argues that infants have an intrinsic motivation to interact socially with people. It is through these exchanges that infants begin to become aware of others' mental states, e.g. their goals, intentions, and subsequently develop a Theory of Mind. Finally, in addition to the endogenous factors, there are convergent or supporting exogenous factors. These exogenous factors are the roles played by the socializing agents. Thus in chapter 2, the role social interaction plays in the development of the infants' understanding of people's gestures, actions, verbalizations, and facial expressions that lead to an understanding of people's minds will be discussed.

If infants are born with predispositions to recognize that they are similar to other people and also an innate ability to interact with them, then these innate factors would only be adaptive if infants were sensitive to people, that is, if infants could identify people from among other animate and inanimate objects in the world. I will focus on the type of input the domain specific principles use to make this identification. Human infants show a preference to attend to human stimulation, such as their faces, voices, and emotions. Although infants with autism apparently have no difficulty in processing these stimuli, they do not show a preference for human stimuli early in life; rather they treat social stimulation much as they would nonsocial stimulation (Karmiloff-Smith, 1992). Because infants with autism have difficulty with some aspects of Theory of Mind development, it would seem that a preference for human stimuli, (rather than the ability to perceive and process them), and a predisposition to interact with people are some of the precursors to Theory of Mind development.

Many of the questions infancy researchers are posing about infants can be answered through studying infants. However, this is not an easy feat. Infants do not talk, nor do they cooperate much, and consequently trying to find out what infants perceive and know, or what their perceptual or conceptual understanding of things is, and whether these notions are innate or acquired, demand quite innovative methodologies. Every area in infant development has its own method and equipment for data collection. In order to make sure that infant behavior is observed reliably, infant responses in various paradigms are video recorded so that the many fast moving and subtle infant behaviors can be examined over and over again, in order to reach a reliable conclusion between the coders. Sometimes the sequence of infant responses (e.g. gaze, vocalizations, and point, cf. Legerstee and Barillas, 2003) is of interest and sometimes behaviors by themselves, such as eye movements to measure whether infants have become familiarized (habituated) to a particular stimulus, is chosen as the dependent variable. Such micro-analytic coding of behaviors demand advanced computer technology and refined statistical analyses. Although various methods of infancy research will be highlighted throughout the book, in chapter 2 a detailed discussion of the pertinent methods will be presented in order to facilitate comprehension of the various studies discussed in the subsequent chapters.

In chapter 3, I will examine the development of the animate/inanimate distinction. Such research is important because it sheds light on the structure of the human mind. Namely, if infants treat the psychological differently from the physical right after birth, then this may indicate that infants have domain specific rather than domain general mechanisms. Many theorists argue that infants are born with domain specific principles to process information of people, which are different from those which they use to process information of physical objects (see Carey, 1985; Chi, 1988; Gelman and Spelke, 1981; Legerstee, 1992). This indicates that from birth infants distinguish between animate and inanimate objects. If infants have domain specific mechanisms, then one can expect to find prerequisites to Theory of Mind development, and continuities in inferential processes. However, if infants have a domain general mechanism then it is argued that infants progress from perceptual to conceptual knowledge. That is, development proceeds from knowing the physical attributes of people to knowing their mental states. As indicated earlier, this discontinuous position is a somewhat difficult theoretical stance to adopt and defend, because one has to discuss how and when infants change from perceptual to conceptual knowing. In chapter 4, I will discuss this distinction, in both theoretical as well as methodological terms.

If one argues for a continuity of the psychological and inferential processes, then infants must have a concept of a person (albeit a very rudimentary one) from very early on in life. One can, of course, not have a concept of a person, without having a concept of the self, because a definition of a concept includes more than one entity. Wellman (1993) has indicated that infants need to separate self from others before they can begin to understand that other people have mental states. Thus, they need a notion of a separate self, and an awareness that emotions and feelings are states that can only be shared with social agents (see Hoffman, 1981). Thus if one argues for continuity of mental awareness, which most likely begins with an awareness of emotions in others from birth, then a primitive sense of self should be in existence from the beginning.

In chapter 4, I will discuss the infants' developing sense of self (consciousness). I will draw upon my own work, theories of others, and related publications to present some intuitions and hypotheses about the nature of the self and the mechanisms that lead to the development of consciousness or self-awareness during the first year of life (see Legerstee, 1999; Piaget, 1952; Freud, 1949; Hobson, 1990; Neisser, 1993; Gibson, 1993; Fogel, 1993). Empirical evidence reveals that from birth infants appear conscious of their physical selves, because they are aware of themselves as causal agents bringing about states that did not exist before, e.g. the "I do state" (if I suck, I get milk; if I grab, I hold an object), but also the "being done state" (I am being carried, lifted; I lose my balance, etc.) (Neisser, 1995; Butterworth and Hicks, 1977). Infants also engage in species-specific communicative displays which reveal that they have an early appreciation of the social and mental selves. From very early on, infants engage with others in mutual exchanges of emotions, which gives an insight into the mental states of self and others (Fogel, 1993; Trevarthen, 1979; Tronick, 2003), and they are aware that people can be affected at a distance by their social signals in dyadic relationships (Legerstee et al., 1987). By the end of the first six months of life, infants become aware that people's actions are related to objects external to the dyad. Thus, during the triadic period infants become aware how people are psychologically related to *other* objects (than the self), about which they now begin to communicate and to share information.

In summary, it is argued that from birth infants are conscious of the physical selves and are familiar with their own faces and voices; they are also conscious of their social and mental selves. They are on their way to becoming representational agents and unique mythical entities. The development of the various aspects of the self supports a constraint constructivist model.

If one posits that infants perceive the self as an independent and social agent, what is the process by which they acquire information about people that will lead to an understanding of more complex mental states and the development of a Theory of Mind (Bruner, 1999; Hobson, 1993)? In chapter 5, I will discuss this question. Earlier on I argued that dyadic interactions allowed infants a glimpse into others' minds through sharing of emotions. Hobson (1990) suggests that infants are biologically endowed with the ability for nonverbal interaction, which allows them to perceive "other minds" through social exchanges. Thus unlike what Piaget (1954) and others have suggested, communication is not a tool that facilitates the development of a symbol using mind. Rather, these authors and others (e.g. Vygotsky, 1978; Kaye, 1982) argue that social interaction is the origin of the mind. These statements would support the hypotheses proposed in chapter 2, that (1) the ability to recognize conspecifics as similar to self and (2) the ability to interact with them in communicative exchanges are endogenous factors that prepare infants to develop a Theory of Mind. Evidence from autistic infants corroborates with this view. As indicated previously that infants with autism do not have a Theory of Mind because of their inability to share emotional states with others (Camaioni et al., 1997; Charman et al., 1997).

Not only must infants recognize conspecifics and their behavior and distinguish them from self, other people, and inanimate objects, but the affective/social exchanges infants engage in with their caretakers contribute greatly to infants' developing Theory of Mind (Legerstee and Varghese, 2001; Legerstee and Weintraub, 1997; Legerstee, Van Beek, and Varghese, 2002; Tager-Flusberg, 1989; Reddy, 2003). Affective states are social signals that provide information about another person's intentions, and provide a direction for one's own actions (Montague and Walker-Andrews, 2001). As indicated earlier, infants with autism do not preferentially orient to human faces and voices. Nor do they engage in mutual eye gazing, shared attention over objects, and imitative learning (Charman et al., 1997; Mundy and Sigman, 1989). Gaze alternation and pointing to affect another's attention (mental state) is not produced nor comprehended by autistic children (Baron-Cohen, 1989; Charman et al., 1997; Camaioni et al., 1997). These behaviors in normally developing infants have been suggested to reveal that infants perceive people as purposeful and intentional agents (Legerstee and Barillas, 2003). Thus social interactions would seem essential in the acquisition of a Theory of Mind. If we do not interact with other people, either verbally or nonverbally, how can we get to know what they think, feel, desire, and believe? Thus in chapter 5, I will describe the earliest social interactions infants engage in. There is a rich amount of literature that reveals the early expectations infants have about the communicative behaviors of people. These early communicative interactions are *dyadic in nature*. Infants relate to people through mutual eye contact, imitation, and the sharing of emotions. Thus, in dyadic communication, infants show that they are motivated to share with others what they have in mind, to achieve mutual awareness (Bruner, 1999).

As ontogeny progresses infants' means of relating to the social world undergoes a key transition. From engaging exclusively in *dyadic* interactions early in development (either with people *or* objects), infants begin to take part in *triadic* exchanges at around the first year of life (Bakeman and Adamson, 1984; Carpenter et al., 1998; Desrochers, Morrissette, and Ricard, 1995; Feinman, 1982; Fogel, 1993; Legerstee et al., 1987; Legerstee et al., 2002; Legerstee and Weintraub, 1997; Leung and Rheingold, 1981; Scaife and Bruner, 1975; Trevarthen, 1979). As a consequence, infants engage in a variety of behaviors that indicate that they perceive human actions to be related to external events (Baldwin and Moses, 1994; Baron-Cohen, 1991; Franco and Butterworth, 1996; Legerstee, 2001a; Legerstee and Barillas, 2003; Messer, 1997; Tomasello, 1995). These emerging triadic exchanges constitute infants' first attempts to *simultaneously* integrate object interests and person engagements within their focus of attention. In chapter 6, I will discuss these triadic exchanges. There is disagreement of what these triadic interactions mean in terms of the intentional stance in infants. To those who take the discontinuous view, these triadic abilities index for the first time an awareness of intentions in others. Infants begin to perceive people as intentional agents whose perspectives may differ from their own (Tomasello, 1995).

However, theorists who argue for a continuation of inferential processes argue that the triadic period indicates the beginning of a more complex awareness of mental states in others, one involving objects. This more advanced awareness of mental states is partially brought on by changes in physical development (e.g. cortical maturity, a more advanced visual system that allows infants to perceive events external to the dyad, and maturing motor abilities, e.g. the ability to coordinate two actions) to which parents are reacting (e.g. they hand infants objects while talking about them) (Legerstee et al., 1987; Bakeman and Adamson, 1984). I will describe in chapter 6 how, by 5 months, infants for the first time bring things outside the dyad to the attention of the interlocuteur in order to make these events a topic of conversation. Tuning into others' attention is marked by the development of coordinated attention. Coordinated attention is one of the most elementary ways infants begin to share attention with others over objects. As discussed in chapter 5, mutual sharing of attention not involving outside objects can already be noticed during dyadic interactions. But when infants begin to alternate their gazes between people and objects between 5 and 7 months of age, when infants begin to look at people's faces during ambiguous situations, or when they are being teased, infant monitoring of the gazes of people announces a more advanced awareness of the mental states of people.

Thus, in the first six chapters of the book I describe how the endogenous factors with which infants are born enable them to recognize conspecifics as similar. This hypothesis is supported by the finding that at birth, infants have particular expectations about communicative interactions with people, which is expressed first in dyadic face-to-face communication, and subsequently in triadic interactions.

I will devote chapter 7 to the social interactionist account. I will examine in detail the social interactionist view introduced in chapter 1, that an understanding of people and their mental states is deeply influenced by the interactions infants have with social partners. I will examine the mechanism these theorists put forth in the development of the infant's understanding of people. Because of the importance of social interaction for the infant's developing Theory of Mind, I will provide a historical perspective on parent–child interactions (e.g. psycho-analytic theory, attachment theory). I will also focus on what caretakers do to enhance their infants' understanding of the social world. Concepts such as mutual attunement and affect mirroring will be discussed and empirical data to highlight their effectiveness will be presented.

In chapters 8 and 9, I will provide empirical evidence to show how variations of the social milieu affect variations in the development of certain socio-cognitive processes. Even though nativists, "as if" social interactionists, and dynamic systems theorists seem divided (oppositional) on the type of precursory abilities they are willing to attribute to infants, all emphasize the importance of sensitive responding of the caretaker in developing a Theory of Mind. These authors stress that the quality of mother–infant relationships is important for infants' social, emotional, and cognitive growth (Fogel, 1993; Freud, 1949; Stern, 1977; Field, 1995).

As indicated earlier, the endogenous factors influencing the development of ToM in infants are the innate abilities to perceive others as similar, and an innate sense of emotional attunement to engage in acts of communication with them. These endogenous factors interact with the exogenous factors in the ontogenetic process. Just like the endogenous factors, the exogenous factors, such as the socio, emotional, and cultural information that is transmitted to infants during social interaction, play a determining role in the development of a Theory of Mind. Many argue that sensitivity to species-specific interaction patterns may be essential for the development of a Theory of Mind in pre-linguistic infants (Bruner, 1999; Tager-Flusberg, 1989). Consequently, the quality of the social relationship between caregiver and infant must influence (1) an awareness and sharing of emotions during the first 4 months of life, (2) sharing of attention over objects during the subsequent months, and (3) an awareness that when people emote positively while attending to objects, they may want or desire this object (primitive desire reasoning). I will present research to show that these capacities are acquired sooner in infants whose parents scaffold these activities than parents who do not.

In Chapter 10, I will summarize the purpose of this book and evaluate whether the questions provided in the introduction and the theories that have given rise to these questions can be adequately supported by empirical evidence. I will provide a test of the three theoretical approaches that I have referenced recurrently throughout the chapters because they have put forth some interesting hypotheses about the type of innate mechanism that link the infants with the environment. This study supports the argument that an awareness of others' mental states cannot occur purely endogenously via maturation.

Throughout this book, I will argue that infants are born with a sense of people, and that this predisposition gives infants a head start in the acquisition of a Theory of Mind. I will provide much empirical evidence to support this view. However, I am well aware that others may interpret this evidence differently. I see this as a positive thing because these different views provide the impetus for further research. I agree with others that we need more empirical evidence in order to continue to enrich our view of the infants' precocious social cognitive capacities.

2 Endogenous and exogenous influences in development

Human beings acquire information both from biology and culture in the acquisition of various social cognitive milestones (Kaye, 1982; Tronick, 2003). Just like other animals, humans have innate predispositions that not only contain the blueprint for physical maturation but, unlike many animal species, human infants have domains that contain sets of representations that sustain a specific area of knowledge such as language, number, and physics (cf. Karmiloff-Smith, 1992), but also sociality (cf. Legerstee, 2001b). The domain responsible for an understanding of people may not develop like other universal endogenous developmental processes, often involuntarily and without planning. I like to argue that the development of an awareness of the mental states of others requires considerable *social interaction* in order to develop into the complex capacity that it is. However, not all environmental and social interactions are beneficial or important for ToM development. Therefore, the specific social domain contains knowledge of people, but also domain specific constraints that propel infants to focus on input that is specific to people and their mental states. Thus the *endogenous* processes or predispositions facilitate engagement in pre-linguistic dyadic communication. During these interactions, infants share emotions and imitate the expressions of people, thereby enhancing mutual awareness and promoting identification with social partners. The endogenous processes allow infants to adapt to, and to learn from, the external environment, to optimize and also to recognize *exogenous factors* that are especially important for ToM development. Exogenous factors interact with the endogenous factors, and play a formative role in the development of an understanding of the mental states of people.

The endogenous and exogenous processes also propel infants into the subsequent *triadic* state, where infants begin to communicate with conspecifics about objects and interesting events. During the triadic state, infants show and request objects, they point out interesting events in the environment with gestures and vocalizations, and they show that they are aware when others reference, want, or desire objects.

24

In this chapter, I will discuss the factors that facilitate the development of ToM. I will argue that the development of an awareness of mental states requires a significant amount of developmental processes and time. Infants have endogenous factors that give them a head start in the developmental process and prepare them to take advantage of species-specific exogenous factors.

Endogenous factors

"Like me"

As indicated in chapter 1, infants' *innate* abilities to recognize that they are similar to other people, that they are of the same species as humans and different from other animals and physical objects, are important factors in the development of a Theory of Mind. Such particular attention biases permit infants to build more refined representations about people from birth that are necessary precursors to a Theory of Mind. As ontogeny progresses, infants are attuned to perceive increasingly more complex behaviors in others, and as a result of the identification with their conspecifics adjust to their social displays and internalize them. Hence, rather than just being shaped and reinforced for producing closer approximations of adult behaviors, infants are innately programmed to identify with conspecifics and to interact with them. Through such social interactions infants' understanding of other minds becomes consolidated.

Preference for human stimuli

Support for the fact that infants recognize their conspecifics may be found by looking at the special attraction infants have for social stimuli. From birth, infants actively use their visual and auditory systems to acquire information about their surroundings and themselves. Infants are visually attracted to movement, contour, contrast, certain levels of complexity, and curvature (Banks and Salapatek, 1983; Haith, 1966). Newborns seem to prefer these parameters when they are arranged in face-like rather than in abstract ways, because they track a human schematic face significantly more than a scrambled face or a blank face (Goren, Sarty, and Wu, 1975; Johnson and Morton, 1991). Using preferential looking paradigms of two-dimensional stimuli, researchers have shown that by 2 months, infants discriminate between the faces of mothers and female strangers (Barrera and Maurer, 1981), and by 4 months, they distinguish among the faces of a man, woman, and a baby (Fagan, 1972). The results suggest that rather than having to construct a notion of a human face out of the various physical parameters mentioned above, infants may be born with some kind of template for "faceness" (e.g. primal specification of some structural characteristics of the human face called "CONSPEC" by Johnson and Morton, 1991, p. 105). However, newborns spend more time looking at their mothers' faces than at strangers' faces (Bushnell, Sai, and Mullin, 1989; Field, Cohen, Garcia, and Greenberg, 1985). This demonstrates that they are able to recognize their mothers' faces as familiar and suggest that this activity cannot be regulated by sensory information alone (e.g. "CONSPEC", Johnson and Morton, 1991); it must also involve information stored in memory, that is, some of this information is represented by infants.

Auditory perception also appears to be well developed in newborns. Unlike the visual system, the auditory system is stimulated in utero (DeCasper, Lecanuet, Bushnel, Granier-Deferre, and Naugeais, 1994). Preferential sucking paradigms have shown that newborns attend preferentially to human speech over other sounds (DeCasper and Fifer, 1980). At one month, they make fine distinctions among speech sounds (Eimas, Siqueland, Juscyk, and Vigorito, 1971) and discriminate between linguistic contrasts not available in their mother tongue (Trehub, 1976). Newborns also retain information about syllables (Juscyk, Kennedy, and Juscyk, 1995) and, just as with human face stimuli, infants at birth recognize the voices of their mothers (to whom they were familiarized in the womb) from those of female strangers (DeCasper and Fifer, 1980). These findings suggest that infants are prepared to recognize and represent human stimuli.

Taken together, the available evidence indicates that infants are perceptive to stimulation emanating from people. They recognize social stimuli from among nonsocial stimuli. Because infants have demonstrated that they represent information of visual and auditory stimulation of people, this sensitivity for social stimuli may already be at a more structural rather than simply a perceptual level.

It appears that infants with autism do not show such preference for human stimulation; these infants also have shortcomings in the development of a Theory of Mind. These findings support the idea that an early preference for human stimuli can be regarded as precursors to Theory of Mind development.

Imitation and cross-modal perception

The special awareness infants have for people is evident in their preference for human stimuli, but also in the various *social responses* infants produce when facing people. For instance, soon after birth infants *imitate* gestures of people, but not of inanimate objects that simulate these gestures (Legerstee, 1991b). This indicates that imitation is a social mechanism to learn about people. According to Meltzoff and Brooks (2001, p. 173), "this sensitivity to human acts and ability to map equivalences between self and other provides leverage for understanding the beginnings of social cognition." It does so, because when humans behave, or imitate the behavior of the infant, they reflect how infants behave, and consequently how they feel and what they intend. Through this recreation, infants begin to focus on the meaning of these behaviors rather than on the physical features. Thus the ability to re-create the behaviors of others make these behaviors significant. It allows for imitative learning to take place. Imitative learning or intentional imitation occurs when infants learn to separate the means from their goals, thereby demonstrating an understanding of something about human intentions (see chapter 3, and the study on "Imitation in 10-month-old infants," for a demonstration of this type of imitative learning).

The earliest evidence of infant imitation can be found in neonatal reproduction of mouth opening and tongue protrusions, proprioceptive types of behaviors that infants can only feel themselves produce, but not see (Meltzoff and Moore, 1977; Maratos, 1973). How is this type of imitation possible in young infants? According to Piaget (1954; see also Berkeley 1709/1963) the senses are not coordinated at birth. Thus an object heard cannot be identified with an object seen. These modalities (the visual, auditory, and others) become coordinated in infancy through experience through touching, grabbing, and shaking things, infants come to perceive that the rattle is a round, shining sound-producing object, rather than a series of unconnected stimuli. Until infants come to recognize correspondences between information perceived through different modalities, stable sensori-motor schemas of three-dimensional, solid, sound producing, textured objects cannot be formed and hence cannot be thought about (Mandler, 1992).

Adults use language when communicating between the senses. They tell the visual sense that the sound that woke them up in the middle of the night was produced by the basketball player in front of the house. Because infants do not have language, how do infants communicate from one sense to the other? Meltzoff and Moore (1977) argue that neonatal imitation is made possible through cross-modal matching. Cross-modal matching, or "active intermodal mapping," is an ability that allows the infant to communicate between the senses through an abstract representational system that is not modality specific. When infants perceive human acts in one modality (e.g. visual, auditory), this information is stored in amodal form (not modality specific). This way it can be recognized and used by other senses. In the case of imitating proprioceptive acts, such as mouth opening and tongue protrusion, the infant can reproduce (tactile modality) the act seen (visual modality).

Cross-modal mapping is also used in speech perception (Legerstee, 1990). In order to imitate infants must perceive and then reproduce the vocal sounds of the actor (just like the infants do with facial movements). The speech infants hear has multimodal qualities. When adults speak, the voice not only emanates from the mouth, but the lip movements match the pattern of the spoken language (Sullivan and Horowitz, 1983). The perception of speech sounds by adults and infants has been shown to be influenced by both auditory and visual properties of the vocal act (Dodd, 1979; Grant, Ardell, Kuhl, and Sparks, 1986; Kuhl and Meltzoff, 1982; MacKain, Studdert-Kennedy, Spieker, and Stern, 1983; Summerfeld, 1979). For example, in certain linguistic contexts, visual information corresponding to one phoneme combined with auditory information of another may lead to the perception of a third in children and adults (McGurk and MacDonald, 1976). In addition, 4- to 5-month-old infants seem sensitive to the visual and acoustic properties of speech (Kuhl and Meltzoff, 1982). The authors revealed that they serendipitously observed vocal imitation while studying intermodal perception in 18- to 20-week-old infants in the study referred to earlier. Not only did the infants look longer at the face that articulated the non-vocal component of the speech sound they heard, but they imitated the vowel as well. Thus the infants who heard /a/ vowels responded with /a/ vowels, and those who heard the /i/ vowels responded with /i/ vowels. However, Kuhl and Meltzoff (1982) did not vary independently the visual and auditory components involved in reproduction of the speech signal, and therefore it is not clear whether the infants were imitating the sound produced by filmed faces or the mouth movements (the proprioceptive movements). Only the imitation of the mouth movements would imply cross-modal mapping (e.g. the kinesthetic reproduction of a visually perceived target). We addressed this concern (Legerstee, 1990). We presented 3–4-month-old infants with the vowel sounds /a/ and /u/. For one half of the infants, these sounds were paired with an adult who silently articulated the same vowel; for the other half, the adult articulated the opposite one. Only the infants who were exposed to matched auditory and visual information were observed to imitate the vowels (see figure 2.1). Clearly, infants paid attention to both the sound and the mouth movement.

Thus, according to Meltzoff and Moore (1983), imitation allows infants through cross-modal matching to perceive others to be "like me." This "like me" awareness is the starting or building block for social cognition and not an end-point after months of postnatal learning.

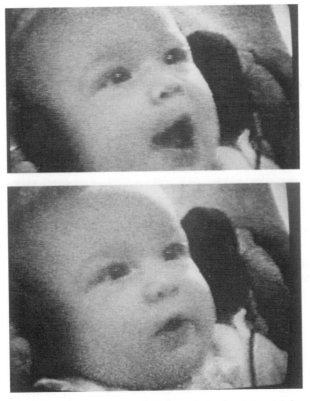

Figure 2.1 Three-month-old infants imitating /a/ and /u/ sounds.

The finding of Legerstee (1991b), namely that infants imitate actions of people and not of inanimate objects, not only informs about the endogenous ability of infants to perceive others "like me," but it also suggests something about the imitative response. Rather than being a reflexive response, that can be elicited by certain stimuli (those that seem to move toward the mouth, are self-propelled, or have a particular form, shape – copies of social stimuli such as tongues, mouths, hands, and faces), imitation is a social mechanism that "offers a unique channel for early communication, one in which both the timing and form of the exchange gives both partners the opportunity to share reciprocally in the exchange" (Meltzoff, 1985, p. 28). Thus, infants expect causal relations among social entities, rather than mere contiguities of perceptual features (associations). That is, infants expect people to be responsive, to reciprocate in social interactions. Infants do not have such expectations of inanimate objects and consequently they are restrained to only imitate people and not inanimate objects (e.g. banging of the door). Through imitating the behavior of adults and through noticing the adult imitating certain behaviors of the child, the social significance of many socio-cultural acts internalized in adults come to be internalized in the infant (Barresi, 1984; Locke, 1980; Vygotsky, 1962). Thus, whereas the recognition of others as similar to self is an endogenous factor, imitation is an innate mechanism that facilitates such recognition because through imitation, and the innate ability to map equivalences between self and other, infants learn about the meaning of their own and people's actions.

Imitation actually is a nice example of a mechanism that facilitates the interplay between exogenous and endogenous factors in the developmental process of learning about the human mind. Although infants' inferential processes allow infants to perceive others to be "like me," social interaction plays a role in facilitating an understanding of people right from birth. As indicated earlier, social interaction plays a greater role in an understanding of the mental states of people than perhaps in any of the other domains (Tager-Flusberg, 1989). How else can infants learn about people's minds unless they are exposed intimately to them from an early age?

Emotional awareness, mutual sharing of emotions, innate sense of attunement

The early demonstrations that infants imitate only the gestures of people, and not of inanimate objects that simulate social acts, supports the idea that infants perceive people to be similar. The question is, what is this similarity based on? As suggested, this similarity cannot be physical or perceptual, because when animate and inanimate objects are equated on physical characteristics (for a review of these studies see Legerstee, 1992, chapter 3) infants still discriminate between the two classes. Meltzoff and Moore (1997) argue that infants perceive others as similar to self because they recognize equivalences between perceived and executed acts as a function of cross-modal mapping. Thus the perceptual mechanism of cross-modal mapping is the starting state for the Meltzoff and Moore (1977) infants.

In my view, infants perceive others to be "like me" because they are born with an affect sharing device (AFS) that is made up of three components that interact together; they are (1) self-inferential processes that allow infants an awareness of their own mental states through the perception of their own emotions, and (2) inter-personal awareness that allows infants to recognize the emotions of others, and (3) innate sense of emotional attunement. Infants are born with the ability to perceive global happy and unhappy emotions (Izard, 1971). Neonates discriminate and imitate these emotions (Field et al., 1982). When infants are in an emotional state they have particular mental experiences (Reddy, 2003; Hobson, 1989). Thus, the earliest simple mental states are associated with feelings and emotions. When infants engage with others who reflect their emotions back to them, infants, through the workings of the AFS, attribute the same mental experience they have to others.

The ASF allows infants to communicate and develop in interaction with others pre-verbally. Through the innate sense of emotional attunement, infants recognize whether the emotions of self and others are on the same level; whether they are congruent. If they are, infants identify with people and through this understanding develop shared representations. Attuned interaction reduces and prevents the overlapping of shared representations, thereby fostering social and cognitive independence (Vygotsky, 1978).

Tronick (2003) proposed that infants have an intrinsic *motivation* to interact with other people, e.g. to have relational intentions (see also Bruner, 1999; Fogel, 1993). There is empirical evidence to support these suggestions. From birth, infants produce organized actions that are specific for interacting with people. During these mutual conversations infants gaze almost continuously at their partners while sharing emotional states through vocalizations and emotional gestures of the face, body, hands, and arms (Fogel and Hannan, 1985; Legerstee, Corter, and Kienapple, 1990). These proto-conversations have a definite turn-taking structure (Jaffe et al., 2001) which appears as the result of both maternal and infant pause and vocal outbursts (Kaye, 1982; Legerstee and Varghese, 2001; Trevarthen, 1979; Tronick, 2003). During this "turn-taking" and through the sharing of their affective states infants are revealing their "intersubjective" nature (Trevarthen, 1979). Thus infants possess capabilities to perform simple inferences such as "if I smile, I feel happy; if you smile, you might feel happy as well"[1] (see figure 2.2).

Meltzoff and Brooks (2001) argue that the "like me" mechanism with its tools such as cross-modal matching and imitation could bring about early awareness of emotional states in others, and thus make intersubjective sharing possible. The idea that a perceptual mechanism such as cross-modal mapping links the infant with the environment suggests that infants begin life without cognitive structures to support simple mental states in infants. Thus Meltzoff and Moore (1977) propose that cross-modal mapping, the recognition of equivalences between perceived

---

[1] Markova, Cognitive seminar, 2004.

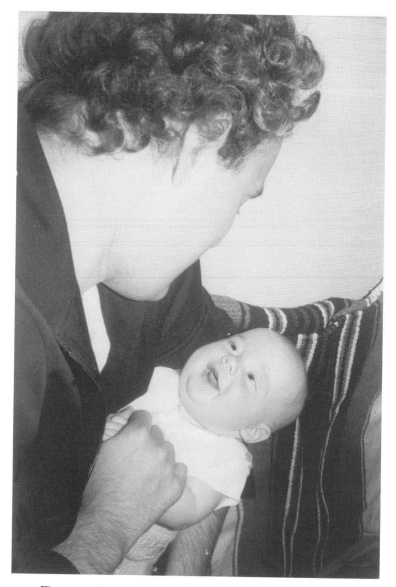

Figure 2.2 Five-week-old infant sharing emotions with gazes, smiling, and cooing.

and executed acts rather than some kind of inferential ability, links the infant with the environment. If this is so, then it would seem that the authors argue for a discontinuous development of mental life, one where infants progress from a perceptual to a conceptual state. Thus through imitation and sharing of acts, infants progress to eventually sharing mental states. Hence in the AIM model (Meltzoff and Moore, 1977) infants progress from perceiving acts to conceiving what led to these acts (e.g. to an understanding of the underlying mental states that were responsible for these acts).

I am in favor of a continuous proposal for the infant's understanding of the mental world. Sharing of emotions requires the ability to represent the specific emotional state. Through mechanisms of cross-modal matching *and* affect sharing infants are able to identify emotions amodally and mentally from birth. What that means is that infants represent any social stimulation (intra- or interpersonal environmental) in an amodal way so that information from any source can be applied not only across senses or situations, but also across people.[2] Stern (1985) argues that rather than imitating exactly what the infant does, the caretaker imitates the infant's emotions through various modalities; e.g. voice, face, rhythmic movements all respond in an attuned way to the infant's emotions. According to Fogel (2001), all psychological experience depends on a relationship with the environment: although emotions are experienced with respect to the body's encounter with a relational dynamic, they are experienced within individual bodies. An adequate theory of infants' conception of mental states must agree with Flavell's (1999) persuasive argument "that because older human infants are making genuine mental state attributions in a few short months, ... it is not unreasonable to suppose that they might be doing some precursor or early version of the same thing now." Indeed, it would be hard to imagine how infants could learn to make mental state attributions later if wholly incapable of anything like it earlier.

The proposition that infants have intra- and interpersonal inferences would offer an alternative explanation of the autistic inability to share emotions. It could be argued that, instead of having a missing module, autistic individuals have difficulty performing interpersonal inferences due to the fact that they are self-biased.

The idea that infants share emotional states with others during turn-taking in early conversations as a function of the AFS (innate abilities for intra- and interpersonal inferences and attunement) (e.g. "if I smile, I feel happy; if you smile, you might be happy as well") is not always

---

[2] Ibid.

appreciated by others. For instance, Tomasello (1999) argues that such interpretation would attribute to the child an awareness of others as subjects of experience (e.g. an understanding that people have internal states, can have intentions), which he feels does not happen until around 9–12 months of life. Interestingly, like many who propose that infants have the ability for primary inter-subjectivity (Meltzoff and Gopnik, 1993; Meltzoff and Brooks, 2001; Legerstee, 1997a; Trevarthen, 1979), Tomasello also believes that infants are born with the ability to perceive others "like me," which he calls (and I agree) "a uniquely human biological adaptation which is present in the first months of life" (1999, p. 309). This ability allows infants to align themselves with their interactive partner. He also uses neonatal imitation as an example of this phenomenon. However, for Tomasello "like me" does not allow infants insights into people's mental states, at least not until 9 months of age. That is, he argues that only at around 9 months of age do infants begin to use different means to attain the same goal, which (à la Piaget, 1954) puts the infant in the category of an intentional being. It is only at that moment that the infant through the "like me" mechanism begins to perceive others also as intentional beings (here he departs from Piaget, 1954 who proposes that infants do not perceive others as intentional beings until the end of the sensori-motor period). For Tomasello (see Carpenter et al., 1998) the constellation of triadic behaviors or joint attentional abilities (infant interaction with people involving objects) appear simultaneously at that time (but see contrary evidence in chapters 6 and 8) and herald the beginning of the infant as a psychological being.

As discussed above, it is clear that not all theorists believe that infants go from a period where they are behaviorists to one where they become psychologists, and if they do believe that infants progress from sharing actions to sharing mental states (cf. Meltzoff), they may not see the 9-month period as revolutionary in this regard. It is interesting that Tomasello (1999) criticizes the starting state nativism stance of Meltzoff for not explaining how the process of "like me" is related to the learning system, in particular how the "like me" stance is responsible for the emergence of complex joint attention behaviors at 9 to 12 months. It would seem to me that Tomasello (1995) does not provide an explanation either. In fact there is no empirical research, nor a detailed theoretical analysis by Tomasello, that has focused on the first 6–9 months of life. Nor is there an explanation in Tomasello's account of how the infant progresses from being a behavioral to a psychological organism during the first 9 months of life.

Tomasello (1999) does not believe that the complex dyadic interactions in which infants engage during the first 2 months of life involve "turn-taking," during which infants share their affective states, thereby revealing their "inter-subjective" nature (Trevarthen, 1979). He proposes that Trevarthen sees this inter-subjective nature as the result of an innate sense of "the virtual other," which would seem an "innate sense that others are 'like Me.' " In support of Trevarthen, Bruner (1999) also argues that infants from birth "seem motivated to bring things at the focus of their experience to the attention of others." Bruner calls this "mutual awareness" and argues that this ability provides evidence that infants have an innate capacity to appreciate that humans share the same world.

It is interesting that although many researchers are quick to label the infant actions toward physical objects as goal directed (e.g. the 4-month-old infant reaches for an object that is closer than the one out of reach: the reach is goal directed; von Hofsten, 1982) they are less inclined to attribute a goal to the social interactions infants engage in at such an early age (see Tronick, 2003, for an excellent discussion on this topic). It is difficult to believe that infants can have intentions to reach for one of two inanimate objects, but not an intention to communicate their feelings with interlocutors. Like Trevarthen (1979), Bruner (1973) also proposes that infants are born with particular behaviors that are pre-adapted to achieve their goals and which are different for the social and nonsocial domain. The *endogenous* or innate action pattern infants use to interact with people are elicited by appropriate social stimulation, but are not under the control of reinforcement. Instead these skilled social activities, albeit rudimentary, are planned actions and are, from the beginning, under the control of mentally represented intentions. It is these representations that propel infants toward their goals. Thus rather than developing representations through acting on the world at the end of the sensori-motor period (cf. Piaget, 1954), Bruner puts intentions at the onset of skilled activity.

It should not be surprising that human infants have innate action skills that facilitate their interaction with conspecifics. Many nonhuman species have innate responses that are specific to their own species. Gotlieb (1991, p. 6) calls these actions species specific perceptions. He argues that "usually patterns of stimulation are provided by other members of the species to which others react."

Schaffer (1971) said almost a quarter of a century ago, "from birth, the infant is equipped with a species-specific cognitive structure which ensures that he is selectively attuned to certain types of environmental stimuli" (p. 37). In later writings, Schaffer speaks of the infants' "social pre-adaptation, when referring to predispositions to selectively attend to particular kinds of stimuli and to structure its responses in particular ways" (p. 192). He also proposed that ... "on the auditory as on the visual side, infants arrive in the world especially attuned to stimulation provided by other people" (p. 193). Emde (1989) agrees that "the infant comes to the world with a biological preparedness for participating in social interaction" (p. 38) and he also stresses the role of affect in relationship experiences. Astington (2001) further observes that infants seem to be tuned into people right from the start, although she argues that innateness does not necessarily mean that a function is there right from birth. Tager-Flusberg (1989) was more specific in her acclamations. She argued that sensitivity to species-interaction patterns is essential not only for social interaction, but for the development of a Theory of Mind.

Exogenous factors

Together, the endogenous stepping stones are viewed as one of the essential prerequisites to the infant's understanding of people and their minds (Hobson, 1998). Other developments are viewed as external convergent or supporting (*exogenous*) factors. As I have argued earlier, the role that *social interaction* plays is seen as an essential convergent influence in the infant's understanding of people's gestures, actions, verbalizations, and facial expressions, but also their intentions, desires, and beliefs. Although I will discuss the various theories that address the social interactions infants engage in in later chapters, it is important to outline the theoretical model here in order to properly frame the empirical research in the following chapters. Suffice it to say that the endogenous and exogenous factors interact in the developmental process and facilitate the development of a Theory of Mind.

Endogenous and exogenous factors and their interaction

The finding that infants have specific modules or predispositions that give infants a leg up in learning about people (Legerstee, 1991b; Trevarthen 1979; Bruner, 1975) supports the view proposed earlier that an understanding of the physical and the psychological develops separately. If initially the development of the physical and the social are driven by domain specific rather than domain general principles, then changes can occur independently in each domain rather than simultaneously. Evidence for such reasoning is supported by the finding that object permanence occurs earlier in the social rather than the physical domain. For instance, Legerstee (1994b) conducted a study to investigate the development of search for objects that differed in animacy (people versus toys) and familiarity (mother versus stranger, laboratory versus home toy) in infants 6, 8, and 10 months old. The results showed that when infants were required to search for their mothers and familiar objects who interacted with them under similar conditions (games of hide and seek) the infants looked for their mothers earlier than for inanimate objects.

Most theories emphasize that endogenous and exogenous factors interact in the developmental process (e.g. classical cognitivists, social-cognitivists, dynamic-systems theorists, constraint-constructivists). However, there are those who focus uniquely on either the endogenous processes (modularists) or the exogenous processes (e.g. environmental behaviorists). Actually, even within the interactionist positions, authors may still emphasize the endogenous over the exogenous factors (or vice versa) in their conception of development.

Although most developmental theories emphasize how infants' cognitive structures change through interacting with things in the environment, they differ in the amount of preparedness they attribute to this development. As asked in chapter 1, how do the theorists link up the infant with the environment? If these linkages are provided by reflexes then these theorists are on the low end of the "preparedness" spectrum, and on the high end of the role of development (either through associative learning or construction), and if these linkages are modules, then these theories are on the high end of the preparedness spectrum (and on the low end of subsequent development or construction). The trade-off is that the more the infant has innate modules (endogenous capacities) for the acquisition of a certain kind of knowledge, the less the infant can benefit from experience (exogenous factors).

Piaget and cognitive structures

As explained earlier, according to Piaget (1954), infants are at birth devoid of any cognitive structures. Infants come equipped with reflexes and biological mechanisms of assimilation, accommodation, and equilibration. Thus infants do not have domain specific (endogenous) knowledge that gives them a head start. Instead, through exercising their reflexes, infants develop cognitive structures that in turn allow for more advanced actions on the environment. These actions Piaget called action schemas. As a consequence, human infants go through a lengthy period during which they do not think. Only near the end of the sensori-motor period, by about 18–24 months, do infants become able to represent the world in a conceptual manner. At that time, the action schemas change into mental schemas allowing infants to form concepts of things that can be recalled. Thus, during the second year of life there is a gradual shift from subjective understanding to an objective understanding of things. Piaget called these first two years in the infant's life the sensori-motor period. During this time infants only possess *perceptual* knowledge. During perceptual differentiation, infants rely on immediate sensory stimulation that distinguishes people from things. During conceptual differentiation, infants rely on more enduring traits to discriminate between the two classes. These enduring traits are available to the child in the absence of perceptual stimulation. Thus, conceptual differentiation implies that infants represent this knowledge mentally rather than perceptually. They can think about people and things and recall them when they are absent. It is only when infants understand that people and things continue to exist when not perceptually discernible that infants are beginning to separate themselves from the external world and to place themselves within a common space with other objects (Bremner, 1988) (see chapter 4 for a more detailed discussion of perceptual and conceptual awareness). The end of the sensori-motor period, then, marks the beginning of thought. According to Piaget, infants at this stage are becoming social and their responses intentional. It is only at this particular point that people are differentiated from objects on their social dimensions rather than physical ones.

As a consequence of accumulated evidence of infant awareness of the internal states of others at an age Piaget had not predicted, Piagetian constructivist theory was challenged. Many theorists incorporated and acknowledged the newly discovered precursory abilities to a Theory of Mind during infancy, although they remained primarily constructivist (e.g. Flavell, 1988; 1999). Recently, more contemporary theories have been developed that challenged Piaget's theory, either by proposing that an understanding of a Theory of Mind is innate (Fodor, 1983; Baron-Cohen, 1991; Premack, 1991) or by arguing in favor of an integration of nativist and constructivist principles (Chapman, 1992; Karmiloff-Smith, 1998; Legerstee, 2001a; 1998; 1997a; Wellman, 1993).

Behaviorism and cognitive structures

The view that infants do not have cognitive structures at birth, but are instead equipped with reflexes that connect the infant to the world, is similar to the behaviorist assumption that infants are born with minds that resemble blank slates, i.e. *tabula rasa*. Behaviorism, like Piagetian theory, proposes that infants start life with domain general, biologically specified processes, such as physiological perceptual systems and a general learning mechanism that operate according to the laws of associative and imitative learning and conditioning.

Because Piagetian and Behavioral theorists propose that infants at birth do not have innate structures to make sense of input (endogenous factors), infants initially view the world full of chaotic stimuli that are perceived through unintegrated sensory modalities. Although there are some similarities in the way the Piagetian and Behavioral theorists view the infants at birth, there are many important differences that distinguish the theories. The Piagetian child constructs an understanding of the mind after living two years relying on perceptual experiences. The Behavioral theorists never talk about the mind in their theorizing, and consequently there is not a whole lot of talk about the developing Theory of Mind.

The two schools have also different views about *the motivational* level of the child. Whereas the Behavioral child is viewed as a passive recipient of environmental stimulation with a hedonistic nature, whose behaviors are conditioned through reinforcers, the Piagetian child is an active creature who is affectively motivated to interact with the world. Already during the reflexive stage (0–1 months), the inquisitive infants, through the biological processes of assimilation and accommodation, transform their reflexive actions into action schemas through actively interacting with the environment. When that happens, cognitive structures develop that then give rise to more advanced interactions with the physical and social worlds.

Nativism and cognitive structures

Baron-Cohen's nativist account of the development of Theory of Mind proposes that infants are born with specific precursors to Theory of Mind. He hesitates to call these modules (in the Fodorian sense), preferring the term "neurological mechanisms" that mature at different developmental times as a function of neural maturation (endogenous factors) rather than as the result of an interaction with conspecifics (exogenous factors). According to Karmiloff-Smith (1992, p. 6) one should not confuse modules with domains. A domain consists of representations of a specific area of knowledge, e.g. linguistic, physics etc., but "a module is an information processing unit that houses this knowledge as well the computations on it." Thus modules are much more rigid and less plastic; as a consequence, modules provide the infants with more information at the beginning, but they are less amenable to change. Empirical evidence has shown that the mind and its intellectual processes have a large range of reactions to environmental input. This suggests that the ontogeny of the structure of the mind and its resulting products are much more variable than the modular position suggests.

Baron-Cohen's (1991) model accounts for the development of intentionality in infants based on the maturation of the three endogenous factors without crediting the social milieu for an influence in this process.

The three neuro-cognitive mechanisms mature between birth and 18 months. They are the intentionality detector (ID), which is a primitive perceptual mechanism that interprets directional (motion) stimuli as being volitional. Anything that is self-propelled is agent-like until knowledge is updated and corrected. The eye direction detector (EDD) detects the presence of eyes or eye-like stimuli and infers from the direction of the eyes whether gaze is directed to self or to other (social or nonsocial object), and infers that eye direction leads to seeing. Both the ID and the EDD function from birth to around 9 months and infer intentions from dyadic situations. The operation of these two modules leads to the maturation of the shared attention mechanism (SAM) between 9 and 11 months, allowing infants to perceive meaning in triadic relationships. SAM makes ID's output available to EDD. Infants become able to infer the other's interest about a third object during joint attentional interactions. The final module to mature at 1.5 to 2 years of age is the Theory of Mind mechanism (ToMM). The ToMM provides infants with the ability to represent epistemic mental states (pretending, thinking, knowing, believing, imagining, dreaming, guessing, deceiving etc.).

The module most important for the early perception of intentionality is the ID which allows the infants to "read mental states of goal and desire into a wide range of stimuli" (p. 517) that appear to move by themselves. However, the idea that intentionality is activated by a certain pattern of motions, such as self-propelled motion or motion with respect to a particular goal, is an interesting hypothesis. It is contradicted by findings that soon after birth, infants interact differently with animate and inanimate objects even when the motions of the two objects are kept constant (Spelke, Phillips, and Woodward, 1995). For instance, Legerstee (1997b) showed that when people and objects interacted contingently with 3-month-olds, infants smiled and cooed at people but not at the inanimate objects (toys that were surreptitiously manipulated by an experimenter). Secondly, there are many apparent self-propelled items (cars, airplanes, and sneezes) that are not animate. Thus movement alone will not work in identifying animates. In addition, Baron-Cohen's assertion that the modules mature without the help of social partners is not supported by empirical findings. Muir and Hains (1999) write in a detailed paper assessing Baron-Cohen's (1991) theory, "what stands out is that infant sensitivity was revealed only by a change in affective behaviour (e.g., smiling), while their visual attention seems to be captured by any of the novel adult behaviours." This suggests different bases for the responses: looking may be driven by more general learning mechanisms, whereas smiles and vocalizations have a potential social significance. Thus, it would seem that rather than using infant looking behaviour to infer infants' understanding of socio-cognitive capacities such as Theory of Mind development, infants' social responses need to be taken into account. These social responses are only elicited by social objects that move independently and not by inanimate objects (Legerstee, 1992; 1997b). These findings highlight the suggestion that interacting with people is essential for the development of ToM in infants.

Dynamic systems and cognitive structures

The idea that the environment is important for development is also supported by dynamic systems theorists who argue that "a fundamental property of any developing living systems is that it is open to and inter-active with its particular environment" (Schore, 2000, p. 158). They further propose that the infant *actively* seeks and modulates its behavior in relation to this environmental input, which input in dynamics systems theory refers to the social environment. Thus, rather than a tabula rasa on which the environment makes its imprints, dynamic systems theorists see infants as active organisms that come prepared to participate in human relationships in order to expose themselves to socio-emotional learning that is required for growth of endogenous factors (see Fischer, Shaver, and Carnochan, 1990). This interaction between exogenous and endogenous factors and its quality, influences the future route of self-organization (e.g. the emergence of new developmental forms) such as the development of awareness of people's minds. Fogel's (1993) immensely captivating book is devoted to developing through relationships. Fogel argues per-suasively that "an attempt to comprehend the human mind and self that is not grounded in theory of personal relationships may sprout and grow but it is unlikely to yield edible fruit and attractive flowers: Human cognition and the sense of self are fundamentally and originally relational" (p. 4). Relationships are viewed as dynamic systems which are created out of repeated interactions between caretaker and infant. As a result, these relationships develop stable and consensual frames, until something happens within the relationship, perhaps as a result of the creativity of co-regulation, and the dyad shifts to a different level in the relationship.

Constraint constructivism and cognitive structures

Constraint constructivists also see the infant as an active organism that contributes to its own development from birth. Rather than proposing that infants are born with a module to perceive mental states in others, constraint constructivists suggest that infants have domain specific pre-dispositions (*endogenous factors*) that direct them to the necessary input for Theory of Mind reasoning. A full fledged ToM is constructed through interacting with people (*exogenous factors*) (Karmiloff-Smith, 1992; Tager-Flusberg, 1989).

In my view, normal socio-emotional and cognitive development is based on the infants' abilities to perceive that from the beginning they are similar to other human beings. Subsequent development is a function of this perception of similarity, and the interaction infants have with their conspecifics. The infants' innate predispositions are specific to understanding social objects and different from those infants use to act on inanimate objects. In chapter 3, the infants' ability to differentiate between the social and nonsocial world will be discussed in detail.

Infant methodology

Before presenting empirical data in support of the various theoretical positions and hypotheses discussed so far in this book and which will be presented in the following chapters, it is important to briefly introduce the major paradigms for studying infants, e.g. the "whys and the what's" (Bornstein and Lamb, 1992, p. 61). In other words, we need to focus on how an understanding of infant abilities has and is being arrived at.

Much of Piaget's work on infants was conducted with his own three children. Although Piaget's experimental manipulations were very ingenious, his method was primarily observational and involved the infants' active manual responses. The problem with this approach is that there may be confounds between physical and intellectual capacities with such methods. For instance, Piaget (1954) assessed object permanence in infants through a manual search task. In order to be successful on this object permanence task, infants had to lift up a cloth with one hand and pick up the hidden toy with the other. Such coordinated actions requiring infants to retrieve objects are sensori-motor behaviors that are too complex for infants less than 8 months of age, and can therefore not be used reliably to assess conceptual knowledge in younger infants. Over the past forty years, alternative methods have been developed specifically to study infants. These new infant methodologies focus on other and more passive response systems of infants such as their looking and sucking rather than on active manual participation. These measures are used to determine whether infants discriminate between various visual and auditory stimuli. For instance, in preferential looking paradigms, infants are presented with two stimuli side by side. If infants look longer at one stimulus than the other, it is agreed that infants discriminate between the two stimuli. (Of course, one needs to counterbalance the positions of the stimuli among the infants to make sure that infants do not have a particular bias looking to one stimulus over the other or looking in a particular direction over the other.) Thus if we want to find out whether infants discriminate between two different faces, we present infants repeatedly with one of the faces until the infant looks away. It is of course possible that the infant is tired or has fallen asleep and therefore looks away. However, if the infant regains interest and increases looking when presented with the other face, it is likely that the infant discriminates between the two stimuli.

A method that relies less on spontaneous preferences is the habituation paradigm. After infants have looked at a particular stimulus, they decrease looking; in other words, infants habituate to the stimulus. Habituation can also be used as a discrimination measure. The infant is presented with a particular stimulus and, when the infant looks away, another stimulus is presented. If the infant dishabituates (increases looking) then it is possible to assume that the infant discriminates between the two stimuli. The idea is that if infants do not discriminate between the two stimuli, infants should not dishabituate.

Another way to assess preference or discrimination of stimuli is to use the non-nutritive sucking paradigm. This paradigm is useful for auditory stimuli, e.g. when the stimuli are not visible. Infants are allowed to suck on a pacifier wired to a recorder and are presented with auditory stimuli. For instance if we want to find out whether infants discriminate between the phonemes /ba/ and /pa/ we may (after having acquired a sucking baseline from the infants) present the infants with the phoneme /ba/ /ba/ /ba/. We will notice an increase from baseline and then a decrease in sucking (habituation). The infant is then presented with the phoneme /pa/ /pa/ /pa/. If infants' sucking recovers, then it can be said that infants discriminate between the two sets of phonemes.

The problem with these methods is that although we can deduce preference from this kind of discrimination, if infants do not show preference, e.g. do not differentiate in the amount of looking or sucking for one stimulus over the other, this does not necessarily mean that infants do not discriminate between the two classes. Infants may prefer them equally. By changing subtle features of the stimuli, the reasons why infants fail to discriminate can be further investigated.

Habituation techniques can also be used to test infant expectations or beliefs about physical and social events. Infants tend to look longer at novel than at familiar events (Spelke, 1985). In a typical experiment, infants are presented with two events, a possible and impossible event. The possible event is consistent with the belief examined in the experiment and the impossible event violates this belief. Thus, if infants have a belief that objects continue to exist when occluded by another object, then they look longer (are surprised) when this belief is violated. Using this violation-of-expectation paradigm, Baillargeon and her colleagues (1993) showed that already by 2 to 3 months infants are aware that objects continue to exist when out of sight. This experiment, and many others conducted by Elisabeth Spelke and her colleagues, indicated that soon after birth infants were sensitive to some elementary laws of physics.

Habituation paradigms can also be used to test infants' understanding of social principles. I had shown in earlier work that when infants are presented with people and inanimate objects (e.g. graspable toys), the infants will communicate with persons but try to grasp the toy (see Legerstee, 1992 for an overview of this work). In a subsequent study I wanted to find out whether this differential responsiveness was the result of what the infants saw (e.g. reacted to the physical difference between the stimuli) or whether these responses were a consequence of something deeper, e.g. whether infants used social rules to make this distinction, namely that one communicates with social stimuli, but acts on inanimates. To test for this hypothesis, I familiarized infants with a scene where an adult was talking to something hidden behind an occluder (Legerstee, Barna, and DiAdamo, 2000). After familiarization, infants were presented with two stimuli, a person and a broom. During this test event, infants looked longer at the broom than at the person. This demonstrates that infants found it surprising that people would talk to inanimate objects. These findings suggest that infants understand that people communicate and interact at a distance with other people, but not with inanimate objects.

Thus, habituation studies, when properly controlled for alternative interpretations such as task specific learning and when sufficiently replicated, can provide evidence for an awareness of social understanding soon after birth, and the existence of domain specific principles that facilitate and propel learning.

If infants learn through interacting with people, and if the quality of these interactions influences this development, then infants must not only be studied in interaction paradigms, but the dependent measures obtained during these interactions must be analyzed in such a way that the individual contributions of the participants are being revealed. Thus, if one argues that "child development is shaped by a cumulative experience of a co-constructed interactive process between parent and child" (Hui-Chin Hsu and Fogel, 2003, p. 1061), then one must not only devise a particular method that emphasizes this dyadic relationship, but one needs to measure this relationship between the exogenous and endogenous factors with statistical analyses that reveals something about the reciprocity of the interaction. Sequential loglinear analyses can reveal interesting contingencies between the interactive strategies of mothers and the communicative behaviors of their infants which high-lights the reciprocal nature of these dynamic communicative interactions (Fogel and Hannan, 1985; Legerstee et al., 1990; Legerstee, Van Beek, and Varghese, 2002). Despite the significance of the reciprocal nature of parent–child interaction, the extent to which the dyadic interactions are symmetrical, asymmetrical, and unilateral needs to be determined and the effect of the communicative history of the dyad (recent or not) on the self-organization processes of the dyadic system needs to be revealed. Guided by dynamic systems theory, Hsu and Fogel (2003) examined the stability and transition in mother–infant face-to-face communication during the first 6 months of life. Three important methodological and statistical requirements had been implemented: (1) the development of a coding system that used the behaviors of both interactants as the unit of analysis, (2) the use of a design that revealed the dynamic process of the commu-nicative dyad as it develops over time, and (3) the use of a statistical procedure that allowed the researchers to examine the influence of "cumu-lative history" on the presently observed communicative interactions. The results of these ambitious methodological and statistical techniques allowed the authors to reveal the relational, dynamical, and historical nature of mother–infant communication during the first 6 months.

In the next chapter I will not only focus on infants' interactions with people, but I will provide empirical evidence that infant interactions with people are different from those they have with inanimate objects. These findings suggest that infants appear born with specific responses for animate and inanimate objects.

3   Animate/inanimate distinction

Relationship between social and nonsocial cognition

In chapter 2, I argued that infants are born with innate domains that contain representations about people, as well as particular principles on how to interact with them. If that is true, then it follows that infants must have different domains that contain representations of physical objects. That infants have specific domains for interacting with people and objects should not be surprising. People and inanimate objects differ in significant ways, and consequently the rules and regulations on how to interact with the physical domain should be different from those we use to interact with people. This suggests that an understanding of the social and the physical develops differently. In the present chapter, I will discuss the development of the animate/inanimate distinction in infants.[1] Not only does knowing how the animate/inanimate distinction develops in children shed light on the sociality of infants, but as introduced above, it addresses the larger theoretical question of how social and nonsocial cognition are related (Gelman and Spelke, 1981; Glick, 1978). According to domain general theorists, cognition is unitary and people and nonsocial objects come to be known through the same cognitive processes. In brief, Piaget (1952) proposed that infants have abstract domain general principles that initially reveal people as an object among all objects. Through interacting with people infants come to understand them as subjects among objects. However, in chapter 2, I have provided evidence to show that researchers who have begun to study people do not regard the social domain of knowing as similar to the classical developmental models of cognitive knowing (e.g. Glick and Clarke-Stewart, 1978). For example, whereas the movement of things is predictable from knowing how the physical forces act upon them, people can move themselves (Glick, 1978; Hoffman, 1981). In addition, people seem far more complex to deal

---

[1] Parts of this chapter have been published in Legerstee, 1992; Legerstee, 1997a, b.

with than inanimate things. Physical objects can be specified because they present stable and predictable reactions; social events are subtle and their unpredictability is often beyond complete specification (Gellman and Spelke, 1981). Given the differences between the physical and social domains, we might expect knowledge about the two domains to be processed differently.

In disputing this idea, domain general theorists argue that infants react differently to people and objects because of perceptual differences between them. They propose that if some of the physical stimuli of people such as self-propelled movement (Premack, 1991; Gergely et al., 1995; Rakison and Poulin-Dubois, 2000), eyes, hands, or sounds (Johnson, Slaughter, and Carey, 1998; Johnson, Booth, and O'Hearn, 2001) or contingent movement (Watson, 1972; 1985), were associated with non-social objects, infants would not respond differentially to the two classes. One way to examine these predictions is to conduct studies in which these variables are controlled (Legerstee, 1992; 1994a; 1994b; 1997a; 1997b; Legerstee, Barna, and DiAdamo, 2000; Legerstee and Barillas, 2003; Legerstee and Markova, 2005). In the present chapter, I like to provide such empirical evidence. This evidence shows that infant discriminations of people and inanimate agents runs deeper and does not depend purely on superficial physical phenomena.

Definition of the animate/inanimate distinction

In 1981, Rochel Gelman and Elisabeth Spelke wrote a fascinating paper in which they gave a detailed account of what a mature concept of people and objects should contain. They noted that although people and objects are similar in that both have physical properties (size and shape), the two classes are different because only people communicate, grow and reproduce, move independently, have feelings, intentions, and thoughts. Not only do people and objects have different properties, but they are perceived differently. When looking at people, we may initially notice their appearance and their behavior, but we tend to focus primarily on their mental states such as emotions and intentions. Objects do not have inner states and therefore we would only pay attention to the physical characteristics of objects and their functions. As a consequence of these differences, adults interact differently with the two classes. They communicate with people but act on objects. When communicating with people, interlocutors expect them to reciprocate verbally or with actions, whereas they do not expect inanimate objects to reciprocate. In order to get nonsocial objects to move, one has to manipulate them. Adults also focus on the emotions and intentions of people, but on the physical attributes of inanimate objects. Thus adults understand that people have mental states and self-generated movement and can communicate. More importantly, however, they develop different relationships with people than with non-social objects.

Relationships with people are complex, involving emotions and social rules. These emotions can be strong and may enhance or interfere with subsequent cognitive processes. The emotions aroused when interacting with physical objects are usually less intense, and are the result of whether one is successful or not at accomplishing a task (Hoffman, 1981; Legerstee, 1997a).

Theoretical perspectives on the animate/inanimate distinction

Because the ability to differentiate people from other things is foundational for human development, theorists as diverse as Piaget (1954), Rheingold (1961), Watson (1972), Bruner (1973), and Trevarthen (1979) have described in detail how *infants* come to distinguish people from things. Although, for modular theorists, infants are precocious cognizers and consequently differentiate between people and nonsocial objects veridically, it would seem that many attributes adults use in their discrimination of people and nonsocial objects are later developments for children and are constructed through interaction with environmental stimuli. They are later developments because they are initially not necessary for the child to begin the road of ascribing psychological properties to people. As discussed earlier, the innate representations infants have of people allow them to identify people as similar to the self, with emotions and intentions, but not with complex biological processes such as the ideas that people grow and reproduce. These concepts are being constructed with age (Gelman and Coley, 1990; Gelman and Markam, 1986).

Piaget's view on the animate/inanimate distinction (animism)

For Piaget (1954) the question of how infants develop an understanding of the animate/inanimate distinction has been addressed in his studies on communication, animism, and causality. Because infants have no initial cognitive structures (no innate knowledge), infants at birth are neither social nor cognitive creatures. They gradually learn to differentiate between self, other people, and inanimate objects during the first two years of life, at which time they develop expectations about the behavior of people and recognize that people have intentions. Thus, the traditional Piagetian assumption proposes that an understanding of the social and physical world needs to be constructed through acting on it during the infancy period. Consequently, prior to the concrete operational stage, infants confuse mental and physical events (animism) and they do not differentiate between external and internal states (e.g. talking and thinking). However, empirical evidence has challenged Piaget's position on animism (see Rakison and Poulin-Dubois, 2000; Legerstee, 1992; 1997a; 2001b for reviews).

New research has shown that even preschoolers can distinguish between the mental and the physical when verbal tasks are being used (Carey, 1985), and that infants as young as 18 months begin to treat human behavior as intentional and distinct from that of nonsocial objects when nonverbal tasks are used (Meltzoff, 1995; see also Rakison and Poulin-Dubois, 2000).

Research with younger infants, using traditional perceptual methods that relied solely on infant gazes to assess their sensitivity to changes in various configurations of people and nonsocial objects (e.g. line drawings, pictures, and video recordings of objects and faces) (cf. Muir, Cao, and Entremont, 1994), initially supported Piagetian theorizing. These authors hypothesized that the reduction of social information to "simpler" forms would bring out the essential feature cues of "social meaning," thereby making recognition of the meaning easier. However, recent research has suggested that the removal of dynamic and temporal components of social stimuli disadvantages infants by removing information that is essential for an awareness of sociality. By having infants judge two-dimensional information rather than observing infants in social situations one removes essential social cues. This makes the tasks more difficult for infants, and instead of measuring social awareness, one measures the infants' information processing capacities (Moore, Hobson, Lee, and Anderson, 1992).

Social interactionists showed that when infants were observed with people and nonsocial objects in natural settings, a completely different picture emerged. Already in the second month of life, infants treated people as social objects, smiling, vocalizing, and imitating their actions, whereas they treat nonsocial objects as things to be looked at and goals for attempted reaching (Legerstee, 1992; 1991a; Legerstee, Corter, and Kienapple, 1990; Legerstee et al., 1987). Such differential responsiveness has also been found in infants with Down syndrome, at an age when the infants had approximately the same mental age or level of perceptual-cognitive sophistication as the nondelayed infants (Legerstee and Bowman, 1989; Legerstee, Bowman, and Fels, 1992). This empirical convergence is certainly interesting (see figure 3.1).

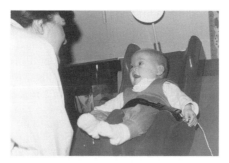

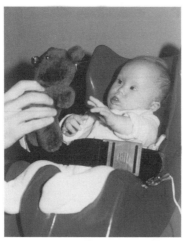

Figure 3.1 Six-month-old infant with Down syndrome smiles at mother and grasps for toy.

Young infants also expect people to act reciprocally. Infants as young as 5 weeks will get upset when people refrain from responding, but not when physical objects remain immobile (Legerstee et al., 1987); and they will imitate mouth opening and tongue protrusions modeled by people, but they do not react this way to objects simulating these gestures (Legerstee, 1991b). In addition, 3-month-old infants have different relationships with people than with nonsocial objects. If people are responsive to infants, 3-month-old babies become happy (i.e. coo, smile etc.) and take in subsequent information faster (i.e. habituate to a multimodal stimulus) than if objects act contingently to infant actions. However, if people act in a random way, infants become distressed and fail to habituate to subsequent cognitive tasks. In contrast, if nonsocial objects respond at random to the infants' actions, this does not upset the infants, and it does not seem to affect their subsequent interactions with the external environment (Legerstee, 1997b). Thus, even for very young infants, relationships with people evoke more intense emotions than interactions with nonsocial objects, and only the relationships with people seem to affect their motivation to learn.

Not only do these results show that infants react differently with social and nonsocial objects, but the results suggest that "infants use dynamic information in the perception of a world of spatially connected, separately moveable, whole, permanent objects, in the first 5 months of life, long before theories based on static assumptions have led us to believe" (Butterworth, 1990, p. 63).

Motion theorists

What accounts for the manifestation of differential responsiveness to people and nonsocial objects in such young babies? Many recent attempts to explain how the infant's differential responsiveness to people and nonsocial objects comes about have focused on *movement*. One of the most obvious differences between people and things is contained in the word "animate." Human beings are seen as the origin of motion, as internally motivated, sometimes as a center of consciousness (Legerstee, 1998). That is, they are seen as having an internal locus of causality (DeCharmes, 1968). Piaget (1954) acknowledged this distinction in his writings when he discussed different developmental patterns in favor of person over nonsocial object permanence toward the end of the sensorimotor period. He explained this difference by proposing that infants noticed people to be independent sources of causality and not nonsocial objects, and consequently people are more cognitively motivating to infants than objects and should therefore produce more rapid accommodations than nonsocial objects. It could be argued of course that the finding that infants have a different onset of a conceptual understanding for people over objects, and subsequent different developmental paths for animate and inanimates, provides evidence for specific domains from which this knowledge is generated. However, Piaget argued that this type of difference in development was the result of "horizontal decalage," e.g. a difference in performance rather than competence. He argued that although infants acquired a level of competence for the two classes simultaneously (supporting a domain general approach), they would show this competence (e.g. object permanence) sooner for people (performance), because people were more attractive stimuli to infants (see Legerstee, 1994a; 1994b). Rakison and Poulin-Dubois (2000, p. 1) also argue for domain general learning and focus on motion as the initial cue which infants use to differentiate between people and inanimate agents. The authors list the type of motion that differentiates people from objects into the following properties: (1) onset of motion (self-propelled vs. caused motion), (2) line of trajectory (smooth vs. irregular), (3) causal action (from a distance versus contact), (4) pattern of interaction (contingent vs. noncontingent). Human movements contain most of these four characteristics, and although most theorists emphasize one of the four characteristics over the other, it is understood that the pattern of human interactions is contingent, is self-propelled, have irregular lines of trajectory and are more often caused from a distance.

By using motion characteristics to argue that infants differentiate between people and objects, researchers not only argue for a domain general mechanism but they are essentially saying that infants use surface features to distinguish between people and objects. That is, they argue that infants use perceptual aspects rather than conceptual aspects. As pointed out in chapter 1, various theorists propose that some type of conceptual understanding of people is present at birth (as a result of domain specific knowledge), whereas others argue that infants convert perceptual attributes or features into conceptual knowledge later on (domain generalists).

In the remaining part of the chapter, I will discuss in some detail theories that have addressed the animate/inanimate distinction. Because I am interested in the foundation of the animate/inanimate distinction and its relationship to Theory of Mind reasoning later on, I will focus on theories that have put in place specific principles or modules used by infants to differentiate between people and objects during the first year of life.

Contingency analysis – Watson A contingency theory has been presented by Watson (1972; 1985) to explain how infants adapt to their social and nonsocial environments. In a seminal paper written in 1972, called "Smiling, Cooing and the Game," Watson proposed that infants had to learn to differentiate between people and objects. He argued that infants were born with an innate module, e.g. a contingency detection mechanism (CDM). During the first 3 months of life, the CDM is preset to prefer perfect contingencies, which enables infants to differentiate between self and the external environment (e.g. the infant puts head on pillow; infant touches mother, etc.). It is not until 3 months of life that the CDM begins to prefer imperfect contingencies. If infants perceive imperfect contingencies between their behavior and rewarding environmental responses, they smile and coo. Thus by 3 months of age, any contingent response stimulus (social and nonsocial) will elicit attention and positive affect in infants. In contrast, any non-contingently acting stimulus may elicit inattention and neutral affect in the infant. However, if infants have had contingent experiences with the stimulus in the past and the nature of the stimulus becomes momentarily ambiguous or uncertain, fear and negative affect may arise. However, according to Watson (1985) it is the perception of intermittent contingencies that allows infants to differentiate between people and objects, because in the natural environment only people respond in intermittent ways to infant actions.

That infants are sensitive to contingencies has been well supported in the literature. Watson (1972) and Watson and Ramey (1972) showed that infants can learn about contingencies involving nonsocial objects when in a controlled environment. They tested whether infants would increase the movement of a leg, attached to a rotating mobile, in order to make it move. They exposed 2-month-old infants to ten minutes of non-contingent mobile rotations on each of fourteen consecutive days. When the infants were subsequently brought into the laboratory and allowed to control the movements of the mobile they failed to learn the task (transfer effect). This was in contrast to the experimental infants. Their prior exposure to a contingent mobile over the same 2-week period facilitated learning of a subsequent contingency task. In another experiment, Watson supported his assertion that by 3 months, infants become more aroused by "imperfect, but clear contingencies," by showing that the infant's kicking response increased when (a) 50 percent of their responses were reinforced, and (b) they received six non-contingent responses per minute, but that virtually no increase in the kicking response was shown after continuous reinforcements.

Thus, according to Watson (1972), infants use imperfect contingencies to separate people from objects, and because infants do not prefer imperfect contingencies until 3 months of age, they do not differentially respond to people and objects until that age. In chapter 10, I will be discussing a study that would refute the idea that infants prior to 3 months of age are not sensitive to intermittent responding (see Markova and Legerstee, in press), and in the present study I am refuting the idea that infants are equally sensitive to contingencies of both people and physical objects (e.g. dolls) (Legerstee, 1997b).

In follow up studies using both social and nonsocial stimuli, it has been shown that transfer effects were obtained with social stimuli in both naturalistic settings (Dunham and Dunham, 1990), and after training practices (DeCasper and Carstens, 1981). Studies using nonsocial stimuli have failed to produce consistent evidence for transfer effects (Finkelstein and Ramey, 1977; Gekoski and Fagan, 1984; Millar, 1972; Ramey and Finkelstein, 1978). It is possible that these differences are related to the many methodological differences of the nonsocial contingency studies. However, if this is so, then transfer task failures should be equally evident when social stimuli are used, since these studies had different methods also. A more plausible hypothesis has been proposed by Dunham et al. (1989, p. 1494). In that study, 3-month-old infants who had received a contingent reinforcement schedule where the experimenter vocalized and touched the infant's feet each time the baby vocalized responded with social behaviors (smiled and cooed), and on a subsequent transfer task showed more initial interest and habituated quicker to a multimodal stimulus than infants who had received non-contingent stimulation. These infants appeared distressed and showed little interest in a multi-modal stimulus on the subsequent transfer task. However, infants in the control group, who were confronted with a continuously rotating mobile (nonsocial object), did not produce negative or positive affect and on the transfer task showed more interest in the multimodal stimulus than infants in the non-contingent social group. The authors suggested that the "use of *social* stimulation during the contingent/non-contingent pre-treatment phases of the paradigm may be of critical importance in the transfer effects that were obtained."

If by 3 months infants are more sensitive to contingent responding of people than of objects (when the reinforcement schedule is controlled), then infant social behavior cannot be a generalized response to activity levels as suggested by Watson (1985). Rather the infants' affective states may be the result of the dynamics of the communicative exchanges infants have with their social partners. This has important implications for social and cognitive development of infants because it suggests that certain social experiences can produce changes in 3-month-old infants that generalize (transfer) to cognitive functioning. It can be expected that if experienced continuously, inadequate interactive signals of either the infant or the caregiver could have long-term consequences for further development.

To find out whether infants react differently to contingently respond-ing people and objects and whether these interactions affect their subse-quent cognitive performance, infants need to be observed in an experiment that will pit various levels of contingency of people and objects against each other in one experimental paradigm. Some time ago I conducted such a study (Legerstee, 1997b). The responses of 3-month-old infants to persons and objects that interacted with the infants at two levels of contingency were contrasted in two experiments. In Experiment 1, contingent responding of people and objects was con-trolled. In Experiment 2, the facial/vocal dynamics were controlled as well as contingent responding. In both experiments, contingent interaction had different effects on infants, depending on whether the "actor" was a person or an object. In addition, the contingency and person/object variables influenced infants' states of attention to a non-social stimulus on subsequent transfer tasks. Specifically, infants who experienced contingent interactions with people exhibited positive affect and exposed themselves to subsequent higher levels of stimulation than infants who experienced non-contingent interactions with people. These infants exhibited negative affective states and exposed themselves to very low levels of subsequent stimulation. In contrast, infants who experienced contingent and non-contingent interactions with objects did not show such variation in emotional expressions. Instead they produced primarily neutral facial expressions in all conditions and did not show very high nor very low levels of interest for the multimodal stimulus on the subsequent transfer task.

By responding differentially to people and objects despite similar contingent movements and face-like features of both the person and the object (a doll), infants indicated that they had rudimentary categories of the two classes that did not rely on these features. Watson would perhaps explain the results by arguing that the perception of contingency initially defines the category 'social' for infants, but that the history of contingency learning (variable social reinforcement versus immediate nonsocial reinforcement) from birth to 3 months creates a difference in 3-month-old infants' reactions to nonsocial objects. However, it is difficult to see how infants can form social and nonsocial categories from birth to 3 months through a process of differential conditioning. Although by 3 months of age infants may have had ample practice playing contingency games with people, it is likely that in the natural world infants would have had little experience with objects to perceive and analyze "perfect and clear contingencies" given their limited motor abilities (e.g. reaching and grasping) to manipulate and act on objects independently.

Watson (1972, p. 1087) himself states that during the first two to three months, the combination of slow response recovery and short contingency memory prohibits the infant of becoming aware of contingencies between his behavior and its stimulus effects in the physical environment.

Motion alone is not enough – Gelman The results of the Legerstee (1997b) study suggest that rather than having an innate ability to perceive contingencies, infants have domain specific knowledge by which to recognize people and thus separate them from inanimate objects. For instance, Gelman, Durgin, and Kaufman (1995) argued that infants are born with domain specific structures which draw infants' attention to the various details that distinguish animates from inanimates. The animate structures specify that people (and other animates) are capable of self-generated movements and the inanimate structures specify that objects need agents to move them. However, Gelman does not believe that the distinction between people and objects is made on a perceptual (spatio-temporal) level, because, as she argues, perceptual information is usually ambiguous or incomplete. Rather, the structures allow infants to interpret movement of objects differently depending on whether the movement is made by animate or inanimate objects. Gelman and colleagues (1995, p. 183) wrote: "If we encounter a round object in the desert with needles we may think it is a cactus until it begins to move, then we realize that it is an echidna and would not maintain that it was a cactus on what it looked like initially." Thus, according to Gelman, infants interpret perceptual information from both movement and external features when drawing conclusions about the animate/inanimate distinction. However, even if infants are aware that animates can move by themselves and should look a certain way, it would seem that in order to classify animates as human, they need to appreciate that humans act according to certain social rules. Various authors view the ability to perceive intentions in others as a prerequisite to a conceptual understanding of people. They argue that it allows for a clear differentiation between the social and the physical (Frye, 1981).

Rakison and Poulin-Dubois (2000) agree that in addition to various forms of movement, psychological features (goal-directed vs. no aim) and an influence of mental states (intentional vs. accidental) are used by infants to make the animate/inanimate distinction. However, according to the authors, the psychological features are extracted from sensory input before 2 years of age. Infants possess an associative learning mechanism that, when triggered by sensory input, establishes correlations between two characteristics and thus brings about expectations in the child about the properties of either animate or inanimates. Subsequent experience facilitates the recognition of people as prototypes of animates due to repeated observations.

Although I have argued elsewhere that both physical and psychological characteristics are important in developing a concept of animacy (Legerstee, 2001a, b), it is difficult to see how psychological categories can be created through the establishment of an association between two perceptually observable characteristics without the introduction of constraints on such learning. It would seem a mystery how children come to have a concept of an intentional agent by observing a self-propelled object moving toward a goal, if we consider that there are many ambiguous stimuli (e.g. remote controlled toy cars, etc.) (see also Gelman et al., 1995). From an evolutionary point of view, it would seem unsound that infants at birth come equipped with a representation of a relationship between two physical variables, rather than a notion of people as psychological beings; it would seem that perceiving people as psychological is more adaptive to a social animal.[2]

In addition, perceiving people as social before the second year of life, rather than as a self-moving contingently interacting object, would explain why infants interact socially with others and not with contingently moving objects (Legerstee, 1997b). Infants must be extracting some type of information not available in physical objects, such as emotional sharing (cf. Hoffman, 1981) that makes it attractive to engage in communicative interactions with people only.

To conclude, the perception of movements (Rakison and Poulin-Dubois, 2000; Premack, 1991) or bodily acts that are "like me" (Meltzoff and colleagues) has been provided as the basis for the animate/inanimate distinction in infants. These positions essentially assume that there is a time in the life of the infant that they are asocial creatures. What is the evidence for such proposition? On the theoretical front Baldwin (1902, cited in Hobson, 1990) proposes that very early in life infants respond to "suggestions of personality" in the behavior of others and thereby differentiate people from other things. Thus, for Baldwin, experience of others is grounded in specific ways of "instinctive" communication.

How would "suggestions of personality" be identified in young babies? In chapter 2, I discussed the idea put forth by others (cf. Bruner, 1973; Fogel, 1993; Schaffer, 1984; Trevarthen, 1979) that infants are born with certain predispositions to respond to people. Indeed, on the perceptual level, infants react differently to people and objects soon after birth (see Legerstee, 1992, for an overview), suggesting that infants are born with a preference for social stimuli and an ability to interact with them, but they also recognize people as similar to the self because they imitate people, but not inanimate agents simulating these gestures (Legerstee, 1991b). Thus infants noticed the movements of social and nonsocial stimuli but only imitated those produced by social objects. Note that the Legerstee (1991b) study contradicts the idea that the appearance of any "self moving object" provides infants with the notion that they are facing a social object. This imitative responsiveness of infants to people and not to physical objects not only suggests that imitation is a social response, but it would support the contention put forth by Gelman and Spelke (1981, p. 54) that "the infant implicitly 'knows' that he and another person can act in

[2] Gabriela Markova.

kind." This is particularly important in face to face interaction during the early days. Infants do not only imitate the non-affective facial gestures (tongue protrusion and mouth opening as presented in the laboratory), but they also imitate human emotions during natural interactions (Field, Woodson, Greenberg, and Cohen, 1982). Thus, in addition to revealing a preference for people over inanimate objects, infants perceive similarities between the human model and the self and consequently engage in communicative matching with them. By imitating the emotions of others, infants share affect, and become aware of equivalences between their own and others' mental states. This early, simple recognition of people as similar becomes multifaceted through more sophisticated forms of affective exchanges. It is through these inter-subjective forms of interaction that a more complex conceptual understanding of a person is constructed (Chapman, 1992; Legerstee, 1997a). Thus through a process of self-organization and the role of adults as co-regulators, infants advance in emotional awareness which would seem essential to the infants' own intentional behavior and an awareness of mental states in others (Freeman, 2000; Fogel and Thelen, 1987).

In summary, as explained in chapter 2, infants are born with endogenous processes to perceive people as similar to them. This recognition is not based on movement, facial features, hands, or cross-modal equivalences; rather, it is based on affective awareness. It is this innate affective awareness that allows infants to perceive others to be "like me." Subsequent sharing of emotions allows infants to recognize their own mental states as well as providing a glimpse into the mental states of others. The importance of affective sharing is underscored by empirical evidence demonstrating the negative consequences when caretakers lack emotional sensitivity in their interactions with infants. In chapter 7, I will discuss how lack of sensitivity to infant emotions confuses infant objects relations (Freud, 1949; Mahler, Pine, and Bergman, 1975) and delays subsequent social and cognitive competence (Legerstee and Varghese, 2001; Legerstee, Van Beek, and Varghese, 2002). In the remaining part of this chapter I will discuss studies that appear to support the idea that infants differentiate between people and objects soon after birth.

Infant abilities to differentiate between people and objects: the first 6 months

The finding that infants can imitate proprioceptive actions (which they cannot see themselves perform) during the first 8–10 months of life contradicts the accounts of classical constructivists (Piagetian) and social learning theorists (Bandura, 1962). As discussed earlier, according to these theorists, infants do not have endogenous processes or cross-modal perceptual abilities to recognize that they are like other people. Instead, infants have to learn through manual indices (touching the face of their caretaker and then the self) (Piaget, 1954), or conditioning (Bandura, 1962) that their faces are similar to that of their conspecifics. As a result, infants would only become able to imitate proprioceptive actions such as facial features by the end of the first year.

As noticed, between birth and 3 months, infants discriminate in their responses between people and objects when perceptual cues are controlled for. Infants' responses to people appear social in nature (Legerstee, 1992). Cognitive developmental theorists but also learning theorists would view such data merely as preferential responding to some type of stimulation originating from people but not from objects. Although so far I have discussed infants' appreciation of the differences between people and objects in paradigms where the different perceptual stimuli were controlled, it is still possible that infants were responding to the perception of some other, partially confounding stimulus dimension.

As discussed earlier, when presented with people and objects, infants communicate with people and manipulate toys (Legerstee et al., 1987; 1990). To determine whether this finding was the result of a more profound awareness of people rather than of perceptually available indices, I conducted a study in which the responses of 4-month-old infants to hidden people and objects were investigated in a game of hide and seek (Legerstee, 1994b). The results showed that infants vocalized toward the occluder behind which the person had disappeared, but reached toward the occluder behind which they had seen the inanimate object disappear (the object was hidden by an invisible experimenter). The fact that infants used different types of responses to bring the objects back to view suggests that infants were aware of the properties (internal workings) of people and things in the absence of perceptual cues. Infants appreciated that people can reciprocate and that their actions can be caused at a distance but that inanimate objects need contact.

Although these naturalistic studies indicate that infants were competent social perceivers during the first months of life and differentiate in their responses between animate and inanimate objects, they do not show what infants' expectations are about the behavior of *others*. In particular, it is unclear whether infants expect others to talk to people and to manipulate objects. If infants perceive *others* to be like the self, then any changes that occur within the infant correspond to similar changes infants perceive in others. I addressed this particular question in the following study (Legerstee, Barna, DiAdamo, 2000; see also Molina, Van de Walle,

Condry, and Spelke, E. S., in press). We habituated one group of 6-month-old infants to a person who talked (see figure 3.2a) and another group of infants to a person who reached while facing an occluder (see figure 3.3a). Thus the infants only saw people talk and act toward an occluder (see figures 3.2a and 3.3a).

The hypothesis was that if infants construe people as entities who are self-propelled and capable of independent movement (agents), who can interact from a distance, then infants would be surprised (measured by longer looks) if it was revealed that people were talking to a broom (figure 3.2b) rather than a person (figure 3.2c). After habituation, infants were shown what the person had acted/talked toward, namely, either a broom or a person. Infants who previously had been habituated to an actor talking and smiling looked longer when they were shown a broom in the subsequent test event (figure 3.2b). Infants who previously had been habituated to an actor reaching, looked longer when they were presented with a person (see figure 3.3b). What do these results reveal about the infants' understanding of the psychological states of people? I like to argue that the infants' differential responsiveness during the test events may not indicate that 6-month-old infants understand human actions as the result of the person's thoughts or beliefs, but it does suggest that they construe the actions such as talking and reaching as goal directed instead of just movements. In this experiment, this understanding relies on two factors. First, the infants' own ability for intentional action, e.g. they talk to people in order to communicate a message to them, and they manipulate objects in order to get them to move. Second, the infants' abilities to make inferences about the behavior of people. Infants had to infer that the adult's actions were indeed directed toward something they could not see, but they also had to remember this experience when they eventually saw the person and objects alone.

The materialist argument against continuities

The interpretation of the data in the Legerstee et al. (2000) study indicating that 6-month-old infants use inference (rather than an associative mechanism; see also Rakison and Poulin-Dubois, 2000 discussed above) to determine what object the actor was acting upon was criticized by Gergely (2001). Although Gergely admits that our experiment "is a well-designed habituation study with proper controls and clear-cut results indicating that 6-month-old infants expect people to talk to persons rather than inanimate objects, and to physically manipulate inanimate objects rather than persons" he took issue with the interpretation put forth. Gergely pointed to the data *he* had collected with this

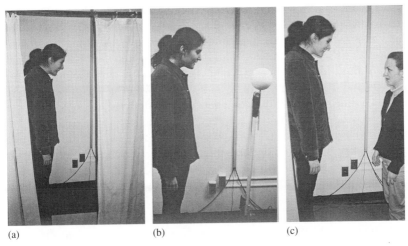

(a)   (b)   (c)

Figure 3.2 (a) Person talking to occluder, (b) Person talking to broom, (c) Person talking to person.

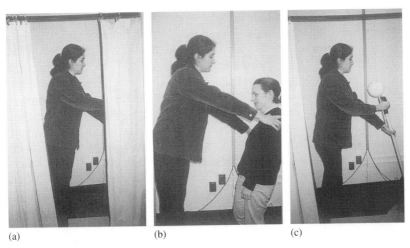

(a)   (b)   (c)

Figure 3.3 (a) Person reaching behind occluder, (b) Person manipulating person, (c) Person manipulating broom.

colleagues (Csibra et al., 1999; Gergely et al., 1995) to argue that 6-month-old infants do not use theory driven inference. How valid is this argument? In his studies, the authors habituated 6- to 12-month-old infants to a display of a small circle that had to move over an obstacle in order to reach a larger circle. In the test phases, infants were shown the same display without the obstacle. Infants either saw the small circle move straight toward the large circle (rational event, new action) or they saw the small circle jump over nothing to reach the large circle (non-rational event, old action). The infants looked significantly longer at the non-rational old action, compared to the new one. Gergely argued that 9- and 12-month-old infants, but not 6-month-olds, were able to evaluate the rationality of the agents' goal directed actions. "As our controls make it clear, this inference to a novel means action is not based on previous associations, but stems from the infants' emerging naive theory of rational action which assumes that agents pursue their goals in the most efficient manner available to them given the constraints of reality" (Gergely et al., 1995). Thus, according to these findings, somewhere between 6 and 9 months infants become sensitive to two broad types of motions (self-motion vs. caused motion), two types of trajectories (goal directed vs. random), and two types of contingency motion (at a distance vs. direct physical contact). In the natural environment, self-propelled, goal-directed motions are associated with animates (people and animals), whereas inanimate objects are set in motion and do not pursue goals. A critical issue not answered in the study of Gergely and colleagues is whether infants have started to associate each type of motion with a specific object (Legerstee, 2001b; Poulin-Dubois, 1999). Experiments where infants view inanimate objects moving in particular ways (e.g. Ball, 1973; for a review see Spelke et al., 1995) can only clarify the infants' knowledge of physical principles. If one interprets the differential attentional pattern infants display to inanimate objects which move in different ways as an indicator that infants infer that "agents pursue goals in the most efficient manner," then this implies that infants are confused about these movements because they attribute animate properties (goals, agency) to non-living things. This is called *animism*. It would seem that in order to provide evidence of an awareness of goal directness/agency, infants should be tested in one paradigm where animate and inanimate objects are pitted against each other. Only these paradigms can be used to shed light on how infants perceive animate objects (of which a person is the prototype for infants; cf. Carey, 1985), and inanimate objects. Woodward (1998; see also Leslie, 1984) showed that when a hand and a rod moved toward a goal (toy) at either the left or right side of the screen, infants dishabituated to the hand, but not to the rod, when the goal changed, while the path on which they traveled remained the same. On the contrary, they dishabituated to the rod, and not to the hand, when the path changed while the goal (toy) remained the same. Together, the above studies show that during the first 6 months infants encode the behaviors of animate and inanimate objects differently. They attribute goal directness to people only.

Infants perceive intentions in people and not in inanimate agents: infants at 10 months

In a now landmark study with 18-month-olds, Meltzoff (1995) revealed that when people and a surrogate object failed to complete a task (e.g. pulled a dumbbell apart) infants only completed the movements of people (e.g. they pulled the dumbbell apart) but not those of the inanimate agent. Because the infants imitated what the actors intended to do, without seeing the end state performed, they must have known that there was more to the physical actions the person produced. That is, infants were aware of the internal states of people that drove these actions and knew that the observable actions were only part of the intended acts. The finding that infants completed the intended acts of people and not of surrogate objects suggests that their attribution of intentions is specific to people.

Meltzoff's (1995) study provided a useful paradigm to assess an awareness of others' intentions in imitation research, and stimulated further investigations aimed at determining the onset and the meaning of this ability. For instance, Bellagamba and Tomasello (1999) replicated the finding for 18- but not for 12-month-olds. Only the 18-month-olds completed the target acts without having seen them modeled before. In addition, when infants were only shown the end state (e.g. the separated two parts of the dumbbell in the same location), neither 12- nor 18-month-olds reproduced the target acts as often as they had after seeing the unsuccessful or completed acts. In a later article, the authors argued that the task may either have been too complex for these young infants, or that perhaps more demonstrations were needed for successful completion of the task (Carpenter et al., 1998).

There is some evidence that, at least by 15 months, infants are able to complete the unsuccessful actions modeled to them. Johnson et al. (2001) presented infants with a stuffed orangutan puppet that was handled by an experimenter out of the infant's view, to embody the behavior of an intentional agent (the presence of a face, eyes, self-generated movement, and contingent behavior). Because the infants completed the unsuccessful actions of the orangutan puppet, the authors proposed that 15-month-old infants have a conceptual representation of a mental agent, which can be evoked by faces, hands, and displays of reciprocal behaviors.

While Johnson et al.'s (2001) findings may shed light on infants' sensitivity to some key features, such as the presence of a face and independent and reciprocal responding, the lack of a person condition against which the inanimate agent condition should be compared leaves open the possibility that at 15 months infants respond to others on the basis of physical acts. In a recent study, conducted with my student Yarixa Barillas (Legerstee and Barillas, 2003; see chapter 5), we found that 12-month-old infants produced intentional actions, such as declarative pointing, to people but not to a non-human agent (an independently reciprocating toy dog, with contingently blinking eyes).

From the available evidence so far, it is not clear whether imitation with objects in infants younger than 18 months (cf. Meltzoff, 1995) reveals an understanding of the intentions behind people's actions. Not all forms of imitative behavior at that age necessarily entail an understanding of others as intentional agents. *Mimicry* involves blindly reproducing the demonstrator's behavior, without understanding the goal, whereas *emulation* refers to reproducing the end result without regard for the demonstrator's actual behavior or behavioral strategies and goals (Bellagamba and Tomasello, 1999). *Stimulus enhancement* occurs when infants manipulate objects simply out of curiosity after the adult has picked up an object and does something with it. Mimicry, emulation, and stimulus enhancement are types of social learning that do not require an understanding of others as intentional agents. Intentional imitation occurs when infants show that they are aware of the person's intentions behind the action. Most of the classical studies on infant imitation toward the end of the first year of life do not reveal whether infants are engaging in simple mimicry or intentional imitation, because these studies did not incorporate the necessary controls. Thus, together, the findings do not provide a definitive answer to whether infant imitation reveals the intentional stance in infants.

Inspired by Meltzoff (1995), in a recent study (Legerstee and Markova, 2005) we used the re-enactment paradigm to investigate whether 10-month-old infants would complete unsuccessful actions of people and inanimate agents. No research had investigated the relationship between imitation, the concept of intention, and the concept of animacy in 10-month-old infants. In the present experiment, the inanimate agent embodied some of the characteristics that have been said to imply the presence of a mind (cf. Johnson et al., 2001), such as the physical stimuli of a face, hands, and independent movements. Consequently, in our test situations, we presented infants with a human and non-human model (a dog). Both demonstrated either a completed or an unsuccessful act to determine whether "infants interpreted the behavior of social and non-social agents in purely physical terms, or whether they too read through the literal body movements to the underlying goal or intention of the act" (Meltzoff, 1995, p. 846). To find out whether the infants naturally perform the actions without modeling and to control for stimulus enhancement, infants were also presented with a baseline, during which either the human or the non-human model manipulated the test items without showing the target act. Thus, the infants' tendency to perform the target act was compared in several situations: (a) After they saw the test items being manipulated but the target act was neither shown nor attempted, (b) after the target act was demonstrated completely, and (c) after an unsuccessful attempt to perform the target act was demonstrated.

We hypothesized that because infants between 9 and 12 months have been shown to (1) imitate complex and novel actions with objects (Kaye and Marcus, 1981; Killen and Uzgiris, 1981; Meltzoff, 1988), and (2) perceive people and not inanimate agents as intentional beings (Legerstee and Barillas, 2003), 10-month-old infants should complete the unsuccessful actions of people, but not those of inanimate agents.

Thirty 10-month-old infants were administered three tasks, (1) a put in task, (2) a take out task, and (3) a brushing task. Each task had a baseline and a completed action, and a baseline and an unsuccessful action demonstration. These tasks were administered by a person and an inanimate agent. The person (E) exposed a clear view of her face. She was instructed to display a friendly but neutral facial expression, and not to speak so that she could not reinforce the responses of the infants and so that she remained comparable in responsiveness to the inanimate agent.

The inanimate agent also had a neutral/friendly facial expression. The inanimate agent was a large stuffed brown and beige animal dog (Big Dog, BD). BD possessed a face, arms, hands, and exhibited independent and reciprocal movements, features thought to identify mentalist agents to infants (Johnson et al., 2001). BD was of the same height as the human agent when sitting down. BD wore a sweater that covered his body and front paws. The long sleeves of the sweater had been removed. They were worn instead by E. She stood behind a white curtain that separated her from BD. The curtain had strategically located openings through which E could put her arms. Thus hidden behind the curtain, with her arms covered with BD's sleeves, E was able to manipulate surreptitiously the test objects, making it appear as if BD performed the actions independently. In order to monitor the accuracy of her actions in the BD condition, E observed her actions on a video monitor on her left side. E wore gloves in both the human and non-human conditions. She was trained to perform the same actions in the same manner for the E or BD condition. Ten-month-old infants are less physically able to perform the relatively fine hand–eye coordination required to reproduce the target acts than the 15- and 18-month-old infants who reportedly were successful in the re-enactment paradigm. In the studies by Meltzoff (1995) and Johnson et al. (2001), coding focused on whether the infants produced the target act or not. As suggested by Kaye and Marcus (1981), a microanalysis of imitative behaviors needs to be employed in the coding scheme, in order to capture the imitative approximations toward the target act (see also Moerk, 1989). Consequently, we developed a detailed analysis of the various imitative infant behaviors, with the goal to provide some insight into the behavioral strategies underlying infants' imitative responses. All coding was done from videotapes. Infant responses were assigned a score ranging from 1 to 5, depending on the extent to which the infants' responses approximated the target act (e.g. putting an object into its container, taking it out from its container, or brushing with the brush on the plate) as follows: (1) No approximation to the target act. The infant does not produce any of the component actions of the target act. Infant just picks up objects, puts objects in mouth, bangs objects, throws objects on floor, etc.; (2) slight approximation to the target act. The infant approximates the modeled action, e.g. lifts up the toys and puts them down but does not let the objects touch each other and is low on complexity of component acts; (3) higher order component acts. Infant may lift up and put down the test objects, as if to put one object into or take it out of the container, or as if to brush the plate. Objects may touch each other, but target act is not reproduced; (4) very close to reproducing target act. Test objects touch, toy is moved above the container, and may even be clumsily dumped into, taken out of, or touched several times on container/ plate; (5) full and immediate production of the target act. The following figures show the infants' imitative responses to the person in the completed put in task (figure 3.4), and to the inanimate agent in the completed take out task (figure 3.5) and the unsuccessful brushing task (figure 3.6) respectively.

Recall that the purpose of the present research was to investigate whether infants would imitate completed and unsuccessful actions of people only, or whether they would imitate these actions also of inanimate agents that embodied the behavior of an intentional agent (the presence of a face, eyes, self-generated movement, and contingent behaviors). We found that infants imitated the completed actions of both the person and the inanimate agent. Does this mean that infants ascribe a purpose and a goal to both the human and non-human model? Apparently, some accul-turated non-human primates imitate the actions of others. For example, the habit of potato washing may have been transmitted through imitation in Macaques (Nishida, 1986). Regardless of whether the data on primates is reliable or not (Tomasello, 1996), the reproduction of visible actions cannot be a valid indicator of an awareness of the model's mental state. In order to demonstrate such abilities, infants would need to infer what the model intended or wanted to do. The ability to infer what the model's

Figure 3.4 Infant imitating action in completed put in task in person condition.

Figure 3.5 Infant imitating action in completed take out task in inanimate agent condition.

Figure 3.6 Infant imitating action in unsuccessful brushing task in inanimate agent condition.

intentions were was assessed in the unsuccessful action tasks. In contrast to imitation of completed acts, imitation of unsuccessful acts cannot be the result of perceptual cues, because the target of the unsuccessful act remains invisible. We found that completing the unsuccessful acts was constrained to people only, and did not generalize to a broader category such as the inanimate object that looked and acted like a human. The data support developmental trends evident in the early months. From an early age, infants categorize people and objects as distinct as indexed by their differential responsiveness to each entity (see Legerstee, 1992; 1997b; 2001a; Rakison and Poulin-Dubois, 2000; Spelke et al., 1995 for a review).

Taken together, the results of each of the three tasks revealed that during the unsuccessful person condition, the infants completed the target act, whereas during the unsuccessful inanimate agent condition the infants did not. This differential responsiveness in the human and non-human conditions provides an argument against the idea that infants complete actions of people as a result of emulation learning. If the infants had reproduced the target acts during the unsuccessful test trial without regard for the behavioral strategies or goals, then the infants would have behaved similarly in both the person and inanimate agent condition. These findings suggest that by 10 months, infants perceive people, and not inanimate agents, as intentional beings that have purposes and goals.

The animate/inanimate distinction: cue based or domain specific representations

What the various experiments with people and inanimate objects have shown (for reviews see Legerstee, 1992; 2001a; Spelke et al., 1995) is that when physical features (such as face and movement) of the animate and inanimate objects are controlled, infants still differentiate between the two classes. During their first months of life, infants communicate with responsive people, but not with dolls (equated on movement, size, and novelty with the person) (Legerstee, 1991b; Legerstee et al., 1987). Between 2–3 months, infants expect people to share affective states with them, but they do not have such expectations about inanimate objects (Legerstee and Varghese, 2001; Legerstee et al., 1990). By 5 months, infants recognize their own faces and voices as familiar stimuli and differentiate them from those of peers and inanimate objects (Legerstee et al., 1998). By 4 months, infants will call for people, but reach for toys that have disappeared behind an occluder (Legerstee, 1994a), and by 6 months infants expect people to communicate with persons and to manipulate inanimate objects (Legerstee et al., 2000). By 10 months, infants perceive intentions in the actions of people, but not in those of inanimate agents (Legerstee and Markova, 2005), and by 12 months, infants can be conditioned to follow the gazes of people and inanimate agents, but they point to people only in order to direct their attention to interesting events (Legerstee and Barillas, 2003, see chapter 5).

In my opinion, infants interact differentially with social and nonsocial objects, and have different expectations about them, because they have innate predispositions that contain representations about each domain. This domain specific knowledge gives infants a leg up in the developmental process. Infants subsequently learn about the two classes through both frequencies of occurrences of particular actions and constraints on the particular relations among these occurrences. Although the precise nature of these constraints is unclear (they can range from innate intuitions to precise rules), infants could not have concepts without these endogenous factors. They need associations to detect new input and domain specific principles to guide the inquiry (Keil, Smith, Simons, and Levin, 1998).

In this chapter, I have relied on perceptual as well as conceptual evidence of the animate/inanimate distinction to show that when the physical differences of people and inanimate objects are controlled, infants still discriminate between the two classes. I have further shown that infants' represented knowledge of people allows them to predict how people will act in particular circumstances. This represented knowledge, partly present in domain specific modules, and partly acquired through associations, reveals the infant's growing awareness of people. This increasingly sophisticated social understanding prepares the child for the acquisition of a Theory of Mind.

4   Self and consciousness

I know that I exist, the question is, what is this "I" that I know?

Descartes

Although infant differential responsiveness to people and objects and their relatively advanced social relationships lend credence to the idea that infants have developed a concept of people, an important feature of a concept of a person is that it is distinguished from the self. "One's concept of self is a concept of a person; one's concept of persons cannot be a concept applicable only to a single individual (one-self), for the reason that in this case it would no longer constitute a concept" (Hobson, 1990, p. 165).

The ability to identify with others and to distinguish between self and other plays an important role in inter-subjective relationships. Human adaptation involves an understanding of others, but also an understanding of the self as different from others. Indeed, the self cannot be viewed in isolation from our view of others, but relies deeply on how we represent people. Thus the self is perceived in relation to the other (Fogel, 1993). As discussed in chapter 3, the "other" can of course be the physical as well as the social environment. Infants discriminate between self and inanimate *agents*, and between the self and the other person. The development of a concept of self is seen as a pivotal aspect of social development, and is an important and necessary condition in the identification of others and self as social.

How does a concept of self develop, and when is it acquired? The answer to this question depends on one's theoretical orientation and on how one defines "a concept of self." The concept of self is a multifaceted phenomenon. It involves more than recognition of perceptual features of the self and a differentiation of *animate* and *inanimate* objects in the environment (Legerstee et al., 1998). Thus, an understanding of the self must involve an awareness of the physical, social/mental, and representational aspects of the self (Legerstee, 1998; Legerstee et al., 1998). I would like to state from the start what this argument is not; namely that infants have an adult concept of the self. The concept of self, like other concepts, may have its roots in early infancy, but a mature concept of self is constructed with age and increases in complexity throughout childhood. However, I do not believe that infants ever experience a symbiotic-like phase (cf. Piaget, 1954; Mahler, Pine, and Bergman, 1975). I have argued earlier that infants are conscious of their own emotions and are able to recognize similar emotions in others. This way infants form shared representations of the emotions of self and others, suggesting that infants represent the other as similar in some way, as "like me." Thus there is self – other awareness through the mutual sharing of emotions in infants (Trevarthen, 1979). These shared representations overlap in meaning at times, but they are also distinct. Like Stern (1985, pp. 41–42) I posit that infants from the beginning of life have "biases and preferences"; have a capacity "to form and test hypotheses" and participate in "affective and cognitive processes." This cognitive and affective functioning is unified and is not experienced separately by the child, but it is distinguished from that of others.

In the present chapter I discuss the various aspects of self-awareness in infants, focusing primarily on the earliest representations infants have of the self. Because awareness of the mental self is defined differently and consequently has a different developmental timetable according to different theoretical orientations, I will first provide an overview of how the various theories view the development of self-awareness. Some of these theories distinguish between a perceptual and conceptual awareness of the various features of the self. Therefore, I will begin with discussing this difference from both a theoretical and methodological point of view. However, prior to doing so I will present some philosophical reflections on self-awareness.

Philosophical reflections[1]

Since Descartes (1641/1985), philosophers and psychologists have endeavored to explain human existence. Descartes suggested that he knew that he existed because he thought. However, even if people have immediate evidence for their mental selves, how can they be sure about the existence of their own body, the external world, and even more challenging, how can they be sure about the thoughts and emotions of others? How is it possible to know that what one thinks one perceives of *others* are not simply aspects of one's *own mind*, of one's own imaginations?

---

[1] Portions of this essay have been published in Legerstee, 1998.

The problem of self-awareness is solved neither by adopting a position that eliminates the bodily dimension nor by a position that contests the notion of self-awareness or the mind. Materialists and behavioral neuroscientists propose that the mind is a wholly physical phenomenon. But how do the senses and experiences (e.g. Churchland, 1991; Hume, 1739/1888; Locke, 1710/1975; Watson, 1928; Watson, 1985) lead to self-awareness? Rationalists and empiricist epistemologists, monistic and dualistic mind–body positions are not really able to address the problem of self-awareness as long as they do not address the genetic (in the Piagetian sense of developmental) dimension of this problem. Developmental psychology in general and infancy research in particular have produced a vast literature to address these issues and are able to complement, falsify, or verify philosophical reflection (Teo, 1997). These genetic epistemologists propose that there are several levels of the self – such as the physical, the social, and the mental – that are internal to the mind (e.g. innate) and of which humans become conscious during their first year of life.

Evidence about the development of a self-concept in infancy has, however, proved difficult to find, perhaps because of methodological problems, and consequently many theories that have been developed in this area are speculative. However, in order to interact meaningfully with others, one has to identify oneself as human and similar to others. Thus, the development of a concept of self is fundamental for sociality, for social interaction, and consequently for Theory of Mind development.

Perceptual versus conceptual methods

Before engaging in a more in-depth discussion about the ontogeny of the self by presenting the theoretical positions and the empirical findings that have investigated the development of self, I would like to discuss briefly two issues that I have referred to in earlier chapters, but that need to be analyzed now; namely conceptual and perceptual awareness. I will first discuss these terms from a methodological point of view. I subsequently discuss the theoretical works that address these terms in their frameworks.

In this chapter, the distinction between perceptual and conceptual awareness refers to the different experimental paradigms that researchers employ to assess awareness of certain aspects of the self. Some methods only allow us to infer a perceptual awareness from infant responses, whereas others allow us to interpret that infants possess a conceptual understanding of self, one that is stable, and provides infants with a sense of uniqueness. Experimental paradigms that provide information on perceptual self-awareness in infants often rely on the products of the infant's perceptions of, or direct experience with, environmental stimuli that identify the self. For example, mirror studies can only claim that infants are familiar with certain aspects of the physical self (Legerstee et al., 1998). Such studies provide little direct information about the mental self. Even studies where 18-month-olds wipe off a rouge spot from their forehead can only talk about self-perception or self-recognition. These studies usually rely on the emergence of *other* symbolic types of behaviors *at that age* (language or the tendency to display self-conscious emotions such as embarrassment when noticing the red spot) to argue that mirror self-recognition reveals a conceptual awareness of the self (Lewis and Brooks-Gunn, 1979). Chimps and orangutans also display a form of self-recognition after repeated exposure to their own face (Gallup, 1982). It is possible that these great apes, just like infants, use contingency (when I move so does the image) to identify aspects of the physical self. It is more difficult to show when infants' sense of self is a mental or conceptual ability.

Studies that aim to provide evidence for a conceptual or representational awareness of the self must show that infants are aware of the self in the absence of immediate sensory experience. In this case, infants' identifications of self are products of their mental capacities (e.g. inferences, representations, etc.). Infants would be able to draw on this knowledge when perceptual stimulation is not available. For instance, in chapter 5, I discuss how infants demonstrate that they are aware of being the object of attention during the first months of life, because they respond "with deep-seated emotions" when a person looks at them. It could be argued that infants understand that people show by their gaze direction to what they are psychologically connected. If true, such awareness would be evidence of a mentalistic conception of people, and of the self. I will elaborate on a conceptual awareness of the self later on in the chapter.

In summary, in order to provide evidence for the theoretical assumptions discussed below, it is important to distinguish between a perceptual method, e.g. one that can only assess what the infant sees, hears, e.g. perceives in the environment, and one that relies on what infants infer from internal representations of the self.

Perceptual versus conceptual – theoretical orientations

Many theorists argue that perceptual self-awareness is a precursor to a conceptual awareness of the self (e.g. Berkley, 1975; James, 1890; Mahler et al., 1975; Merleau-Ponty, 1942; Piaget, 1954). These theorists propose that infants go through a period in development where infant awareness of self is related only to what infants perceive of themselves through external or internal physical stimulation. This type of self-concept is not stable or enduring, because it does not exist in the absence of such stimulation. With development, these earliest perceptions about the self are overturned and changed into a more appropriate (realistic), representational awareness of self. When that happens, infants have an enduring self-concept, one that can be accessed through introspection (Piaget, 1954; Barresi and Moore, 1996; Perner, 1991). These positions argue that during the first stage the infant is a behaviorist and during the second stage the infant is a psychologist. The problem with the perception/conception distinction is how one can differentiate between these two cognitive processes (the conceptual or high functioning mode and the experiential or low-functioning cognitive mode) and at the same time explain the emergence of both modes of processing from the same origin: as resulting from interactions among innateness and experience (Pascual-Leone and Johnson, 1998).

Not all authors make the perceptual/conceptual distinction. Many propose that a primitive sort of self-awareness or consciousness exists at birth, and that with development a more complex consciousness develops (Butterworth, 1995; Gallagher, 1996; Gibson, 1995; Kant, 1781; Karmiloff-Smith, 1992; Legerstee, 1997b; Meltzoff, 1990). Whereas the perceptual/conceptual divide proposes that infants develop from an experiential/perceptual-motor to a qualitatively different mental/conceptual awareness of self (Legerstee, 1998, pp. 628–630), those that argue for a continuum in conscious awareness propose that infants develop from primary consciousness, which includes primitive representations of the physical/social as well as the mental aspects of self, to a higher order consciousness, which entails a fully developed concept of self. These theories may also propose that the internal representations of the self become enriched through considerable construction that takes place through interacting with the social *milieu*, thereby creating a strong self-identity and understanding about the self.

Piaget and the self

Piaget (1954) has argued that before infants can understand the self as an independent object, they need to have an understanding of other objects. Because Piaget's theory with regard to the development of a mental self remains influential in more recent theorizing about self-awareness and Theory of Mind, in particular when considering the relationship between perception (action) and conception (representation/operation) (see for instance Frye, 1981), current theories of representation must be contrasted with that of Piaget. Piaget argued that during the first developmental stages (the reflexive, the primary and secondary circular reactions), the infant is in an *adualistic* stage and does not differentiate between self and the environment. Adualistic here means that infants are self-centered; they are not aware of their sociality and mental states, nor are they aware of the environment. The infant's world is basically solipsistic. Infants' actions during this period are repetitive and always centered on the infant's own body. Thus when infants pick up a rattle, the interest of the infant is not focused on the sound the rattle produces, rather infants perceive the rattle simply as an extension of their own arms and continue the actions in a kind of circular, repetitive way for their own pleasure. In a sense the infant is the center of the universe and for the first 8 months of life is pretty well undifferentiated from other objects. During the stage of secondary circular reactions, the actions are also continued for the pleasure they bring, but now the infant perceives that the sound is produced by the rattle, and consequently continues to shake the rattle in order to continue to be able to hear the sound. Although self/other differentiation begins around this point, it is not until stage 6 (around 18 months) that infants become able to represent themselves as different from others and to view themselves as an independent object in space. This is the onset of conceptual knowledge; infants change their subjective understanding of the world and their selves to an objective understanding. Thus Piaget proposes that perceptual awareness precedes and is qualitatively distinct from conceptual awareness and argues for an initial state of dualistic confusion (Piaget, 1954) or of "normal autism" (Freud, 1961; Mahler et al., 1975). After the initial adualistic state, infants enter a state of dualism where a differentiation between self and other social and nonsocial objects are made. Indeed, psycho-analysts such as Mahler (Mahler et al., 1975) argue that at birth the infant is in a symbiotic state (undifferentiated). This state is maintained by caretakers who respond to every whim of their infants. With maturation (at around 10 months of age) most caretakers begin to introduce a "delay of gratification" into their responsiveness. It is then that infants begin to become aware of their surroundings and their self-existence (id/ego differentiation).

Mirror studies initially supported the idea that infants progress from a lack of self-awareness to the existence of one. It was found that infants treated mirrors as objects, playing with them and patting them, and that only by around 18 months did infants begin to view "themselves" in the mirrors. Whereas previously they had touched the mirror, infants now began to touch the red spot on their head that had been surreptitiously put there, or infants became shy (seeing "a spot" on their head) and turn away or cover their faces. However, as indicated above, mirror self-recognition can only be interpreted as perceptual awareness of the self. There are many other ways for infants to identify the self, as is revealed in the theories below.

Bio-social theories and self-awareness

Whereas mirror recognition at 18 months has been heralded as a conceptual awareness of self, many authors place this development earlier. For instance, Hobson (1998) traces the history of thinking about the "self-concept" and argues for a differentiation between what are variously called the ecological versus interpersonal self or "I–It" versus "I–Thou" relations. Hobson argues that infants have a biological propensity to engage in deep emotional (mental) interpersonal relations with others (inter-subjectivity). These social interactions are a precondition for self-reflection and self-consciousness, for indexical thought, and for an objective view of the world. Hobson argues that autistic children have an ecological (I–It) self but not an interpersonal (I–Thou) self. Autistic children lack the biological basis for coherent, affectively patterned experiences and interpersonal relatedness and consequently fail to engage in subjective interactions. They are therefore not aware that they exist in the minds and hearts of others.

Trevarthen (1979) proposes that infants are not only acting and thinking selves as traditional cognitive theorists propose, but like Hobson, Trevarthen argues that infants have an innate need to relate to others. These innate intuitions express themselves during social interactions when infants engage in sensitive and responsive sharing of emotions with their conspecifics. The infants' innate sense of people allows for an interpretation of the affective states that are exchanged during face-to-face communication in terms of emotions, goals, and intentions. All of this implies an awareness of emotions/mental states in self and other.

For Fogel (1993) social interactions play a special role in the development of the self because people not only react, they interact and elaborate on the infant actions. Thus the self is dialogical; the self is experienced as a function of participatory cognition rather than imaginative cognition. As a result of this participatory cognition infants detect self-referent information, but also the individual relationship with the environment (Fogel, 1993, p. 148).

Tronick (2004) argues that infants strongly seek states of interpersonal connectedness, and that failure to achieve connectedness wreaks profound damage on their emotional, mental, and physical health. This is because lack of connectedness with others results in a failure to create meaning. More precisely, lack of connectedness, or the formation of a dyadic state of consciousness, results in a failure to establish or expand the state of consciousness of the self.

Thus, research on the development of inter-subjectivity in infancy reveals that the roots of a conceptual awareness of the self can be identified in early infancy. Maternal affect mirroring and infant species specific sensitivity to her signals reveals a mutuality of affective sharing that suggests that infants are aware of their own communicative contributions. In fact, infants expect others to engage in communication with them, because as the "Still-face" studies show, they become upset and withdrawn when their partners refuse to interact with them (Legerstee et al., 1987; 1989; Legerstee and Varghese, 2001; Tronick, 2004). Thus through interacting with people we *experience* how we are perceived. It allows us to reflect upon ourselves, to analyze our own behavior and thinking, and to encourage self-adaptations. Affective regulation is not only within the infant, or only within the caretaker, it is dyadic, it is co-created (Tronick, 2002). Through you I feel my emotions, I value my actions, and I perceive my "self." Thus the self develops as part of a mutually regulated exchange between caretakers and the infant. Hence, social relationships involve special communications in which the individuals modify their participation on the basis of an evaluation of the other's mental and emotional state (Fogel, 1993).

Ecological theories and self-awareness

Like Trevarthen (1979), and Fogel (1993), Neisser (1993) argues that an important source of information for early self-perception is found in social interactions. Neisser distinguishes between several kinds of selves: the ecological self, the interpersonal self, the extended self, the private self, and the conceptual self. He argues that this initial division is necessary, because there are many different kinds of information on which self-knowledge is based.

Neisser proposes that in the beginning infants have an implicit awareness of self which consists of the ecological self as experienced perceptually through visual flow during movements, through bodily sensations and interactions with physical objects; and the interpersonal self, which is perceived through interaction with others. Like the bio-social theorists, Neisser argues that the interpersonal self emerges early in life and is specified by emotional signals that are directed to the infant by communicative partners. In turn, infants perceive information about the self through systematic effects they have on their partner's behavior. Thus information about the interpersonal self is derived from social interaction.

Neisser proposes, however, that these early selves are directly perceived rather than represented, and that an awareness of the representational or conceptual self does not occur until the second year of life, and corresponds to the infant's successful performance on the mirror recognition task.

Neisser's theory draws on the ecological theory of Gibson (1969; 1995) who proposes that information about the self is veridically perceived. Thus unlike the classical cognitive developmental view in which perception begins with a retinal image that needs to be interpreted, Gibson argues that perception is an activity: "It is the obtaining of information from a dynamic array in the environment surrounding the perceiver. This activity begins immediately at birth (and to some extent before)" (1995, p. 5). Gibson claims that the first awareness of the infant's own body comes through proprioceptive experience, which includes both internal (muscle and joints) receptors and external (visual and auditory) senses. An awareness of self can be specified by simultaneously feeling the muscles and seeing the arms and legs move. The physical and social selves are the first levels to be perceived through bodily movements and social emotional forms of communication respectively. Thus the theory of direct perception proposes that proprioceptive specification of self (internal and external) is possible long before the infant can move around the environment. Consequently, consciousness, which includes a sense of awareness of self as separate from environmental stimuli, appears at the onset of development for this developmental theory rather than at the end of the infancy period (2 years of age).

If the information about the self is directly perceived at birth, does that mean that information about the self includes an awareness of the mental self? Neisser argues that infants in the interpersonal stage engage with others in emotional communication and are influenced by the social overtures of others. If this is true, then infants perceive the mental states of others and the self. Emotions are mental states and infants through interacting with people during periods of emotional attunement indicate that they give meaning to global kinds of emotions initially, such as happiness and sadness (Izard, 1978; Field et al., 1982). According to Bremner (1998, p. 207), "... a social relationship involves a special form of interaction in which the individuals modify their contributions on the basis of assessment of the other's mental and emotional state. Such relationship is a precursor to a Theory of Mind because it is aimed at investigating a particular aspect of knowledge of self and others, knowledge of the 'mental self' and 'mental other'." Based on these arguments it would appear that Neisser's (1993) mental self develops simultaneously to the interpersonal self, namely at the beginning of the infancy period, rather than at the end of the sensori-motor period.

Constraint constructivism and self-awareness

According to the constraint constructivist position, infants from the beginning are conscious of their social and mental selves. Partly, such awareness is the result of the infants' gradual process of modularization which is founded on the infants' domain specific attention biases toward human faces, voices, and movements that facilitate Theory of Mind representations (Karmiloff-Smith, 1992). Partly also, because of the infant's primordial "like me" experiences, which they obtain through imitation, but also through intra and interpersonal awareness, the innate sense of emotional attunement. Through imitation infants may detect bodily equivalences between self and other, because infants not only imitate people, but they are imitated by them as well. However, through their innate sense of emotional attunement infants perceive emotions (simple mental states) in others and recognize these to be similar, or different, from their own emotions (e.g. the self) (Wellman, 1990; Hobson, 1993; Trevarthen, 1979; Tronick, 2003).

What empirical evidence is there to support these theoretical propositions and ideas? Below, I will document some of the available data to reveal that neonates are conscious of their bodily, social, and mental selves.

Consciousness of the physical self

Consciousness of the bodily/physical self would refute the notion that infants begin life unable to separate self from others. Numerous studies have demonstrated that infants are aware of their surroundings and perceive themselves as physical agents. Infants become distressed when hearing a recording of the cries of another infant but not of their own (Dondi, Simion, and Caltran, 1999). Also within the first week infants use visual information to control their posture (Berthenthal and Bai, 1989; Butterworth and Hicks, 1977), and they explore their own bodies, and accommodate their open mouth to their approaching hand (e.g. Butterworth and Hopkins, 1988). Infants also engage in visually guided reaching (Hofsten, 1980). The fact that infants only reach for three-dimensional objects rather than two-dimensional representations of them (Rader and Stern, 1982) indicates that this behavior is not unconscious or reflexive, but that infants perceive the distance of the object relative to their self. Similarly, when infants respond with avoidant reactions to looming objects and not to objects approaching on a "miss" path (Ball and Tronick, 1971; Yonas et al., 1979), they reveal that they are aware that object knowledge and self-knowledge are inseparable.

Further knowledge of the self is evidenced when infants augment non-nutritive sucking to bring a picture into focus (Kalins and Bruner, 1973) and increase the movement of a leg, attached to a rotating mobile, in order to make it move (Rovee-Collier and Fagan, 1981). Infants also appear able to exert control over the environment. Eight-week-old infants can learn to produce interesting events by pulling strings attached to their arms. If the strings are detached, infants get upset and kick harder in order to reproduce the events. Thus, by two months infants show some sense of personal agency, revealing an awareness that they can control the environment in the physical realm.

Awareness of face and voice as familiar and social stimuli

Young babies know that they are separate entities, and are actively involved in investigating the cross-modal equivalences and spatial congruencies that lead them to perceive and learn more about their bodily and social selves during the first months of life. When do infants begin to recognize their face and voice as their own? Between 18 and 24 months of age, when infants see images of self or others, they use pronouns to refer to these images (e.g. me and you) (Legerstee and Feider, 1986). Younger infants have limited linguistic skills. In order to reveal whether infants know that the face they see and the voice they hear are familiar to them, researchers have focused on the infants' recognition of these features.

Face recognition is taken as an important aspect of self-recognition. It is assumed that if infants recognize their own face, they would have an internal representation of their face to which they compared the face in the mirror. The face reveals our emotions and allows us to communicate nonverbally with others. Gallup (1982) demonstrated that recognition of one's own physical features is crucial for the development of an awareness of self in higher primates. In a variety of studies, he found that after three days of experience with mirrors, chimps would change from making threatening gestures to self-directed behaviors such as picking food from their teeth. After ten days of mirror experiences, Gallup first anesthetized the chimps and then painted red marks on their face. When the chimps recovered, they apparently recognized their facial features, because they touched the spots more than marked chimps that did not have mirror experiences. Studies using Gallup's procedure with infants reported that self-recognition as indexed by touching the rouge-spot on their faces did not occur until infants were at least between 18 and 24 months old. Michael Lewis and Brooks-Gunn (1979) asked mothers to apply the rouge-spot surreptitiously while pretending to wipe their infants' faces. The authors predicted that if infants had an idea of what their "self" looked like, e.g. knew who the child in the mirror was, then they would notice, when put in front of a mirror, that the red spot was on their forehead rather than on the face of "another child" and wipe the spot off their own nose. Nine-month-old infants did not touch the spot, between 15 and 17 months infants began to remove the spot, and between 18 and 24 months most infants wiped the spot off their noses.

The rouge task has been criticized methodologically because it is not a suitable task for young infants (competence/performance confound). If infants are born with a biological ability to perceive others as similar to the self in some way, either through the sharing of emotions during the first months of life (Legerstee, 1992; 1994a; 2001a; Fogel, 1993; Hobson, 1989; Reddy, 2003; Trevarthen, 1979; Tronick, 2003) or as expressed through imitating others' acts with the help of cross-modal abilities that allows infants to link proprioceptive acts with perceptual ones as in neonatal imitation (Meltzoff and Moore, 1977; Meltzoff and Gopnik, 1993), then it would suggest that one of the reasons older infants rather than younger infants perform successfully on the mirror task is the result of a better understanding of what the task demands, and a decreasing confusion involving the reflective properties of the mirror (Loveland, 1986).

There are various ways to study the development of self-recognition in infants. In a recent study, Bahrick et al. (1996) showed that infants as young as 5 months recognized their facial features as familiar stimuli. They looked less long at their own previously filmed facial image (indicating familiarity) than at that of a same-aged peer. Although the study by Bahrick et al. (1996) does not show whether infants recognize their face as belonging to self, the findings are of interest because the authors controlled for proprioceptive contingencies. Instead of having babies look in the mirror, in which case they could have distinguished between the faces of their peers and their own faces because of differential contingencies between the visual stimulation of the mirror images and the proprioceptive feedback from their own body motion, the authors showed the infants previously recorded video images of self and a peer. They further controlled for other differences between the infants by dressing them in yellow robes. Because the infants only had featural differences to go by in their differentiation of the faces of peer and self, the authors provided evidence for recognition of the face in the study rather than self-awareness.

The finding that infants recognize their own features suggest that infants perceive some of their facial features as familiar, but it does not reveal whether infants attribute these features to the self nor whether the infant perceives these features as social. A recent study I conducted with

Figure 4.1 Five-month-olds discriminate between moving and immobile faces of self, peer, and dolls.

my students (Legerstee, Anderson, and Schaffer, 1998) showed that some information about the self may be represented in 5–8-month-olds (Legerstee et al., 1998). The paradigm used was a modified version of the one used by Bahrick et al. (1996). All infants received two visits. During the first visit, infants were filmed in interaction with their mothers in order to obtain visual and auditory material of a smiling and cooing baby. Of the 5-minute interaction tape, a 60-second demonstration tape was cut for the second visit. These demonstration tapes showed babies that moved their faces, and vocalized in a burst-and-pause pattern (three successive bursts of vocalizations for a total of approximately six seconds and a one-second pause during which the babies did not vocalize, repeated for a total of 60 seconds). Burst-and-pause patterns were used in order to simulate human interactional patterns. This pattern has been shown to motivate infants to action rather than to mere visual fixation (Legerstee, 1991a, b). During the second visit, the infants were placed in front of a large television screen and were presented with the demonstration tapes of self, a peer, and a doll. The stimuli were all matched on size and hair color and were dressed in yellow robes (see figure 4.1). To examine the role of movement in the recognition of the faces, the images were presented in static and moving conditions. In the moving conditions, the doll was moved externally by an experimenter so that it swayed sideways and up and down, or internally (an experimenter moved the internal abstract facial features of a hand puppet), and the infants moved as they naturally do when interacting with adults. In the static condition the infants saw a frozen image of self, peer, and doll. The moving and static conditions were presented without sound. The results showed that when 5- and 8-month-old infants were presented with silent moving video images of self, peer, and dolls they looked longer at the peer (novelty preference) and least long at self (familiarity) at both ages. However, whereas the 8-month-old infants also looked longer at the static image of the peer (novelty effect) the 5-month-olds looked longer at their own static facial image. The finding that the younger infants found their static facial image unusual but not their moving image supports the suggestion that recognition of one's own image develops through experience with dynamic facial stimulation during the first 5 months of life. Prior to the experiments, we had asked parents to fill out questionnaires about the amount of mirror exposure their babies experienced. These questionnaires revealed that all infants saw themselves at least once a day in the mirror during caretakers' activities. Parents reported that their infants would look first at their caregiver in the mirror, and would then notice themselves. It was when they observed their own face that they began to coo and smile. Our data showed a similar pattern of responsiveness because the infants smiled and cooed more at their own face than at the peer and least toward the doll. This suggests that infants are aided through mirror exposure to identify their own facial features, which are specified both kinesthetically and visually.

In addition to the visual recognition of the face, infants also attend preferentially to human auditory input and recognize their own vocalizations as familiar sounds. In the auditory conditions, infants of both ages were presented with the social demonstration tapes, but now the visual image was obscured, so that only the vocalizations were heard. The nonsocial sounds were made either by bells or by a synthesizer and matched to the rhythm and frequency (burst-pause pattern) of the infant vocalizations. The results showed that the infants looked longer (novelty) when hearing the peer's vocalizations than when hearing their own (familiarity), and least long when hearing the inanimate sounds. Smiles and vocalizations occurred most frequently when infants heard human voices, with most of the vocalizations occurring when they listened to their own voices. Thus, infants not only discriminated between their vocalizations and nonsocial sounds, but they recognized these vocalizations as familiar and similar to sounds they produce themselves. This indicates that the infants' responses were species-, peer, and self specific.

Consciousness of the social and mental self

The above evidence indicates that infants during the first months of life perceive through various forms of proprioception their bodily movements and voice, and through their responsiveness show an awareness of themselves as objects that have bodies and make sounds. Thus, situations that identify the physical self are continuously specified by acoustic, kinesthetic, and vestibular information. Consciousness of the social self becomes evident when infants interact with their conspecifics (Fogel, 1993; Legerstee, 1997b; 1998; 2001a; Legerstee and Bowman, 1989; Legerstee et al., 1990; Neisser, 1993; Stern, 1995; Trevarthen, 1979). Neonates are able to imitate facial expressions modeled by people. Thus infants are able to use proprioceptive feedback from their own facial expressions to match the facial expressions produced by others (Legerstee, 1990; 1991b; Meltzoff and Moore, 1977). These findings suggest that infants are aware of their own body schema. This body schema is present as a "psychological primitive from the earliest phases of infancy" (Meltzoff, 1990, p. 160). Although the ability to imitate proprioceptive movements need not rely on representation, as shown in earlier works (Legerstee, 1991b) it is not reflexive nor an unconscious type of response elicited by particular stimuli moving toward the mouth (e.g. protruding tongue of an actor). Thus through imitation, the social self (like me) is identified (Legerstee, 1991a, b; Meltzoff, 1990).

Development of the representational self

Awareness of the self continues to develop with age and matures into a self that is able to reflect on its own inner thoughts, but also those of others, in particular about their desires and beliefs. There are various theoretical orientations that explain the meta-representational thought in 4- to 5-year-old children. They fall under the rubric of the modularity theories of Baron-Cohen (1995), Fodor (1992), the simulationist theory (Harris, 1992), and the theory–theory or constraint constructivist theorists (Gopnik and Wellman, 1992; Gopnik and Meltzoff, 1997; Karmiloff-Smith, 1992). I will not discuss these theories here because they do not pertain to young infants. However, the question remains, how does primitive awareness of the self develop into a self-awareness on which children can reflect, and about which they can talk?

Karmiloff-Smith (1992) has developed an interesting theory of how knowledge develops in the child. Karmiloff-Smith proposes that humans are biologically constrained to process certain types of information such as space, time, causality, language, and so on, topics studied in depth by

Piaget (1952; 1954), but that adult knowledge of these concepts is only acquired through active construction. Whereas some types of nativism describe the initial stage of the child's knowledge, the way the mind comes to understand its own representations (e.g. the representational mind) is accomplished through a process of representational redescription (the RR Model). Karmiloff-Smith argues that there is a gradual process of representational redescription of knowledge through the processes of proceduralization and explicitation. Knowledge becomes represented this way in at least four levels labeled as: Implicit (I), Explicit-1 (E1), Explicit-2 (E2), and Explicit-3 (E3). At level 1, representations (sensori-motor knowledge) are not available to conscious access and verbal report; through the processes of proceduralization and explicitation implicit knowledge becomes explicit. At level E2, representations, after being again redescribed, become available to conscious access; however, they are still not available to verbal report. It is only at level E3 that knowledge is re-coded into a cross-system code and can be available to other cognitive domains and to verbal report. It is important to note that moving to a higher level of explicitation is only possible after the child has reached "behavioral mastery" at a certain level in a certain domain.

Although the RR process is the same across all domains (domain general), its operation within each micro domain is constrained by the content and level of explicitness of representation in that domain. As a result, a child's representation may be at level E1 with regards to one domain and at a lower or higher level with respect to another domain. This is in contrast to the Piagetian stage model, where development is the result of maturation through various cognitive stages, which involves changes across the entire cognitive system (but see my Piagetian discussion of horizontal decalage in chapter 3).

Thus Karmiloff-Smith's RR-Model can be viewed as a process that rewrites non-conscious primary level procedural representations (e.g. sensori-motor representations) into secondary representations (e.g. a conceptual form) so that they become cognitively available. These secondary representations are again redescribed until they become accessible to conscious awareness.

Infants are social creatures, aware of their minds and bodies

I began this chapter by positing that some philosophers have argued that self-awareness originates in the mind, whereas others have proposed that this awareness originates from a physical or bodily state. Both theories propose discontinuities between mind and bodily awareness. The problem to be solved for these dualistic infants is to discover that they and other people have bodies or that they and other people have minds. The available evidence indicates that during the first year of life, infants are aware of their own body and (albeit primitive) mental state, and perceive others as having bodies (as revealed through imitation of their bodily acts) and mental states (as revealed through mutual sharing of emotions). There is evidence that the perceptual abilities of infants play a seminal role in the development of the infant's awareness of the external environment and of a primary consciousness of the bodily self (Gibson, 1995). The special preference of infants for social stimuli, and the recognition that they are similar to conspecifics, both in the primary stages of consciousness as well as in the higher forms of self-consciousness, contributes to the infant's sensitivity to humans from the onset (Butterworth, 1995; Fogel, 1993; Legerstee, 1997b; Stern, 1995).

The self as a unique mythical entity

The above account of the development of self has detailed how some of the aspects of self-awareness or a sense of self develop during the first months of life. However, the self represents something that goes beyond the neurological, physical/social, and cognitive accounts. The self is in addition to a mental/social and physical self a unique mythical creature (Kenny, 1988). What is the process by which such uniqueness is created? As documented, from the beginning infants show that they have a primitive awareness of their bodily, social, and mental selves. Some of this knowledge is represented in specific domains. With development the domain specific principles guide infants to identify relevant input to self-awareness. Through this process, which entails infants' interactions with people, infants develop shared and distinct representations of self and others. It is through increasingly more complex interactions with people that new cognitive structures are created that give rise to more profound representations, not only about others but also about the self as a unique entity. That is because during their joint activity, infants and partners not only share the knowledge that each alone possess, but they construct knowledge that neither possessed alone (Chapman, 1992). This generativity of one's own intelligence, which forms the foundation of a unique and mythical self, is not seen as resulting only from equilibrations in the self-environment relationship but also from inter-subjective equilibrations. It is only during this dialectical inquiry that truly novel forms of knowledge, of unique and mythical selves, can be created.

5   Dyadic interactions

Awareness of mental states during the dyadic period

> Before language takes over as the instrument of interaction one cannot
> interact humanly with others without some proto-linguistic "theory of
> mind."
> (Bruner, 1990, p. 75)

Infants (like most other mammals) are social creatures that spend the
beginning of their lives in close proximity to their caretakers. Unlike other
mammals, however, human infants have some special socio-cognitive
capacities that make them particularly social and that differentiates
them from other animals (Tomasello, 1999). That is, because infants
not only come prepared with specific endogenous factors that allow them
to distinguish their own species from inanimate objects, capacities which
higher primates possess also (Tomasello and Call, 1997), but they are
born with self-inferential mechanisms that allow them to perceive their
own primitive mental states via the perception of emotions. This innate
interpersonal awareness enables infants to recognize similar emotional/
mental states in others. It is this very primitive awareness of the mental
world that enables infants to perceive goal directedness and intentionality
in human actions even in the first months of life. Thus it appears that
infants exhibit a natural ability for "inter-subjectivity." This ability is a
precursor or proto-form of Theory of Mind knowledge.

In this chapter, I focus on these first months of life in order to describe
those aspects of sociality that may reveal the infants' early awareness of
mental life. As discussed in the previous chapters, many theorists argue
that unique forms of human sociality involve an awareness of mental states
of others which is only demonstrated by infants during the triadic period
during the latter half of the first year (Tomasello, 1995). During triadic
relationships infants start to include external events and objects in their
interaction with others. It is proposed that the abilities that allow infants to
integrate person and object attention are those that enable infants to
understand that people are mental agents who have independent goals
that can be attained through various means. As a result of this

understanding, infants begin to use adults as social referencing points, and imitate the behavior of people in a way that reflects their understanding of others' intentions. Intentional agents are not only animate beings that use a variety of means for attaining their goals, but they also determine what they will pay attention to. Attention to things *external* to the dyad allows infants to learn symbolic types of behaviors such as cultural artifacts available in the world and language. Tomasello (1999) argues that in order to use artifacts as they were meant to be used, and to participate in social practices as they were meant to be participated in, children have to be able to imagine themselves in the position of the adult users and participants as they observe them. This imagination is possible because of two things. First during the triadic period infants for the first time become intentional agents themselves, and second, as a result of their biological propensity to perceive others as similar, they project this ability onto others.

Although it is possible that attention to objects and the person who attends to them, plays with them, and supplies verbal descriptions for them allows infants to learn about cultural artifacts and their labels, this does not necessarily mean that before the triadic period infants are not aware of mental states of people. In this chapter I will describe in detail what infants do during the dyadic period. I will provide an analysis of the interactions infants engage in before the triadic period in order to clarify whether infants are aware that people have intentions.

One of the reasons that an understanding of mental states in infants is placed so late in development is due to a prevailing uneasiness with the idea that early sociality cannot develop from anything other than asociality. "It is also due in part to our continuing acceptance of the proposition that things mental, being invisible, are graspable only conceptually and with difficulty" (Reddy, 2003, p. 247).

The idea that infants cannot be budding psychologists during the dyadic period is surprising given the empirical findings that infants are already budding physicists during this time. Infants reason about inanimate objects according to three principles: principle of cohesion, continuity, and contact (Baillargeon, 1986; Spelke, 1988). Infants reveal that they are aware that inanimate objects move cohesively, are permanent entities (they exist) and move continuously, and only move when contacted. These principles are not only applied in experiments where the objects are visible, but also where they are hidden. Thus infants appear to draw on their knowledge of objects in the absence of perceptual indices. This surely suggests a conceptual understanding of the properties of objects, on which infants are able to draw when necessary.

Theorists who emphasize that the dyadic period is not pivotal for infant psychological development ignore the behaviors infants engage in during that time. In fact, the problem is that many theorists who argue that the dyadic stage does not involve an awareness of mental activity have not investigated the ontogenetic origins of the infant's social-cognitive skills during that time. In this chapter, I will describe what takes place during the first months of life when infants are engaged with responsive adults, to show that there is indeed a basis from which to argue that during the dyadic period infants are intentional beings with simple mental lives, and an awareness of the intentions of other. These findings contradict accounts proposing that infant behaviors during the first year of life are conditioned responses rather than revealing mental state awareness.

Origin of mental states

In attempting to distinguish the mental from the physical, Brentano (1874/1973) pointed out that the mental is directed at something else (than the self) as object, the mental is thus *about* something, it is *referring* to something. This "something" does not need to exist, it does not really need to be out there. When we imagine the object, or think of an event, we mentally represent it. Thus, Brentano (and various other psychologists) view intentions as the relationship people have with objects. People's behavior is about an object, or about something, if their behavior relates to it in some psychological way (attends to it, refers to it, wants it, etc.). How do children begin to understand that people relate to the world-as-represented (which may be different from the one the children represent)? Bruner (1999, p. 329) examines the intention inherent in acts of *referring* or indicating. Namely, he focuses on

how somebody communicates to another person that there is something particular at the focus of his intention that he wishes to bring to the attention of that other person, in return for which he wants some indication that the other has, as it were, "got the message." On this account, the sender must (a) indicate that he is seeking to draw another's attention to something, (b) indicate what it is that he is trying to draw another's attention to, (c) receive some sign whether he has succeeded or not, and (d) if not, figure out with or without the other's help what further steps need to be taken.

Bruner's definition of the intentionality of referring can be used to analyze communication between two adults, but also between infant and adult. According to Bruner (1999), already at birth infants appear "motivated" to bring what they *feel* to the *attention* of the other during dyadic face-to-face interactions. Thus, almost from the beginning, infants monitor the gazes of their interlocutors in order to share their experiences with them.

Infants perceive adult gazes as an invitation to communicate because they react with social and emotional behaviors when adults establish eye contact with them (Legerstee et al., 1987; Stern, 1985; Bruner, 1999). Bruner (1999) argued that infants know from the beginning that looking is referential in nature because it is always externally focused and object directed (whether social or nonsocial). This is an interesting suggestion because it implies that infants are aware that they are being looked at, just like the infant is aware that they are looking at people (like me). This does not need to imply that the infant is aware to be the representational content (e.g. that the other as looker represents the infant). Such an understanding would require an, at least implicit, meta-representational ability (I know [if you look at me you think of me]). If such sophisticated mental capabilities exist in young infants, then there would be no need for development. Rather this type of simple awareness is a reflection of the infant's mental state, but not a kind of awareness that the infant can access yet (see chapter 4, on levels of representations). This type of awareness is a *precursor* to the later ability to reflect upon this awareness (e.g. Hobson, 1989).

For instance, infants notice that they are the focus of attention of their caretakers, because as soon as caretakers look at them infants begin to engage in emotional exchanges with them (Legerstee et al., 1987; Murray and Trevarthen, 1985; Stern, 1985; Fogel, 1993; Reddy, 2003). These affective exchanges are not just elicited by facial features, because infants do not react with emotional exchanges when facing an inanimate doll (Legerstee, 1992, and see chapter 3). In addition, if adults look at infants but refrain from smiling, infants become distressed. Infants do not get distressed when previously "interactive" dolls become immobile (Legerstee et al., 1989). These behaviors can be noticed as early as 5 weeks in infants (Legerstee et al., 1987). The lack of responsiveness of adults during dyadic exchanges appears to be taken by infants as a violation of the expectation that eye-to-eye contact involves sharing of mutual feelings.

Through alternating their eye contact (looking at and away from their partner) infants regulate their social interactions. This alternation of gaze behavior of pre-linguistic babies is similar in its regularity to the behavior between adults engaged in communication (Perry and Stern, 1976). Mothers treat their infants' 'looking away' as a pause in communication, because they stop talking when infants look away and resume their dialogue when infants re-engage their attention (Legerstee and Varghese, 2001; Stern, 1977).

By 4 months of age, infants show a decrease in their display of affectivity and attention to adults and an increase in their preference for inanimate objects. This interest to things outside the dyad is a result of increased motor and cognitive skills permitting more effective interactions and explorations within an expanding environment. Thus, rather than being a pause in primitive inter-subjectivity, it seems that this object-oriented phase prepares the way for a new mode of communication involving objects external to the dyad. Parents and adults capitalize on this new object attention of infants. They begin naming and describing the items (Legerstee et al., 1987). Infants respond by following adult gazes toward interesting events (see chapter 6). By making the objects part of the conversation, communicative partners show infants the beginning of referential communication. Adamson and Bakeman (1982, p. 219) call this period of development the nonverbal referencing phase, when "gaze pattern, vocalizations, and gestures increasingly serve the referential function of introducing a new topic for discussion, a new message that, that thing over there is what I want to communicate about, to comment on." By focusing on the other's attention, and following their gaze, infants learn much about the objects and things others attend to.

In its most elementary form, gaze following is evident between 5–6 months, but some months later, infants may repeatedly alternate their gazes from social partner back to the object of interest, a behavioral strategy that allows infants to monitor others' attention while also sharing experiences of the world with them (Butterworth and Jarrett, 1991). Infants are in the habit of following the adult's line of regard and expect to find an interesting object; if they don't see one, they turn around and check the adult's face. This behavior is evidence of infants' early inter-subjective representation of the world, e.g. the belief that they share the same world as the other (Bruner, 1999).

Thus, empirical evidence reveals that from birth, infants engage in extensive gaze monitoring of their partners during communicative exchanges in both dyadic and triadic contexts which appears to imply mental state awareness in infants. This would refute the notion that mental state awareness develops between 9 and 18 months (e.g. Tomasello, 1995; Gergely et al., 1995; Barresi and Moore, 1996). The question is: How does this awareness of mental states (even very simple ones) originate in infants? Below I will address this question, albeit it from a somewhat different theoritical perspective than in the previous chapters. That is, I will examine (1) the idea that perceiving intentions in others originates through associative learning, and (2) the notion that perceiving intentions is the result of perceiving "eye-like" stimuli. I will argue, instead, that an awareness of intentions is an inter-subjective phenomenon that can only develop as the result of meaningful social interactions.

Theoretical explanations

Explanation 1 – learning to perceive mental states

Prepared learning theorists argue that infants during the first year of life perceive sociality either in various forms of movement (Rakison and Poulin-Dubois, 2000; Gergely et al., 1995), or as a result of some special attraction to social stimuli (Barresi and Moore, 1996; Piaget, 1954), and that further development during the first 18 months of life is possible through the infant's overwhelming potential for associative learning.

For instance, Corkum and Moore (1995) postulate that infants' understanding of intentions in others does not occur until the end of the second year of life. Although the authors do not propose infants to have a tabula rasa at birth, they do regard them as **asocial** in the Piagetian sense of the word (e.g. infants do not perceive themselves as independent objects in the world until the end of the sensori-motor period, and hence do not perceive themselves, nor others, as social objects). Instead, the authors focus on the infants' abilities for contingency learning. They argue that the triadic period at 9 months, where infants can be seen to follow the gazes of others, does not imply that infants perceive adult attention as an awareness of some object. Rather Corkum and Moore argue that gaze following behaviors have been shaped through reinforcement (e.g. if I turn my head like my mother does then I see an interesting thing). Thus, these are not behaviors that demonstrate an awareness of the attentional/intentional state in others. It is not until the end of the second year, when infants begin to perceive themselves as independent beings and different from others, that they begin to understand where others are looking. This awareness then invokes infants to direct others' attention to something interesting (declaratives).

Legerstee and Barillas (2003) assessed this position. They studied 12-month-old infants to find out whether their communicative gestures, such as gaze following and declarative pointing, indicated that infants perceived people as intentional agents, or whether infant communicative behaviors are merely triggered by specific perceptual cues (e.g. turning of the head) in joint visual attention situations. Two experiments were conducted. In Experiment 1, thirty-two 12-month-olds were successfully conditioned to follow the gazes/head turns of (a) a contingently interacting person, and (b) a life-sized doll (with features of an intentional agent – hands, eyes, face, contingent movements) (see figure 5.1). Infants were then presented with salient (battery operated) toys to determine whether infants would use points and vocalizations to direct the attention of the social and nonsocial agents to these toys. Infants produced significantly more points, vocalizations, and gazes to the person than to the inanimate agent (figure 5.2).

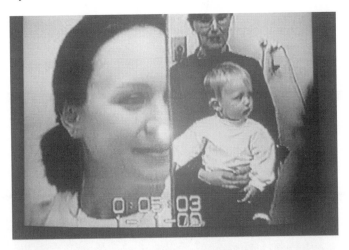

Figure 5.1 Twelve-month-old infants conditioned to follow the gazes/
head turns of a contingently responding (a) person and (b) doll.

Thus when properly reinforced, infants can be conditioned to orient
their gazes in the same direction to which social and nonsocial stimuli
"turned their head." Most infants learned that aligning their head with
the person and inanimate agent predicted an interesting sight. However,
infants did not *transfer* this learned behavior to the production task where
infants tried to direct the attention of people *only* to an interesting sight.
The finding that infants produced communicative gestures to people only
suggests that they attribute intentions to people only.

It should be noted that in Experiment 1, infants directed their communicative bids to a person who looked at the **same** objects as the infants.

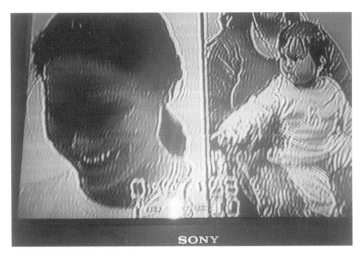

Figure 5.2 Infants produced points to the person.

One could argue that these gestures are imperatives, rather than declaratives used to try to get something from the adult. Imperatives reveal that infants understand people as agents that can make things happen (mechanical agents); declaratives reveal that infants perceive people as having intentions and attention (psychological agents). Declarative points, when directed at an object the person is not looking at, are aimed at redirecting attention and hence involve recognition of mental states.

To find out whether 11–14-month-olds would redirect the attention of the adult, Legerstee and Barillas (2003, Experiment 2) presented infants with an experimenter who emoted and looked at a toy dog on her left (in-focus dog) while another toy dog stood on her right at a 60 cm distance (out-of-focus dog). The session began with the experimenter calling the infant's name; when the infant looked at her, she turned to look at the in-focus dog. In one condition the in-focus dog began to bark and move (5s, 3 trials). In the other condition the out-of-focus dog began to bark and move. Infants directed significantly more points and vocalizations at the out-of-focus dog, than at the in-focus dog, while checking whether the experimenter began to direct her gaze at the out-of-focus dog yet (which she never did!) (see figure 5.3).[1]

Thus by 12 months, infants are aware of the attentional state of the person. (See also chapter 9, Experiment 3, where the same experiment was used to address a different theoretical question involving different infant

[1] Video clips of the additional seven infants (four in-focus, three out-of-focus) can be obtained from the archives of the MPI.

(a)

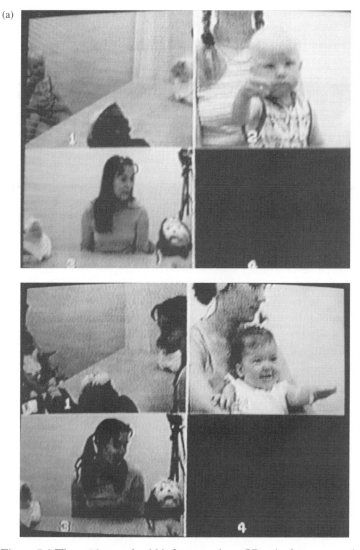

Figure 5.3 Three 12-month-old infants produce GP to in-focus toy and eight 12-month-old infants produce GVP to out-of-focus toys.

behaviors that revealed an awareness of intentions in others.) This suggests that many months before the end of the sensori-motor period infants see people as psychological agents. Infants are tuning in to others and get others to tune in to them. These behaviors are not just expressive kinds of exclamations to enhance the situation or to request the object (cf. Moore

(a)

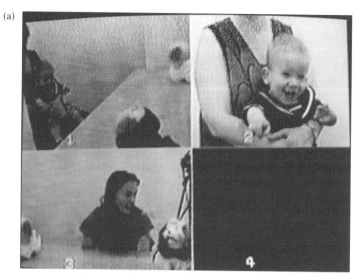

Figure 5.3 (cont.)

and D'Entremeont, 2001). Instead their function is to share interesting aspects of the environment with others. Thus, long before the 18–24 hallmark (cf. Piaget, 1954) infants demonstrate a remarkable level of social awareness. As discussed above, this noteworthy achievement in the social cognitive domain has important precursors during the first year, and probably has cascading developmental effects on the acquisition of a Theory of Mind later on (see also Camaioni, Perucchini, Bellagamba, and Colonnesi, 2004, for a similar interpretation).

Hence the idea that infants do not perceive people as psychological agents until 2 years of age is not supported by available data. More importantly, the prepared learning view does not provide information on how infants develop from knowing the world perceptually prior to 18 months to conceptually thereafter. In other words, how do infants go from understanding the behavioral to the psychological, or from the asocial to the social? It is not clear from this account why the second year of life marshals the onset of mental life in infants, given that symbolic types of behavior, such as referential communication (e.g. decontextualized use of words, Barrett, 1989), occur much before this 2-year hallmark.

Although the authors may be correct in arguing that infants are biologically prepared for social interaction, and have associative learning mechanisms to help them during subsequent development in learning

(b)

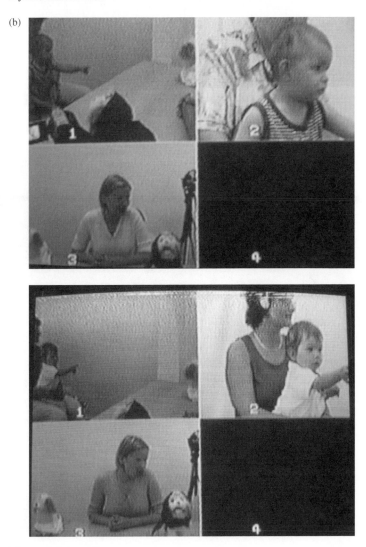

Figure 5.3 (cont.)

about people, this explanation does not tell the whole story. Apparently, chimps also have innate predispositions to interact with their conspecifics and are skillful in analyzing contingencies – but unlike human infants they do not develop an understanding of mental states (e.g. intentions) of their conspecifics (Tomasello and Call, 1997).

(b)

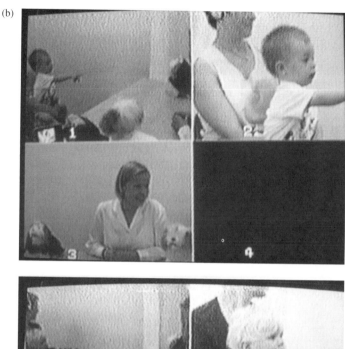

Figure 5.3 (cont.)

Explanation 2 – eye-detection to perceive mental states

Whereas the prepared learning theorists focus much attention on the type of social learning infants engage in as a prelude to an awareness of mental states in people, Baron-Cohen postulates that infants have innate modular neuro-cognitive mechanisms that become active at different developmental periods during the first 18 months of life (see also chapter 4).

(c)

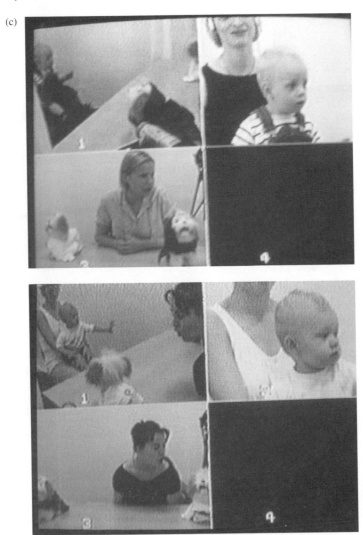

Figure 5.3 (cont.)

Those that are important to perceive mental states are the intentionality detector (ID) and the eye direction detector (EDD) that begin to operate during the dyadic period. The ID interprets all stimuli with self-propulsion and object direction as dyadic representations. Thus ID links an agent (either the self or another) to some object through intentional relations (agent wants object, and self wants object). The EDD provides

(c)

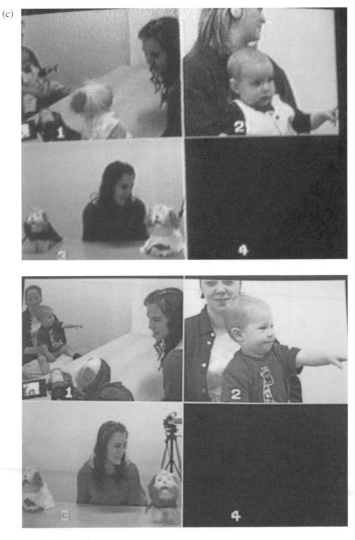

Figure 5.3 (cont.)

the infant with a special attention to eyes or eye-like stimuli (thus not necessarily a feature to detect sociality). The EDD allows the infants to perceive where someone is looking (e.g. agent or self see object). Both the ID and EDD operate primarily during the first 9 months of life. By 9 months of age, the ID and EDD combine into the Shared Attention Mechanism (SAM). This allows SAM to yield triadic representations using the dyadic information generated by ID and EDD (agent sees

object/self sees object). Thus, according to Baron-Cohen, joint engagement is made possible through the maturation of neuro-cognitive
mechanisms (innate modules), and is not dependent on social interaction
and learning. Infants are not born knowing about other persons, nor do
they have to learn about them.

The emphasis on the importance of *the physical properties of the eyes* as
central to inferring simple and more advanced mental states in others is
different from more socially oriented theorists who propose that the "pleasure experienced during direct eye-to-eye contact" implies a mutuality of
awareness, which lays the foundation and is continuous with a more
mature understanding of mental states (intentions) (Bruner, 1999).
Mutual gazing without the sharing of emotions evokes sadness in
infants. Such sadness is not present when infants face the eyes of life-size
dolls (Legerstee et al., 1987; 1990). These findings argue against the idea
that merely "seeing the eyes" elicits socio-cognitive capacities in infants.

In addition, the idea that the timetable of the occurrence of various
social cognitive capacities is not influenced by learning does not seem
supported by available empirical data (see chapters 7, 8, 9, and 10).
Suffice it to say here, there is strong evidence that caretakers who scaffold
infants' focus of attention have infants who produce bouts of joint
engagement sooner and more frequently than infants who do not
experience parental scaffolding (Legerstee and Varghese, 2001;
Legerstee et al., 2002; Legerstee, Fisher, and Markova, 2005; Legerstee
et al., 2004).

Explanation 3 – on being an object of attention

Vasuvi Reddy (2003) provides a compelling account of the early awareness of intentions in infants. She argues that the development of conscious awareness is evident in the first months of life rather than during
the final part of the first year (cf. Tomasello, 1995), or second year
(cf. Corkum and Moore, 1998). Reddy's account has implications for
approaches of other-awareness as well as self-awareness. Reddy proposes
that infants in the first months of life are aware that others are attentive
beings. Unlike classical cognitive theorists and prepared learning theorists, Reddy argues that the awareness of being the object of attention is a
precursor rather than the end result of representations of self and others
as psychological entities. The question is, what is the *quality* of this
precursory ability? It is possible that there is some knowledge about
people and the way they attend to things that is represented in a specific
domain as discussed in chapter 2 (see also Karmiloff-Smith, 1992). After
all, an awareness of the function of attention would seem an important

feature in understanding people. Although early on in life infants are aware that people attend to them, this knowledge may not be available to conscious access. When some months later it does become available, as for instance when infants begin to check the attentional state of people during the triadic period, or begin to direct people's attention to objects, they are still not available to verbal report.

Reddy makes a distinction between being emotionally aware of the attention of others from very early in life, and a subsequent awareness of the objects to which attention can be directed. This awareness can be observed during "primordial sharing" situations of the infant and mother. Reddy focuses on how infants respond to being looked at by others, by having the attention of others directed to them. She argues that already by 2 months, infants react with deep-seated emotions when a person looks at them. There is strong empirical support for this; infants smile when people make eye contact (Wolff, 1987; Legerstee et al., 1987), or when people turn their head toward them (Caron, Caron Mustelin, and Roberts, 1992). Infants also reduce smiling when adults look at a different part of their face rather than at their eyes (Muir and Hains, 1999). Infants increase expressions of emotions when adults coordinate their bouts of expressions with those of the infants' attention (Trevarthen, 1979; Beebe, Stern, and Jaffe, 1979), but show sadness when people refuse to communicate with them (still-face) while continue to look at them (Cohn and Tronick, 1989; Legerstee et al., 1987; Legerstee et al., 1990). However, when people over-stimulate infants with attention and emotional expressions, infants modulate the input by turning away their own gazes (Murray and Trevarthen, 1985; Legerstee et al., 1987; Legerstee and Varghese, 2001). Not only do infants know when people pay attention to them, but by 4 months they try to direct people's attention to themselves through calling when attention is not available (Reddy, 1999).

While redirecting the adult's attention at 4 months of age seems to be good evidence for the infants' awareness of others' attention, it could be argued that infants react to others' attempts to interact with emotional expressions only because they are born with a propensity for the production of some type of behavioral expressiveness, not because they are aware that the adult's attention is directed toward them.[2] This argument would imply that this innate urge to produce these expressive acts, which is usually followed by adult attention, makes infants realize that the other is an attentive being. This would mean that an understanding of attention in *others* could emerge from perceiving being the object of attention. Thus

---

[2] Gabriela Markova, 2004.

there would be a time in the infants' life where they do not know what the purpose of "attention" is, e.g. that they are not aware of the referential role attention plays or of "epistemic intentions" as Bruner (1999) would suggest. In this case, communication and attention are seen as mediated by later developing cognitive abilities that allow for mental state understanding in the first or second year (cf. Tomasello, 1995; Barresi and Moore, 1996). However, according to Reddy (1991) "infant communication is seen as entailing a perception of the other as a psychological recipient and partner" at the beginning of the first year. Reddy proposes that attention and affective engagement are not forced by behavioral acts, rather they are motivated by mental states. Thus Reddy argues that both attention and communication occur simultaneously in the behavioral repertoire of infants and are supported by mental activities.

After the middle of the first year, infants begin to direct the attention of others to specific aspects of the self. Infants may show off, clown, and tease when being paid attention to (Reddy, 1991; 2003; see also chapter 6 for evidence of an awareness of teasing in others). These behaviors are not simply learned routines as a result of contingent reinforcement. Reddy argues that the variety among the behaviors of the infants indicate that infants are consciously aware that people look at them because they act in funny ways. This implies that infants share the same experience with conspecifics. Thus, an understanding of the self as an object of attention is synonymous with an understanding of attention in others and originates from dyadic interactions (see also Hobson, 1993; Bruner, 1999). By the end of the first year, infants' engagement with other people over objects is well documented and will be discussed in the next chapter.

Thus, according to Reddy (2003), infants progress from psychological engagement during dyadic interactions during the first four months of life when they experience others' attention directed to self (e.g. object of attention, or emotional self-consciousness), to doing (representing) the object (showing off, trying to attract attention), to perceiving (aware of being) the object (coyness and embarrassment to being observed), to remembering the object (pride and shame as a result of others' evaluations).

Consequently, it is clear that Reddy postulates a continuous development of an awareness of mental states in infants. According to Reddy the development of an awareness of attention during the first two years of life is the result of a progressive understanding of the differentiation of objects away from the self in infants which deepens their understanding of attention of others. Because the earliest understanding of the self implies an emotional awareness of the attention in others, it involves an understanding of simple mental states. Further development involves a more differentiated view of the self as an object, but also as a represented entity of the intentions in others. Thus with ontogeny infants do not develop a sudden psychological awareness of people; rather the infants' understanding of people as psychological beings becomes richer. These early conscious engagements precede and *informs* conceptual representations of self and other, rather than *derive* from them (Reddy, 2003, p. 397).

When addressing the ontogeny of intentionality, Bruner (1999) argues that infants are from the beginning propelled to make their experiences known to others, to create some mutual awareness of each other's internal states (primitive inter-subjectivity). Infants reveal this intent through mutual gazing. Mutual gazing during the initial months of life, which is exemplified through direct eye-to-eye contact, is a precursor to triadic communication. During triadic communication a third object becomes included into the conversation to which the dyad now jointly attends.

Bruner calls the period where infants recognize that others are attending to something (e.g. the self, an object, or an event) *epistemic intentions*, and the period where they recognize that the person's actions are goal directed *instrumental intentions*. Although both forms can be classified as intentional behavior, it is when infants are able to combine the two kinds of intentions that they are able to perceive meaning: they become able to reflect on what they intend.

The question is, how do infants progress from recognizing epistemic intentions to instrumental intentions; e.g. from recognizing surface properties of other people's acts to the intentions supporting them? Bruner argues that social partners facilitate this transition. Through active scaffolding of infant actions, through treating them as if they have intention-endowed subjective lives, the condition for developing an intention-endowed subjective life has been met. However, this developmental progression would not be possible if infants from the beginning did not have some *innate* capacity to appreciate that humans share the same world, and an awareness of "who and what" is at the focus of the other's attention. Thus, like Reddy, Bruner argues that infants perceive that they are the focus of attention when adults look at them; that they are aware that they are the "aboutness" of the attention of others. This awareness is at the origin of the dyadic period rather than the triadic period or the second year of life. However, this awareness is created through affective social interactions rather than through the workings of innate neurological modules that perceive eye-like stimuli.

Explanation 4 – intention as relationships

Alan Fogel (1993) puts forth a continuous process model in which we come to know ourselves and other people through ongoing relationships:

"infants are participants in these relationships from the beginning of life and they share with their parents in the creation of meaning" (p. 85). Thus, meaning is created jointly during dyadic interactions by the two partners. Infant and caregiver regulate each other's attention and cognitive interests with the social and nonsocial world. During this period, the mother and infant bring together in increasingly complex ways their subjectivity and the history of their relationships. The communication system has a history because during the dyadic interactions, baby and caretaker meet each other with previously developed expectations. During subsequent interactions, their relationship takes on new meanings, because they create new information which then becomes part of the communicative relationship. Variations in the co-construction of these relationships is the result not only of the unique characteristic of each partner but is also created by the history of their relationship (Hsu and Fogel, 2003). It is through relationships that infants self-organize and construct new forms of interactions and an elaborated awareness of the other's mental states. Through the dyadic relationships infants have with their parents they progress toward increasing consensus about shared meaning. This development is not due to independent decisions the participants make "to move on," so to say, as a stage model would predict in which knowledge is fixed in advance (e.g. it is "in" the self or "in" the other), but rather this pattern of developmental change can be explained as propelled by the creativity of mutual negotiations during dyadic interactions.

It is clear that social learning mechanisms such as associative and contingency learning that rely on the chaining of existing old forms of events to explain development can not explain the creation of novel forms of meaning. The dynamics of self-organization of face-to-face communication cannot be explained through a social learning mechanism such as imitation either. Although infants and adults have been found to imitate and match each other's behavior, it is as if adults use imitation to indicate that they agree with infants that they understand and are aware of what their infants are saying, but matching of existing behaviors is not like communication during which themes are created and become elaborated into novel forms of behavior (consensual frames). Rather, early imitation of infants and being imitated by the adult can be seen as an "attention getter" that makes the infants aware of the behaviors of the adult and thereby facilitates identification with the partner, but this mechanism is not sufficient to ensure a full development of social cognitive skills and individuality. Imitation in itself is simply a mechanism that infants use to show what they already know about people (Legerstee, 1991b; Piaget, 1952). Thus copying behaviors of others alone cannot predict the ongoing creativity, elaboration, and extension existent in communicative exchanges between mother and child and hence cannot explain the development of an awareness of mental states in others.

Domain specific knowledge, constraints, and learning about people

The proposals put forth by modularists and the prepared learning theorists have identified important variables infants use in their understanding of people. I agree that concepts of people are acquired through perceptual associations, such as the ability to analyze contingencies they obtain when interacting with other people and through imitation. However, there is little evidence to suggest that infants acquire knowledge about humans based solely on associative learning. Without any constraints on learning, there is little reason to assume that infants could develop a theory of the specificity of people's behavior. In order to do so infants need to adopt mentalist strategies, such as theory driven inferences that work as constraints when interpreting human behavior (verbal and nonverbal gestures, actions, attention/intention).

Furthermore, there is no evidence to suggest that early associations turn into theories from which infants begin to draw inferences later on. In fact there appear to be no descriptions of how theories of inference gradually arise out of frequencies of associations. Indeed, authors of various theoretical backgrounds have emphasized that it would be difficult to postulate how infants could learn to make inferential attributions later if totally incapable of something similar to inferential thought earlier (Flavell, 1999). These theorists have proposed that infants pick up concrete knowledge *and* have intuitive expectations about concepts during their sociocognitive development. These processes allow young infants to interpret people's actions in ways that are precursory and continuous with more mature conceptual understandings of people. Rather than proceeding from a perceptual to a conceptual processing of human behavior, the theoretical and empirical evidence discussed above strongly suggests that infants have representations which guide their search for perceptual or concrete information from birth (Legerstee, Barna, and DiAdamo, 2000).

Thus, the idea that infants learn that people have mental states as a result of some perceptual mechanism such as multimodal integration, imitation, innate attractions to social stimulation, or as the result of the perception of some type of (self-directed) movement, such as contingent responding, is not sufficient. Although these are biologically prepared skills, theorists who put forth these mechanisms as responsible for the acquisition of mental states imply that infants essentially are nonsocial, non-mental entities at birth. During the early social interactions, infants show a wide range of emotional expressions to people compared to inanimate stimuli. Part of this attraction is definitely related to the type of perceptual stimulation infants receive from adults. Adults use (albeit unconsciously) "infant" speech which they direct to infants. This infant directed speech has elevated pitch contours, and other supra-segmental features that captivate infants' attention. Such infant-directed speech appears a universal phenomenon because it is observed in virtually all cultures (M. Papousek, H. Papousek, and Symmes, 1991; Fogel, 2001). Adults also exaggerate their facial features and use many nonverbal behaviors (head nodding, shaking, touch, etc.) to increase infants' attention to them. In addition, adults use highly repetitive and rhythmic play depending on the infant's responsiveness to the adult (Fogel, 1977).

Both Bruner and Reddy, when analyzing the responses of infants who realize that they are the object of the attention of others, conclude that infants are conscious of being looked at. The empirical evidence that has been accumulated on infants' abilities to engage in social interactions seems to support the theoretical orientations of these authors. The evidence is in favor of the idea that infants have a natural ability to appreciate that they share a common world with others, because from the beginning infants can determine what is at the focus of other people's attention.

In sum, the available evidence suggests that mental representations *in part* have their foundations in, and are continuous with, relations between individuals. Hobson (1998) and Fogel (1993) argue, persuasively, that infants start out by relating to other people, and it is in this relation between the infant as experiencer and the world as experienced that one can find the source of "aboutness." Hobson and Fogel, like Bruner, also believe that the transition between these two forms of experiences, child as experiencer and world being experienced, happens through affective communication with others (see also chapters 4 and 7). The infant's natural tendencies to perceive others as similar, and to infer the mental states of self and others through the sharing of some very basic emotions, make it possible that "sophisticated mental capacities arise through the interiorization of interpersonal processes" (Hobson, 1989, p. 296). This is in contrast to what many modularists, prepared learning theorists, some socio-cognitive and classical cognitive theorists argue, namely that interpersonal processes (e.g. mutual sharing of affect) become possible through the interiorization of action schemas or learned associations at the end of the second year.

Watching the infant interact with communicative partners during the first three months of life seems to suggest that infants are motivated to share emotions and feelings, and that they expect their partners to do the same in order to achieve some mutuality of awareness (Tronick, 2003; Fogel and Thelen, 1987). Both Bruner (1999) and Trevarthen (1979) call this mutual awareness "primitive intersubjectivity," and propose that it is a necessary precursor to subsequent, more complex forms of inter-subjectivity, where infants begin to share and refer to things outside the communicative dyad. It appears that "the struggle to share what one has in mind begins early in life" (Bruner, 1999).

6   Triadic interactions – Joint engagement in 5 and 7-month-olds

Infants' understanding of goals involving objects

As discussed in chapter 5, the proto-conversations infants engage in during the first three months of life involve sharing of affect but they do not involve communication about things external to the dyad. Consequently, many authors do not believe that infants are intentional beings, or that they perceive others as intentional.

In this chapter I will elaborate on what I began in chapter 5, namely that in terms of perceiving mental states, the triadic state is a continuation of the dyadic state, except that during the triadic state infants have acquired more complex cognitive structures that allow for more complex interactions involving objects.

The development of triadic social skills

When infants enter the triadic interaction state, they begin to alternate their gazes between people and objects. Monitoring people's facial expressions, their eyes, and the things they attend to is an important mechanism by which infants acquire complex social cognitive skills (Baldwin and Moses, 1994). Such monitoring solidifies infants' developing awareness of the relationship between person and object and deepens the infants' understanding of people as agents with intentions and goals, whose perspectives may differ from their own. For instance, infants begin actively to follow the gazes of others toward interesting events, monitor people's faces when in ambiguous situations, direct people's attention to interesting sights, and use others as social reference points (Baron-Cohen, 1993; Carpenter et al., 1998). Thus, during the triadic period, the nature of communication between infant and caregiver changes in fundamental ways compared to the dyadic period. The triadic social skills, which all involve infant sharing attention with people over objects, are often referred to as joint attentional behaviors (Bakeman and Adamson, 1984; Carpenter et al., 1998; Legerstee and

Weintraub, 1997; Legerstee et al., 2002; Legerstee and Barillas, 2003). There is a vast interest in the infants' understanding of joint attentional behaviors, because of its supposed relationship to language and Theory of Mind (Bruner, 1990; Baron-Cohen, 1991). Although much work has been done to examine the roots of joint attention between 9 and 12 months of age, little research has examined the infants' attentional abilities prior to that age. In this chapter, I would like to examine the development of two examples of joint attentional behaviors in 5 and 7-month-old infants, namely coordinated attention **(CA)** during natural play situations and gaze monitoring during ambiguous situations called goal detection **(GD)**.

Coordinated attention

In chapter 5, I discussed how infant sensitivity to others' gaze emerges during the first 3 months. From the first days of life, infants prefer looking at two-dimensional human faces than at other patterns (Johnson and Morton, 1991). They selectively look at people's eyes when compared to other facial features (Haith, Berman, and Moore, 1977) and respond to shifts in gaze direction (Hains and Muir, 1996; Vecera and Johnson, 1995). In its most elementary form, gaze following is evidenced between 5 and 6 months (Bakeman and Adamson, 1984; Butterworth, 1991; Hood, Willen, and Driver, 1998; Scaife and Bruner, 1975). Through following people's gazes, infants begin to look at the same object or event the other is looking at (Butterworth, 1994; Legerstee et al., 1987).

However, gaze following often involves more than just simultaneous looking. A key characteristic is that both participants share an interest in the object and that both are aware of the other's attention directed toward the object (Tomasello, 1999). In a longitudinal study, Carpenter and colleagues (1998) investigated the abilities of 9–15-month-old infants to monitor, share, follow, and direct others' attention and behavior. The authors found that by 9 months infants began to look up at the eyes of the experimenters. The authors called this behavior "checking" and proposed that this is a measure of children appreciating the intentions of others. They further found that also by 9 months all of the infants engaged in at least one episode of coordinated attention (CA) with the experimenter, and defined CA as "relatively extended episodes, in which adults and infants share attention to an object of mutual interest over some measurable period of time (at least a few seconds)" (Carpenter et al., 1998, p. 5). The Carpenter et al. study was inspired by previous research by Bakeman and Adamson (1984) who observed infants from

6 to 18 months playing with their mothers, their peers, and alone. The authors defined six behavioral categories: unengaged (uninvolved with any person or object), on-looking (observing another person), person (engaged in face-to-face interaction or play with another person), object (involved with an object alone), passive joint (involved with an object with another person without the awareness of the other person's involvement), coordinated joint (involved with an object with another person by coordinating the attention to both object and person). Results showed that the average percent of time infants spend in coordinated joint attention at 6, 9, 12, 15, and 18 months was 2.3, 2, 3.6, 11.2, and 26.6 respectively. Thus there was a gradual increase with age. Interestingly, the authors (1984) did not find a difference between the amount of CA infants produced at 6 and 9 months of age.

Because the consistent production of triadic types of behavior can not be done by chance (Desrocher, Morrissette, and Ricard, 1995; Legerstee and Barillas, 2003), analyzing the frequencies of such behaviors is not of theoretical importance. In other words, if infants produce an average of two CA per episode at 6 months, then this is evidence that such young infants are *able to share attention over objects*.

Goal detection

Simultaneous to sharing attention, infants develop other complex and intentional acts of communication. By the end of the first year, infants begin to monitor people's emotional expressions reliably in order to determine how to act in ambiguous situations (Campos and Sternberg, 1981; Feinman and Lewis, 1983; Moses, Baldwin, Rosicky, and Tidball, 2001), or to determine what the purpose of the actions of others is (Carpenter et al., 1998; Phillips, Baron-Cohen, and Rutter, 1992). For instance, Phillips and collaborators (1992) compared the gaze behavior of 9–18-month-old infants, with and without autism, toward an adult who either engaged in ambiguous tasks (i.e. teasing infants with a toy or blocking them as they played with a toy), or in unambiguous games (i.e. giving the toy to the infant). All infants without autism made immediate eye contact with the experimenter following the ambiguous teasing acts, but only 40 percent did so following the unambiguous giving situation. This pattern was not observed in autistic children who are thought not to detect intentions in others (Baron-Cohen, 1991). Although infants with autism can use specific rules (eyes open, eyes turned toward unobstructed object), to determine where the other is looking, they do not appear to comprehend the psychological state behind the looks. Consequently, infants with autism do not use gaze direction to infer goals and desires in others (Baron-Cohen, Campbell, Karmiloff-Smith, Grant, and Walker, 1995).

It should be noted that Phillips et al. (1992) indicated that they also observed eye contact with the experimenter during ambiguous acts in 6-month-old infants. However, the authors did not report the details of their findings for the infants in this age range.

Theoretical controversies regarding coordinated attention and goal detection

Although there is generally a consensus that joint attentional abilities between 9 and 12 months are evidence of the infants' awareness of people as intentional agents, the theoretical interpretations on how this ability comes about appear to be in sharp disagreement (Baron-Cohen, 1995; Johnson, Booth, and O'Hearn, 2001; Premack, 1990). As detailed in chapter 3, there are various interpretations on how infants come to attribute intentions to others. Briefly, Premack (1990) argued that infants are born with abstract systems to perceive intentional action in objects (social or nonsocial) that appear to move in self-propelled ways. Csibra et al. (1999) and Gergely et al. (1995) proposed that 9-month-olds, but not 6-month-olds, perceive intentionality in the movement of inanimate objects. In those studies, Gergely and his colleagues habituated 6–12-month-old infants to a display of a small circle that had to move over an obstacle in order to reach a larger circle. In the test phases, infants were shown the same display without the obstacle. Infants either saw the small circle move straight toward the large circle (rational event, novel action) or they saw the small circle move over nothing to reach the large circle (non-rational event, old action). The infants looked significantly longer at the non-rational old action than at the novel action. The authors argued that 9 and 12-month-old infants, but not 6-month-old infants, were able to evaluate the rationality of the agents' goal-directed actions. "As our controls make it clear, this inference to a novel action is not based on previous associations, but stems from the infants' emerging naive theory of rational action which assumes that agents pursue their goals in the most efficient manner available to them given the constraints of reality" (Gergely, 2001, p. 580).

Thus, according to these findings, infants between 6 and 9 months of age become sensitive to two broad types of motions (self-motion vs. caused motion), two types of trajectories (goal directed vs. random), and two types of contingency motion (at a distance vs. direct physical contact). In the natural environment, self-propelled, goal-directed motions are associated with animates (people and animals). However, inanimate objects are set in motion and do not pursue goals. A critical issue not answered in these studies (Csibra et al., 1999) is whether infants have begun to associate each type of motion with a specific object (Legerstee, 2001b; Poulin-Dubois, 1999). Experiments in which infants view inanimate objects that move in particular ways (e.g. Ball, 1973; for a review see Spelke et al., 1995) can only clarify infants' knowledge of physical principles. It would seem that in order to provide evidence of goal directedness or agency, infants should be tested in one paradigm in which animate and inanimate agents are pitted against each other.

For instance, Meltzoff (1995) (see also chapter 3) showed that when movement was held constant (the inanimate objects simulated the behavior of people) 18-month-old infants completed the unfinished actions of people but not the uncompleted actions of surrogate objects simulating the human actions. This suggests that infants are aware of the internal states of people that drive these actions, and that the observable actions were only part of the intended acts. Thus it would seem that paradigms using social and physical objects can provide evidence for a conceptual understanding of inanimate as well as animate objects of which a person is the prototype for infants (Carey, 1985). As discussed in chapter 5, Legerstee and Barillas (2003) trained 12-month-old infants during pretrials to successfully *follow* the gazes/head turns of people and inanimate agents toward an interesting sight. However, during the subsequent post trials, infants used communicative gestures such as gazes, points, and vocalizations significantly more to people than to the inanimate objects in order to direct their attention to interesting sights. Thus it would appear that, although some behaviors infants produce during the first year of life can be controlled under associative learning, this does not mean that infants do not perceive people as intentional agents during that time.

Many of the techniques for assessing the roots of infant awareness of goals of people have relied on habituation studies (Woodward, 1998; see also Leslie, 1984). These studies revealed that infants by 5 months of age encode the behaviors of animate and inanimate objects differently. They attribute goal directedness to people only.

As detailed earlier, not all people interpret this behavior as goal directed. For instance Tomasello (1999, p. 69) suggests that although the studies with 5 and 6-month-olds clearly indicate that infants have an understanding that other persons are animates, that move by themselves, "These findings do not imply, nor do any other behaviors at this age imply, that these infants understand others as intentional agents with clearly differentiated means and goals." As discussed in chapter 2, for Tomasello (1995; 1999) goal detection and coordinated attention are behaviors that form part of the triadic joint attention abilities that all occur between 9 and 12 months of age and that announce that infants for the first time have become psychologists. That is, infants engage in joint attention because only then do they understand that they and other people share the same world. Infants at this age begin to look where adults are looking, because they start to understand other persons as intentional agents. In particular: "Intentional agents are animate beings with the power to control their spontaneous behavior, but they are more than that. Intentional agents have goals and make active choices among behavioral means for attaining those goals and they also make active choices about what they pay attention to in pursuing these goals" (Tomasello, 1999, p. 64).

Putting the theories to test

Because of the controversy about the development of an understanding of intentions in others prior to 9–12 months (Gergely et al., 1995; Tomasello, 1995; 1999), I conducted a study to assess the following hypotheses: *first*, because 5–6-month-old infants appear to follow the gazes of their partners quite readily toward an interesting event (Butterworth, 1991), and some engaged in CA (Bakeman and Adamson, 1984), it was reasonable to expect that infants at that age would begin to coordinate their attention. Consequently, infants between 5.5 and 7.5 months were assessed on this ability when playing with mothers and toys. Coordinated attention between a person and object was defined according to Carpenter et al.'s (1998) coding scheme. To my knowledge, there are no studies that have investigated this ability in 5-month-old infants who are beginning to engage in play with people and toys. *Second*, because all infants in the Phillips et al. (1992) study appeared to be able to complete the goal detection tasks, there was no indication how younger infants (e.g. at 5.5 and 7.5 months) would perform on ambiguous tasks in more natural play situations. Consequently, we administered infants at 5.5 and 7.5 months two tasks on goal detection: namely, a natural give and take task, and a replication of the Phillips et al. (1992) tease-and-give tasks. *Third*, in order to test whether 5.5 and 7.5-month-old infants attribute goal-directed behavior to people and not to inanimate agents that appear to move by themselves, they were presented with ambiguous tasks by people, and inanimate agents who were equated on physical features, such as faces, hands, and contingent movement.

Experiment 1 – coordinated attention and goal detection at 5.5 months

In Experiment 1, 5.5-month-old infants were presented with four conditions, (a) a free-play condition to assess CA, (b) a person give and take condition to assess for GD with an adult and (c) a surrogate object condition to assess for GD.

Infants were videotaped while interacting with an adult female stranger in a series of tasks. Filming took place in a 10×12 foot playroom at the infancy laboratory. Infants sat on a red plastic mat facing either their mother or the experimenter. Four digital cameras were used to film the interaction and the films were fed into a digital quad, which provided four images of the experimental scene. These images were recorded on a digital VCR. One camera focused on infant faces, one on adult faces, the other two cameras focused on the infants and their interactions. Four white curtains surrounded the infants and adults to limit possible environmental distractions. Three cameras were placed behind them while their lenses protruded through openings in the curtains. The target object used in the give and take task was a colorful wooden toy with wheels that was fastened on a rod. For the surrogate object task a foam rubber yellow half moon (size 80 cm wide and 20 cm high, with a 20 cm $\times$ 13 cm open half) was positioned upside down, with the open half toward the floor, beside the experimenter.

Coordinated attention task. To find out whether infants would participate in coordinated attention (CA) with the experimenter (E1), infants and E1 were videotaped during a three-minute natural play session. Infants and E1 played with four toys, a rattle mirror, a transparent plastic bear with a round tummy filled with little colored balls that would pop up when the bear was pushed on the head by the mother, a picture book, and a dumbbell rattle. While the infants played with E1, mothers held the infants by the back in the waist in an upright position.

Give and take tasks. During give and take games infants sat on the floor and were supported by the waist by their mothers, while interacting with E1.

Person give and take task. E1 rolled a target object back and forth to the infants, and either gave it to the infants or kept it. Because this give and take sequence was randomized among infants for a total of four trials (two give and two take), the infants did not know when the adult would give or take the objects.

When the actor gave the object the task was unambiguous, because the infant knew the goal of the game. However, when the actor held the object by her side, the situation was ambiguous because the infants did not know whether the object would be rolled back to the infant (as in give). After each give or take task there was a 5 s response period during which the experimenter looked at the infant's face silently while continuing to display a friendly but neutral facial expression (see figure 6.1).

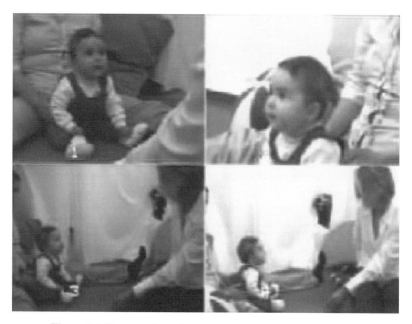

Figure 6.1 Person take task.

Surrogate object give and take task. The surrogate object condition was identical to the person condition, except that now a hidden assistant surreptitiously moved the target object (the same one as used during the Person condition) back and forth from underneath the yellow moon, stopping either by the infant or by the inanimate object, while the experimenter, who sat beside the yellow moon, looked toward the infant with a friendly/neutral face, while her hands were folded in her lap (see figure 6.2).

It was predicted that if infants looked more at people's faces during take than give because of spatio-temporal reasons (e.g. the object was closer to E1 during take than during give) or because infants naturally prefer to look at people (social enhancement) instead of inquiring about the goals of people, then the infants would also look up at E1 in the surrogate object take condition.

Again after each sequence E1 looked at the infants for 5 seconds while smiling. This give and take sequence was repeated twice.

It is possible that looking at others' faces reflects the infants' tendencies to obtain an appraisal of a given event (Feinman, 1982; Walden and Organ, 1988), rather than goal detection. The difference between emotional referencing and goal detection would be that in referencing infants

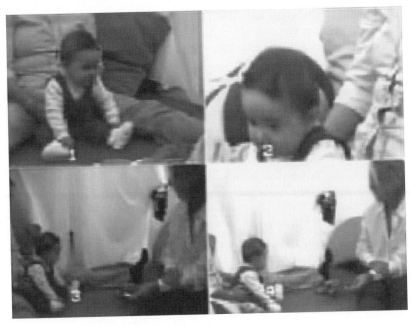

Figure 6.2 Surrogate object take task.

seek information about emotions, whereas in goal detection the infants seek information about a goal (cf. Phillips et al., 1992). We expected infants to reference the emotions of the mother when searching for emotional support, but we expected the infants to try to detect the goals of the experimenter who moved the objects (Carpenter et al., 1998). To control for this possibility infant gazes to mother were coded.

Thus, in Experiment 1 we controlled for spatio-temporal and social enhancement arguments with the surrogate object condition and for social referencing by coding the gazes directed to the mother. Order of conditions (CA and give and take tasks) was counterbalanced among the infants. Order of the give and take tasks were counterbalanced within the semi-structured conditions.

The natural interactions with the stranger were coded for CA. The same definition of joint engagement was used as in the Bakeman and Adamson (1984) and the Carpenter et al. (1998) study, as follows: "The infants' coordination of attention was evinced by alternation of gaze from an object to the mother's face and immediately back to the object" (Carpenter et al., 1998, p. 48). Coordinated attention occurrences continued until one of the participants changed their focus of attention. If the infants produced the response as a result of some other behavior of E1 (e.g. vocalizations) CA was not coded.

Coding for the give and take tasks involved infants looking from target object to E1's face within the 5-second response period. Thus, length of looking was not important as long as the infants looked to the faces of E1 after give or take.

In order to make sure that the give and take actions of the person were not different from those performed by the surrogate object, the tapes were reviewed by seven psychology students. They were told that they were going to view tapes where in some conditions a person moved the target toy, and in another condition a hidden experimenter moved the target toy. Part of the tapes that showed the person and surrogate object were covered so that only the movements were visible. These coders were unable to identify reliably who or what moved the target object.

Results of Experiment 1. Of the sixteen infants, thirteen infants participated in CA during the triadic interactions with people. Twelve out of sixteen infants looked up at the experimenter's face following her take and two infants looked at the experimenter's face following her give. Person take was significantly different from person give. None of the infants looked up from the target to the experimenter's face during the surrogate object condition.

In summary, a significant number of 5-month-old infants in study 1 engaged in joint attention with people and looked up during take with a person but not during give. Such differential responsiveness was not observed during the inanimate object condition. Thus the looks of the infants during take were not the result of a different spatial location of the object in give. The infants were visually attracted to both the person and the object tasks. Infants followed the object movements in both conditions for almost 95 percent of the total time. There was little social referencing during the response time. Two infants turned around to look at their parents' face. There was no fussing by the children during the presentation periods. Thus the person actions and surrogate object movements were not perceptually different to the infants. In the next task, the meaning of these looks in 5.5-month-old infants was investigated further.

Experiment 2 – social obstacle tasks at 5.5 months

In Experiment 2 we tested infants in ambiguous situations, or as they are called in the literature "social obstacle tasks" (Phillips et al., 1992). In one such task, adults give infants an object, and when the infant begins to play with the object the adult blocks the play activity by putting her hands over the object. An example of an ambiguous situation is one

Figure 6.3 (a) Five-month-old looks at ball and reaches for it. (b) Five-month-old looks at face of assistant who moves ball to side of infant.

where infants know what to do, but the adult does something totally unexpected for a familiar situation. Infants were also administered a *mock* task in which the infants were offered the object, but as soon as the infant reached for the object, the adult moved the object out of reach, and held the object beside rather than in front of the infants. Infants also received the give task as control. Fifteen 5.5-month-old infants were included in Experiment 2. Apparatus, set up, and the general procedure was the same as during Experiment 1.

Coordinated attention. To find out whether infants engaged in CA with E1, infants and E1 were videotaped during a three-minute natural play session. E1 used similar toys as during the free play interactions in Experiment 1, while E2 supported the infants by the waist during play.

Block task. Infants sat facing their mother and E1. E1 rolled a ball toward the infant and let her grab it. As soon as the infants grabbed the ball and began to touch and play, the experimenter put her hands on top of those of the infants. During blocking, E1 looked at the infant for a total of 5 seconds with a friendly/neutral facial expression. Infant gaze behavior from target object to E1's face was assessed during these 5 seconds. Infants were given a total of two trials.

Mock task. Infants sat facing E1 and their mother. E1 handed a small ball to the infant (see figure 6.3a). As soon as the infant reached for the object, E1 withdrew her offer, and put the object to the side of the infant (see figure 6.3b). She held the object in that position for 5 seconds while looking at the infant with a friendly/neutral face. Infants had a total of two trials.

Give task. Infants sat facing their mother and E1. E1 rolled a ball back and forth sideways (once) to entice the infant to the object. Then she handed the object to the infant. The experimenter held the ball to make it easier for the infant to touch the ball. During *give* the experimenter looked at the infant for a total of five seconds with a friendly/neutral facial expression. Infant gaze behavior from target object to E1's face was assessed during these five seconds. Infants were given a total of two trials.

The coding procedure for CA episodes during the natural interactions with the experimenter was the same as during Experiment 1. The coding for the conditions (e.g. block, mock, and give) involved infant looking from target object to E1's face within the 5-second response period. In order to determine whether infants would look to mother during these tasks, gazes to mothers were coded during the response times.

Results of Experiment 2. Of the fifteen infants all engaged at least once in CA with the experimenter. The number of infants who looked at E1's face following her block was not significantly different from the number of infants who looked at E1's face following her give. The number of infants who looked at E1's face following her mock was not significantly different from the number of infants who looked at E1's face following her give.

Experiment 3 – social obstacle tasks at 7.5 months

In order to find out whether older infants were more sensitive to the ambiguous tasks, we repeated these tasks with 7.5-month-old infants in Experiment 3. This time we saw sixteen 7.5-month-old infants. Apparatus, procedure, and set up were the same as in Experiment 2.

Results of Experiment 3. Of the sixteen infants in Experiment 3, all participated in CA with E1. Nine infants looked up at E1's face following her block which was significantly different from give and eight infants looked up following her mock which was also significantly different from give. Thus, by 7.5 months infants reliably looked at people during ambiguous acts and not during unambiguous acts.

Experiment 4 – goal detection with people and inanimate objects

An important aspect that separates people from objects is that people are intentional beings and objects are not (Frye, 1981). To investigate whether infant gaze monitoring is specific to people we had infants interact with social and nonsocial agents in the next experiment. The nonsocial agents possessed important features such as eyes, arms, and independent movements, which have been suggested to identify mentalist agents to infants (cf. Johnson et al., 2001). During the sessions infants sat facing a large stuffed animal called Captain Blue Bear (CB). Both E1 and CB were of the same height when sitting down.

The arms of CB had been removed from inside the sweater. A research assistant (RA) placed her arms through the sweater of CB instead, thereby making it appear as if CB had arms and could move independently. Lights were implanted into the eyes of CB which were activated by another research assistant who moved a hidden button attached to the back. Thus, when operated by research assistants CB was capable of contingent and reciprocal actions, which appeared to be self-initiated. Although we had tried to conduct this experiment with the 5.5-month-old infants, we had to abandon this choice because these infants appeared too young for the task. The majority appeared either afraid of the inanimate object or could not be familiarized with it.

Participants were fifty infants (27 girls). Before testing began, infants were encouraged by their mothers to look at and to touch CB, while the experimenter looked on. When infants looked at CB's face the eyes blinked. The familiarization criterion was met when infants seemed habituated with the animal. On average the familiarization sessions lasted for five minutes.

Person and object give and take tasks. The procedure for the person give and take task was the same as during Experiment 1, and the procedure for the CB task was identical to that of the person condition. The infants sat facing CB. The hidden experimenter moved the arms so that it appeared as if CB moved the target toy on a rod to and from the infants. After the give and take tasks, there was a 5-second response period. The procedure was repeated once.

Looking was coded when infants looked from the target object to the face of the experimenter, the inanimate object, or the mother during the 5-second response period. Thus, length of looking was not important as long as the infants looked to the faces of the three stimuli after give or take.

Results of Experiment 4. A repeated measures ANOVA, 2 (Person vs. CB) × 2 (give vs. take), on the frequency of looks during the 5-second response period to person or CB, showed that infants looked up significantly more during the person take action than during any of the other actions. Another repeated measures ANOVA, 2 (Person vs. CB) × 2 (give and take), on the frequencies of infant vocalizations, showed that infants produced significantly more vocalizations during the person than during the inanimate agent condition. Thus, overall infants vocalized more during person give and take, than during CB give and take. This finding suggests that infants vocalized more when interacting with people than when interacting with inanimates regardless of the give or take actions. The finding that infants did not vocalize more when the person took the object than when she gave the object argues against the idea that the vocalizations were imperatives.

In summary, the results of Experiment 4 showed that infants monitored the faces significantly more during take than during give in the person condition. Such differential looking was not apparent in the inanimate agent condition. Thus the looks during take were person specific, which suggests that infants did not focus only on the identical physical movements of the two actors. In addition, there were few looks to the mother during take, indicating that few infants tried to engage in social referencing with their mothers during these conditions. Furthermore, the infants did not vocalize more during take than during give in the person or object conditions. Thus infants did not request that the actor continue her actions during take.

The infants were visually attracted to both the person and the object tasks. Again, infants followed the object movements in both conditions for almost 95 percent of the total time, and few infants fussed during the presentation periods. Thus the person actions and inanimate agent movements were not perceptually different to the infants. Consequently, the results indicated that the end state of the take task was not suggested by the movement patterns alone when considered from a purely physical perspective (see also Meltzoff, 1995). Together, these results suggest that monitoring faces is specific to people and depends on an awareness that people's actions are goal directed.

Experiment 5 – teasing, a glimpse of the mind of others?

We had noticed during the natural play conditions that infants looked up when the experimenter playfully pulled at an object the infants were holding. Reddy (1991) has proposed that an ambiguous act such as "taking" can become teasing when adults smile and muck about with an object. If the child understands that she is being teased during give and take games, then she knows that the adult doesn't really mean to take the object away (e.g. "I thought you intended to take the toy, you laughed, did you change your mind?"). It appears that infants perceive certain humorous actions as playful intentions that have different goals and outcomes by 7–9 months of age (Reddy, 1991).

In the next experiment we investigated whether 7.5-month-old infants begin to appreciate such violation of expectation of the canonical outcome of giving and taking.

A total of eighteen 7.5-month-old infants were seen in Experiment 5. The same camera set up was used as in Experiment 1. The target object used in the give and take task was the same colorful wooden toy with wheels, fastened on a rod, as used in the previous give and take tasks of Experiments 1 and 4. Because infants at 7.5 months look up more during take than give (see Experiment 4), only the take tasks were used by E1; in one condition she had a neutral facial expression and in the other a mischievous one.

Person mischievously smiling and neutral faces during play. During the person mischievously smiling and neutral play tasks, E1 rolled the target object slowly toward the infant. As soon as the infant wanted to grasp the object, E1 rolled the object back while looking at the infant, either with a ***mischievously*** smiling or a ***neutral*** facial expression. We reasoned that if infants understood that the person with the smiling facial expression was teasing, then the goal of the actor (e.g. whether she was going to continue playing or not was ambiguous) and hence infants would continue to check the actor's face. In contrast, during the friendly neutral condition, the goal of the actor should not be ambiguous (e.g. the game is over).

To control for the fact that infants may look more at mischievous faces because they liked smiling faces, infants received also a take task from a surrogate object. In this condition the object was moved surreptitiously by a hidden research assistant from underneath the yellow moon while E1 sat beside her with a mischievously smiling facial expression. This procedure was the same as that described in Experiment 1 with the 5-month-old infants.

Results of Experiment 5. In order to determine whether the mischievous person and the neutral person tasks were not inherently different, the infants' first looks were analyzed during the 5-second response period. Analyses of the first look occurrences showed that the looks did not differ for these tasks. In order to determine whether the mischievous person and mischievous surrogate object conditions were not inherently different, infant looks were analyzed during the 5-second response period. Infants produced significantly more looks to the person than to the object. These findings confirm the results of Experiment 1 that the looks in the take conditions were person specific.

However, in order to find out whether infants checked the mischievous faces more when the person played the game than when the surrogate objects did, we analyzed the amount of checking during both conditions. There were eight infants who looked up in the surrogate object condition. We took the first eight infants who had looked up during the person condition. We compared the amount of checking of these infants. More infants checked the mischievous face during the person than object condition. Thus infants did not just look at people because they preferred happy faces. Only the infants in the person condition continued to check the faces and not the infants in the surrogate object condition.

Between 5.5 and 7.5 months, infants perceive meaning in actions and emotions

In summary, the results of Experiment 5 showed that infants *checked* the faces significantly more during take in the mischievous versus neutral person condition and also more during the mischievous person than during the surrogate object condition. Thus, the looks during take were person specific, which suggests that infants did not focus only on the identical physical movements of the two actors. In addition, there were few looks to the mother during take, indicating that the infants did not appear to reference during these conditions.

The finding that 7.5-month-old infants checked the faces more of mischievously looking people than of people with neutral facial expressions suggests that infants found the actions of the mischievous person ambiguous. With her mischievously looking face, the adult marks her actions thereby increasing ambiguity and providing the infant with a novel interpretation of the give and take game.

Successful social interaction depends a great deal on an awareness of the meaning underlying human attention and facial expressions. As indicated earlier, many researchers would argue that before infants are 9 months of age, they do not perceive intentions in actions of people. In the present studies 5.5 and 7.5-month-old infants were observed during naturalistic interactions with a female experimenter to determine whether infants would participate in coordinated attention with people. We found, while using well-established definitions and coding criteria (e.g. Bakeman and Adamson, 1984; Carpenter et al., 1998), that 5.5 and 7.5-month-old infants reliably coordinated attention with adults over toys.

We also found that these infants monitored the faces of others to disambiguate their goals. Reliably more 5.5-month-old infants looked up during person take than during give. There was no such differential responding in the surrogate object condition. The various controls we implemented indicated that infants' differential responsiveness was not due to differences in movements of the target objects, or the location of the person and the surrogate object (who were located side by side). The looks could not reliably be interpreted as social referencing, or imperative requesting, because the infants did not look reliably more at their mothers who were present (see also Carpenter et al., 1998 for a similar finding with infants between 9 and 12 months).

It could be argued that seeing the target object move on its own during the surrogate object condition must be a surprising or ambiguous event to the infants. However, in the present study, the toy began moving out of the infant's sight. Therefore, there was no cue to indicate how movement of the toys was caused. It was clear that the infants did not attribute the movements of the toys to the experimenter who sat beside the moving toy with her hands folded in her lap, because none of the infants looked at her face during the 5-second response period of either the give or take tasks. These results support the findings of Leslie (1984) and Woodward (1998), suggesting that infants perceive causal relations only between human actions and things.

In order to investigate the meaning of infants' looks at people, we replicated the procedure of Phillips and colleagues (1992) on infant goal detection during social obstacle tasks (blocking and mocking) with 5.5-month-old infants. Although 5.5-month-old infants monitored people's faces during coordinated attention tasks, as well as in give and take tasks, they did so less reliably during the social obstacle tasks. In contrast, the 7.5-month-old infants showed a more robust awareness of the goals of others.

Not only did all of the 7.5-month-old infants participate in CA, but they looked reliably more during block and mock, than during give. Thus the infants in the present study performed remarkably well on the social obstacle tasks in relation to the 9-month-olds tested by Phillips et al. (1992) and Carpenter et al. (1998).

Interestingly, by 7.5 months, infants looked up during take with people, but not during take with inanimate agents that have faces, and interacted contingently with the infant. This indicates that infant perception of goal directed action is specific to people. These findings argue against the suggestions of others that infants rely on self-propelled motion, contingent interaction, or gestures and eye movements to interpret goals (Gergely et al., 1995; Csibra et al., 1999; Johnson et al., 2001). Our results are more in line with the finding of others showing that 5–6-month-old infants attribute goals to humans and not inanimate agents (Legerstee et al., 2001b; Leslie, 1984; Woodward, 1998).

The most revealing finding in this set of studies was that by 7.5 months, infants had an understanding of teasing. These infants read through the literal body movements of people to discern their underlying goals. Reddy (1991) was the first to provide detailed evidence of 7–9-month-old infants' participation in humorous or teasing games with family members. A key criterion in teasing is the creation of ambiguity of whether an act is to be taken seriously (as in the neutral-looking person task where take meant "the game is over") or lightly (as in the mischievously looking person condition where take meant "the game is not over yet"). If infants understand teasing, then they are aware of the ambiguity involved in the game. This ambiguity is created by the adult who smiles in order to convey that she is just pretending. Understanding this type of humor can be seen as a *foundation* to the infants' later understanding that others are behaving in ways that do not always match with reality. Thus, in order for infants to understand teasing, they need to interpret signs of play that override particular actions (Nakano and Kanaya, 1993).

When infants in Experiment 5 were playing games of give and take with people who portrayed either mischievously looking or neutral faces, they continued to check the face of the mischievously looking adult only, as if to determine whether the person was "going to change her mind" and roll the object to the infant again. These infants did not reliably check the person's mischievous facial expression during the surrogate object condition. The positive results suggest that infants paid attention to the social cues of the adult and interpreted the gazes and facial expressions of people differently as a function of who performed the acts. Thus beyond a generalized ability to discriminate or prefer happy compared to neutral facial expressions (e.g. Nelson, 1987; Walker-Andrews, 1997), by 7.5 months infants tend to check people to find out about their underlying motives for action, and not inanimate agents.

In summary, compared to the 5-month-olds, the 7-month-old infants revealed a deeper understanding of the actions of people. They readily discriminated between the movements of social and nonsocial agents, distinguished between ambiguous and non-ambiguous acts, and discriminated between humorous and non-humorous actions. Although monitoring people's faces in these situations may have been partially conditioned, this does not imply that these behaviors are exempt from meaning. Nor do the findings support the idea that infant behaviors are mediated by a central conceptual notion of a mental being that is not isomorphic to people. Rather, the findings point to a rather sophisticated and selective monitoring of people and their object related goals between 5 and 7 months.

How should these early social cognitive skills be interpreted? Carpenter et al. (1998) argued that the demonstration of joint engagement revealed infant awareness of other persons as intentional agents "whose attention and behaviors to outside objects and events may be shared, followed into, and directed in various ways" (p. 118) (see also Tomasello, 1999). Because such joint attentional capacities appear with other triadic behaviors between 9 and 12 months, this period has been called the "9-month revolution" by Carpenter et al. (1998; Tomasello, 1999).

As argued throughout the previous chapters, rather than originating at the end of the first year, an awareness of people's attention can be observed in infants from the first months of life when infants monitor their caretakers' eyes in order to establish eye contact (Bruner, 1999; Reddy, 2003). During that time they smile more when adults look at them and less when adults look away (Muir and Hains, 1999; Reddy,

2003). These young infants not only monitor others' faces, but they seem to regulate the looks of other people, thereby establishing the cyclical framework of face-to-face interaction that allows for mutual sharing of expressions of arousal and affectivity (Fogel, 1993; Stern, 1985; Tronick, 2003). These findings reveal infants' sensitivity to being the object of attention. Between 5 and 6 months, the awareness of attention in others now expands to include objects external to the dyad, and to which other people's attention is directed. By seven months, infants are aware that people observe certain features of them because they engage in teasing with them (Reddy, 2003).

Thus by 7.5 months, infants show that they understand teasing and mocking which suggests an understanding of the meaning underlying ambiguous actions. Adults can only understand teasing if they guess correctly what the other has in mind. Although a concept of humor becomes greatly elaborated with development and becomes more refined with age, the infants' initial origins of the notion of "humor," its found-ation and precursory expression, can be observed during the first year of life. Thus, in certain situations, a behavior with a different goal can have a humorous interpretation, can have a humorous intent.

Taken together, the infants observed in this set of studies monitored people's gazes to discern the meaning of their actions. As many (Reddy, 1991; Bruner, 1990; Flavell, 1999) have argued convincingly, although an awareness of attention and intentions in infants may not be proof that this behavior is *continuous* with a later psychological understanding of the actions of people, it is theoretically unsound to argue that is not. If one accepts that infants are social creatures that know others through their actions to be different from nonsocial objects, then "the split between the meaningless behavior of another and the meaning somehow behind it or added to it, disappears" (Reddy, 1991, p. 153). These theoretical argu-ments favor the idea that infants are likely to be born with an early predisposition to attend to people and to have adults attend to them in order to acquire the various social cognitive skills that allow them to learn about their culture and the people who reside in it.

7 Social influences on infants' developing sense of people

> In contingent responding, people *react* to one and other. However, in affect mirroring, they *are reacting affectively* to one and other.
>
> (Legerstee and Varghese, 2001)

Whereas in the previous chapters the emphasis has been primarily on the endogenous factors that influence infant mental state awareness, in the subsequent chapters I will examine in detail the exogenous influences on the infant's developing sense of people. As discussed earlier, social interactionist theorists put much emphasis on the social factors that influence infants' awareness of people (Bowlby, 1969; Bruner, 1973; Fogel, 1993; Stern, 1985; Trevarthen, 1979; Tronick 2004; Vygotsky, 1978). These authors can be divided into two groups, each differing in the emphasis they put on either the exogenous or endogenous factors when explaining how infants develop the concept of people. Those with a nativist or constraint–constructivist orientation postulate that infants begin life with *an awareness of their own emotional states*. They emphasize the social origins of the self and the infants' innate sense of people. Trevarthen (1979), for instance, maintains that infants have innate capacities to act on the social and physical environments and are instrumental in their own cognitive development. He explains that infant behaviors such as cooing (present in neonates), smiling (appears within minutes after birth), pre-speech movements of the mouth and tongue, eye movements, and attempts to communicate point to the social nature of babies. He further proposes that infants can recognize others as sentient beings that are different from inanimate objects based on their extension of these communicative skills to other humans. Though Trevarthen attributes various innate capacities to infants, he stresses the importance of social exchanges for a developing understanding of people.

In contrast to those authors who postulate an innate awareness of emotion states, there are others who propose that infants are born *unaware* of the emotions of others (and self) but develop these as a result of their interactions with others. Some of these researchers (Bandura,

1992; Skinner, 1948; Watson, 1972; 1985; Gergely and Watson, 1999) emphasize that infants are born with an innate ability to learn through the detection of contingencies and reinforcements. As discussed in chapter 3 (see also chapter 10), Gergely and Watson (1996; 1999) argue that infant abilities to detect contingencies rely on the perfect relations between one event and another. To recap briefly, the contingency detection module analyzes temporal contingencies, sensory relations, and spatial relational information, estimating the degree of causal relatedness between stimuli and events. Imperfect contingencies imply out-of-body sources of stimulation, perfect contingencies imply in-body sources, and non-contingent stimuli are ambiguous (Watson, 1979). During the first three months of life, the module is activated mainly by perfect contingencies, thus allowing the infant to become familiar with her own physical capacities through proprioceptive feedback. After 3 months, the module starts preferring imperfect contingencies, which orient infants toward their social environment (Gergely and Watson, 1999). Although mothers will probably stimulate a baby's cooing with smiles, the probability exists that there are times when she refrains from responding. Her high, but imperfect, contingent responding helps to orient infants to the social environment (Bahrick and Watson, 1985; Watson, 1985). Around 3 months of age, infants also become aware of the emotions of others and, through their interaction with conspecifics, also of their own emotions.

Social interactionists and affect attunement

Even though social interactionists seem divided (oppositional) in the type of precursory or endogenous abilities they are willing to attribute to infants, all emphasize the importance of sensitive responding of caregivers in the development of a Theory of Mind. That is, the *quality* of mother–infant relationships is important for infants' social, emotional, and cognitive development (Bowlby, 1969; Bruner, 1990; Fogel, 1993; Freud, 1949; Stern, 1977; Trevarthen, 1979; Tronick, 2004).

For instance, dynamic systems theorists (Fogel, 1987; 1993; 2001; Fogel and Thelen, 1987; Lewis, 2000) demonstrate how relationship deficits in parenting may interfere with the development of competence in infants. As indicated in chapters 2 and 3, dynamic systems theory considers variability to be an inherent part of development. Because dynamic systems are non-linear, flexible, and multi-causal, small changes in either the context or the organism can result in qualitative and unique organizations of behavior. Thus, as organisms develop, novel behavioral patterns emerge from the process of interaction among multiple independent elements of a particular system (Fogel and Thelen, 1987). Re-organizations (or system phase shifts) result in qualitatively different patterns of behavior that may be driven by changes in contextual elements, such as a decrease in scaffolding of a depressed parent.

In particular, optimal infant–caretaker social interactions facilitate infants' social competence or inter-subjectivity. Optimal social interactions are characterized by sequentially dependent responding (turn taking) between infant and caregiver, during which the dyad can achieve a social communicative state where the infant's optimal level of emotional affect and attention is maintained. Optimal levels of emotional affect would involve a high level of smiling, gazing, and cooing toward the partner. Stern (1985) defines such affective interactions as "mirroring" or "emphatic responsiveness" of caregivers to the infants' expressions of affect. Infants' social competence or inter-subjectivity is defined as a developing awareness of shareable feelings, and is presumed to be the consequence of the affective interactions that infants have with their caregivers.

Dysfunctional mother–infant interactions are characterized by a lack of behaviors that encourage sustained optimal levels of interacting (Seligman, 1975; Field, 1995; Watson, 1985). For instance, depressed mothers spend less time looking at, touching, and talking to their infants, show little or negative affect, and often fail to respond contingently to the infants' signals. Infants in turn show abnormal activity levels and less positive affect. It appears that because of the frequent exposure to the dysfunctional behavior of their mothers, these infants themselves develop a dysfunctional style of interacting (e.g. Field, 1984; 1992; 1995).

Historical perspectives on mother–child interaction

Because of the importance of the social interactions infants experience for the development of an understanding of people and their mental states, I will provide a historical perspective on mother–child interaction in this chapter. Psychoanalytic literature has stimulated modern-day interest in early parent–child relations. According to this theory, early parent–child interactions are the foundation for later personality and character development. Early research shows that deprivation of continuous, one-to-one relations with caregivers has devastating and long-lasting consequences on children's cognitive, emotional, and social development (Bowlby, 1951; Goldfarb, 1943; Ribble, 1944; Spitz, 1963). This is particularly true when deprivation occurs in the first months of life, which has led researchers to propose that there is a sensitive period for the development of social skills. More recent evidence involving Romanian adoptees concurs with these early proposals. Infants institutionalized within the first eight months of life in socially deprived conditions became withdrawn, were unwilling to share toys, and exhibited poor relationships with both peers and siblings. These behaviors persisted several years after their adoption into stable Canadian homes (Fisher, Ames, Chisholm, and Savoie, 1997). The relationship between early deprivation and subsequent dysfunctional behavior points to a need for appropriate stimulation early in life in order to develop appropriate social–emotional skills.

Despite the strength of this aspect of the psychoanalytic theory, several other elements are questionable. For instance, a main tenet of the theory is that analytic object relations become the prototype for future social relationships, depending on the balance between maternal gratification and frustration of the infant's primary organic drives. This view parallels that of classical learning theorists, who propose that infants' love for their caregivers is based on their ability to provide food, which gains reinforcing value. A series of experiments by Harlow (1958; 1961) using infant macaques questioned this view of the mother's role in infant social-skills learning. The development of perception, manipulation, exploration, frustration, and timidity in these primates follows a course that is very similar to that of human infants, allowing for speculation on the impact such separation may have on humans (Harlow and Harlow, 1965). Infant monkeys were raised in isolation from others, except for two artificial mothers. One was made of soft cloth, but did not "produce" any food. The other was made of wire, which afforded little opportunity for cuddling, but provided milk instead. Harlow found that when under stress, the monkeys sought comfort from their terry-cloth mothers. Furthermore, in the absence of the artificial mother, the behavior of the monkeys changed drastically. Vocalizing, crouching, rocking, and sucking – all indicators of emotional strain – increased. When exposed to other young macaques, these primate infants either froze in a crouched position or ran around on their hind feet, clutching themselves with their arms (Harlow and Harlow, 1965). They also showed dysfunctional reproductive behavior, failing to engage willfully in copulation. When these isolation-reared primates did reproduce, they demonstrated dysfunctional, punitive parenting skills. Thus, it is clear that the mere provision of food does not ensure proper social development. Harlow's research formulated a fundamentally different view on the origins of sociability.

Subsequent research began to focus on infants' social origins through attachment theory. Bowlby (1979) and Ainsworth (Ainsworth, Blehar, Waters, and Wall, 1978) argued that infants are born with an innate drive to be sociable and to seek attachment. Although both psychoanalysis and theory of attachment agree that the fulfillment of the infant's need for emotional and social exchange with the caregiver is fundamentally important for future mental health, it is attachment theory that sees the need for sociability as a primary drive. It introduces the idea of the control system of attachment as a crucial mechanism of fulfilling a genetically programmed need to be sociable. This system is organized to maintain a fine balance between the infant–caregiver proximity and the infant's exploratory behavior because it is continually sensitive to the environmental and internal conditions. It will control the type and amount of attachment behaviors displayed by the child, because it depends on the amount of unfamiliarity and threat present in the environment. Different types of attachment patterns can be formed, depending on the quality of mother–child relationships in early infancy. The quality will influence the many aspects of future social–emotional and cognitive development.

A series of empirical studies were inspired by this type of theorizing (Bronfenbrenner, 1974; Davis, 1947; Kagan, 1976; Koluchova, 1972; Rutter, 1971; 1972; Tizard and Rees, 1974). The effects of various forms of deprivation of normal infant–mother relationships were analyzed, and interventions to correct these effects were implemented. The results suggested that the effects of early separations might not be as devastating and irreversible as was previously thought. What needed to be looked at instead was the *quality* of early social interactions, reasons for separations, and availability of other "healthy" social relations. The findings of the above mentioned studies created a context within which the scientific questions became subtler. It is not about whether infant–mother interactions are needed, but what aspects of them are important and how they develop.

Although attachment theory remains a dominant perspective on the importance of early infant–parent relationships for later personality growth, dynamic systems theory appears to address the co-construction of the attachment relationship and its consequences for socio-emotional and cognitive growth more fully. Because relationships form after the parent and child accumulate a history of interactions over time, the current relationship provides the dynamic context for their interactions (Lollis and Kuczynski, 1997). Thus each interaction is influenced and built upon past ones; the shared, co-constructed history shapes the dynamics of the current relationship. Differences in the stability of the ensuing attachment system arise from self-organizing and emergent processes within the system. Fogel (1993), and Fogel and Thelen (1987) described how mother and infant face-to-face interaction (the dyadic system) changes their communicative behaviors as a function of the dynamics of the communicative interactions; that is, the ongoing and expected behaviors of each other. Attachment develops from such dynamic interactions, which is defined as a stable organization of behavioral actions preferred by the mother–infant dyad. Thus, dynamic systems theory is different from traditional attachment theory in that it views attachment as an adaptable process that re-organizes constantly within the relationship and over time.

Contemporary theoretical and empirical works (Bornstein and Tamis-LeMonda, 1989a, b; Field, 1984; 1990; 1992; 1995; Landry, Smith Millar-Loncar, and Swank, 1998; Legerstee, 1992; 1997a; 1998; Legerstee and Varghese, 2001; Murray and Trevarthen, 1985) have concentrated on further analyzing the nature of infant–mother relationships. These theories hold that mother and infant form an affective communication system from the beginning of life.

In chapter 2, I argued that infants were born with endogenous processes to perceive their own emotions (self-inferential process) and those of others (interpersonal awareness). The quality of these affect-reflective "mirroring" interactions plays an important role in the development of the infant's social and emotional development. Accurate feedback confirms the infant's inferences such as "if I smile, I feel happy; if you smile you feel happy too." This coordination of feelings allows for an assessment of interpersonal relationships, and plays a key role in the establishment of infant–mother dialogue that is so crucial to a sense of being responded to, a sense of being understood, and a sense of control and identity (Spitz, 1963). Thus both exogenous and endogenous influences play a role in the formation of the child as a budding "psychologist."

In addition to the infant's self-inferential processes, infants' abilities to perceive stimuli cross-modally play an important part of the infant's developing social awareness (Stern, 1984; Kuhl and Meltzoff, 1982; Legerstee, 1990; Meltzoff and Borton, 1979; Meltzoff and Moore, 1977). When caregivers reflect their infants' affect, they usually respond with a modality that is different from the one used by their infants. Consequently, babies perceive the quality of overt behaviors (shape, intensity, and timing) by transposing them into feeling qualities. By fostering an atmosphere of affective sharing and mutual emotional exchange, maternal affect mirroring makes infants aware that their internal feelings are sharable. According to Stern, once affect mirroring emerges in mother–child exchanges, it becomes a major tool in social–emotional development, as well as in the development of the self.

Parental interactions that involve the sharing of affective states serve as a mechanism of emotional sensitization. The sensitization chain starts with the activation of the infant's internal emotional state. However, if maternal affect mirroring repetitively presents a marked, perceptually distinct external reflection of the infant's affect displays, it gradually sensitizes the infant to the relevant internal cues. This way, infants gain awareness of the distinct emotions and gradually learn to regulate them. In order for this process to lead towards healthy social–emotional outcomes, maternal affect mirroring displays need to be differentiable from their own realistic emotional displays. Ideally, for the mother's affect-mirroring interactions to be appropriate, they should be perceptually and qualitatively distinct. In other words, affect-mirroring emotions should look and feel quite different from the real ones because they are usually an exaggerated version of the parent's realistic emotion expression. Furthermore, mirrored emotions are situated within a specific context of mother–child interaction. Their behavioral outcomes differ from those of the parent's realistic emotions. For example, whereas a parental realistic anger might lead to negative consequences toward a child, the affect-reflective anger expression will not. Finally, affect-mirroring emotions should have a unique contingency relation to infants' activity, being more contingent to the child's behavior than the parent's realistic emotions.

The mechanisms of affect mirroring and interpersonal contingency, through which sensitive and responsive mothers enhance their children's differentiation of their own emotional states from those of others, have an unquestionable heuristic value. What is arguable is their assumption that only after the third month, as suggested by Gergely and Watson (1999) (see chapters 3 and 10), do high but non-perfect contingencies start to orient infants toward external social environment. There is ample evidence suggesting the infants' sociability prior to 3 months (Legerstee, 1992; 1997b; Legerstee et al., 1987; 1990; Spelke, Phillips, and Woodward, 1995). As discussed in chapter 3, infants from very early on differentiate people from inanimate objects. The appropriateness of infants' behavioral responses before 3 months suggests that they have organized knowledge, which they use correctly to classify people as social, and objects as physical (Trevarthen, 1979; Bruner, 1973). It is most likely as a result of these innate endogenous factors that it can be clearly shown that by 2 months non-delayed infants, and by 4 to 6 months infants with Down syndrome (controlled for IQ), treat people as social; smiling, vocalizing, and imitating their actions. At the same time, they treat objects as things to be looked at and to be manipulated (Legerstee et al., 1987; Legerstee and Bowman, 1989; Legerstee, Bowman, and Fels, 1992).

In summary, studies on mother–child interactions show that mothers and infants engage in communication right after birth. Infants make contributions to the interpersonal social exchanges by sharing the affective states of caretakers and engaging in dialogues that entail mutual turn taking (Brazelton, Koslowski, and Main, 1974; Fogel, 1993; Hobson, 1993; Legerstee et al., 1987; Trevarthen, 1979; Tronick, 1989). The quality of the maternal interactions exerts a strong influence on the infant's affective state (Field, 1994; Legerstee and Weintraub, 1997; Malatesta and Izard, 1984). Moreover, optimal infant–caregiver social structures facilitate not only children's emotional, but also their social and cognitive development (Goldberg, Lojkasek, Gartner, and Corter, 1989; Landry et al., 1998).

Thus, research is supportive of the idea that young infants are innately social creatures. From early on they differentiate people from objects and treat the two classes in special ways. Infants engage in active, dialogue-like communication with people and match their emotional states to those of the partner. When this early social responsiveness is supported by caregivers' appropriate and sensitive responding, the infants' socio-emotional but also cognitive development is enhanced.

Affect attunement/affect mirroring and concept of self

As indicated, affect attunement is fundamental to the development of social cognitive development of infants. It is comprised of behaviors that express the quality of feelings of shared affective states without imitating the exact behavioral expression of the mental state (Stern, 1985). These behaviors occur cross-modally. For example, a mother may follow her infant banging a cup on a table saying "Ka-bam! Ka-bam!" The infant's behavior is tracked vocally by her mother. This kind of mirroring is part of affect attunement, but affect mirroring is often used to describe a kind of "affect mimicking." Affect mirroring allows mothers to clarify their children's conflicting emotions. A young toddler who runs around and then falls may feel excitement about her activity, but distress when she scrapes her knee. Whether she laughs or cries will depend on whether her mother shows a distressed or a joyful expression (Stern, 1985). Research illustrates that mothers attune to their infants more effectively than both fathers and strangers (Chada, 1996). Affect mirroring frequently appears automatic and generally mothers are unaware that they engage in it (Szajnberg, Skinjaric, and Moore, 1989).

The caretakers' tendencies to respond sensitively and to attribute meaning to their infants' earliest affective behaviors is important, not only for infants' social–emotional development, but also for their concept of self (Reed, 1995; Neisser, 1993; Fogel, 1993). Through affect mirroring, sensitive mothers will shape and modify their infants' emotional states. They will reflect infants' emotions that are appropriate for the context and adjust their own states in order to modulate those of their infants. This way, infants begin to differentiate their own emotional states from those of their social partners, thereby gradually developing an understanding of the emotions of others as well as a concept of self.

Research with somewhat older infants of abusing mothers confirms the importance of affect mirroring for self-recognition. These children display less evidence of self-recognition (Cicchetti and Schneider-Rosen, 1984), and their language is less likely to involve descriptions of themselves or of their internal states and feelings (Coster, Gersten, Beegly, and Cicchetti, 1989). Recent studies showed that non-abused children show that they have a better understanding of the personal agency and mental states of others than abused children (Verscheuren, Marcoen, and Schoef, 1996).

Affect attunement and the development of efficacy and independence

Support for the idea that affect attunement is important for social and cognitive development comes from research showing that lack of affect mirroring results in dysfunctional social and cognitive competence. According to Seligman (1975), maladaptive attitudes and beliefs in adulthood, such as helplessness, have their roots in early development. If infant actions have *affectively* contingent outcomes during turn-taking episodes, then they develop a sense of control, which is imperative to future social, emotional, and cognitive health. Depriving infants of the ability to learn these affective sequences can result in learned helplessness, as Seligman's research with dogs illustrates. Subjects were unable to escape from differentially emitted shock – continued exposure to an uncontrollable event – thus producing a psychological state called learned helplessness. The dogs were unwilling to escape continued shocks, even when it was possible for them to do so, because they had failed to establish a relation between self-efficacy and environmental events. Seligman argues that an uncontrollable environment has profound consequences for the entire repertoire of behavior: learned helplessness produces a cognitive set in which people believe that success and failure are independent of their actions, and they have difficulty learning that their responses or actions are consequential (Seligman, 1975).

Research has assessed learned helplessness in human infants with similar results (Finkelstein and Ramey, 1977; Legerstee, 1997b; Watson, 1979). As revealed in chapter 3, infants in contingent (controllable) situations responded better to a subsequent learning task than those exposed to random or non-contingent (uncontrollable) situations. Consequently, based on this research, it is believed that the behavior of caregivers not only influences the immediate social–emotional responses of infants, but also their cognitive performance. For instance, Legerstee and Varghese (2001) conducted a study to assess the effects of different levels of maternal affect mirroring on levels of prosocial behaviors and on social expectancies in 3-month-old infants. Prosocial behavior was characterized as infants' high levels of positive affect and increased attention toward their mothers during live face-to-face interactions. Social expectancy was defined as the ability to discriminate between the live and replay conditions of their mothers. Live conditions are those where mothers interact normally with their infants. These interactions are video recorded and, in the subsequent condition, they are replayed to the infants. Whereas mothers in the life conditions usually respond to their infants' signals, mothers during replay look "natural" but their responses are not contingent on those of their infants. It had been predicted that mothers who exhibited high levels of affect mirroring (HAM) would have infants who would join or participate in this interpersonal communication (Stern, 1985), and rank high on prosocial behaviors (smiles, melodic vocalizations, and gazes directed at mother). On the other hand, mothers who displayed low levels of affect mirroring (LAM) would have infants who ranked low on prosocial behaviors. This hypothesis was confirmed. The results showed that 3-month-old infants were highly sensitive to maternal affect mirroring. Infants who had mothers who ranked high on maintaining attention, warm sensitivity, and social responsiveness seemed to reflect back this affect, because they smiled, cooed, and gazed more at their mothers than infants whose mothers ranked low on these behaviors. We further argued that infants who ranked high on prosocial behaviors would rank high on social expectancies. These infants have been exposed to more empathetic interactions during which affective states are shared and therefore should discriminate between the live and replay conditions. This hypothesis was also confirmed. Infants who ranked high on prosocial behavior also ranked high on social expectancy because they discriminated with their responses (smiles, melodic vocalizations, and gazes) between the live and replay conditions. In addition, it could be inferred that infants during the live episode were *sharing* affective states rather than mimicking them, because during the replay conditions, when mothers displayed the same amount of smiles and vocalizations as in the normal condition, infants reduced positive affect. The responses of the infants of LAM mothers revealed a completely different pattern. These infants did not distinguish between the live and replay conditions with their smiles and melodic vocalizations. However, this does not mean that these infants were not able to discriminate contingencies, because when presented with a live interaction first, infants reduced their gazes in the replay condition. However, when the infants were presented with the replay condition first, they did not recuperate during the subsequent live interaction (as the normal infants had). Instead, the LAM infants appeared to avoid further interaction. This suggests that certain social contexts, such as interactions with high affect mirroring mothers, allow infants to form stable expectancies for sharing of affect, whereas other contexts, such as interactions with low affect mirroring mothers, do not, because these mothers are not consistent in their affect sharing.

Field (1995) has developed the "unresponsive mother model" that allows for an interpretation of the results. In this model, infants of responsive and sensitive mothers develop a sense of control or efficacy, while infants of insensitive mothers experience behavioral disorganization, lack of control and efficacy. This model would predict that when infants of HAM mothers are presented with a change in the behavior of their mothers, they do not change their behavior drastically because these infants have developed stable affective relationships with their mothers which results in efficacy. In contrast, when infants of LAM mothers are confronted with a change in the behavior of their mother they become helpless and do not know what to do (Seligman, 1975). These infants have not consistently experienced a synchrony of affect and attention of their mothers, and consequently lack efficacy. Our finding supported these predictions.

It should not be surprising that prosocial infants discriminate between the live and replay conditions because the live conditions mirror the history of affective sharing to which infants of high affect mirroring mothers have become accustomed. Our results are in accord with other studies examining the effect of maternal social responsiveness on infant development in the laboratory with very young infants (e.g. Murray and Trevarthen, 1985; Nadel et al., 1999), and also of studies conducted in more natural play situations (Brazelton, Koslowski, and Main, 1974; Hobson, 1993; Kaye and Fogel, 1980; Landry et al., 1998; Bornstein and Tamis-LeMonda, 1989a; Stern, 1985). These researchers have shown that a parenting style that is responsive and sensitive to children's signals results in infants who rank high on social and cognitive competence.

Many studies investigating the effects of the quality of mother–child interactions have examined the impact of maternal depression on infant behavior (Campbell, Cohn, and Myers, 1995; Cohn and Tronick, 1989; Field, 1984; Murray, Fior-Cowley, Hooper, and Cooper, 1996). However, as Legerstee and Varghese (2001) have shown, mothers who are not diagnosed as depressed may show maladaptive patterns when interacting with their infants. The results indicated that even micro-dysfunctions of non-depressed mothers (mothers had all been screened for depression), such as their lack of affective mirroring of the affective states of their infants, have an effect on the social and cognitive behaviors of their infants. The present findings seem to suggest that infants are sensitive to socially affective contingencies. Other researchers (Legerstee, 1997b; Hains and Muir, 1996; Watson, 1985) have supported the fact that very young infants have this ability. However, these studies did not clarify whether infants responded to contingency or affect mirroring, because the two are confounded in those studies. Maternal responsiveness can be both contingent as well as mirroring affect. In contingent responding, people react to one and other. However, in affect mirroring, infants are sharing affective states with their mothers. The findings, that infants in both the HAM and LAM groups reduced their gazes from live to replay, but that only infants in the HAM group reduced their positive affect, suggest that both groups reacted to a change in contingencies, but that infants of high affect mirroring mothers reacted to a lack of affect sharing by reducing their own affective behaviors.

I like to argue that only if contingent responding is accompanied by sensitive mothering can it have implications for an understanding of people and their mental states. It may be that the simple "perception of contingencies" is important for the development of certain aspects of social cognition, but it is not sufficient to explain an understanding of intentions. Primates are very skillful at analyzing social contingencies, but they do not develop an understanding of their conspecifics as intentional, whose affective states can be shared (Tomasello, 1999). However, the infants in this study were not only reacting to contingencies but also to affect mirroring. For infants to share affective states with others, they need to know that others are similar to them. It is this understanding that is an important factor in the subsequent understanding of others as intentional.

The findings have important implications for theories of social cognition. Researchers focusing on affect sharing of infants often stress the social origin of infants. These authors postulate that infants begin life with an awareness of their own affective states and with an ability to share these states with others (Bruner, 1990; Karmiloff-Smith, 1992; Trevarthen, 1979; Tomasello, 1999). Consequently, they engage in mutual affective relationships from the beginning (Hobson, 1993; Stern, 1995; Trevarthen, 1979). Empirical findings support the idea that infants make independent contributions to interpersonal social exchanges. It appears that even before infants are 3 months old, they match the affective states and behaviors of caregivers, engage in "dialogues," and expect others to engage in mutual turn taking with them (Brazelton et al., 1974; Hobson, 1993, Legerstee, 1991a, b; Trevarthen, 1979; Tronick, 1989). Affective states (smiles, vocalizations, gestures etc.) are social signals that provide information about another person's intentions, and provide a direction for one's own actions (Montague and Walker-Andrews, 2001). It would follow that mothers who provide more information about their own intentions, perhaps through affect sharing initially, have infants that may begin to act intentionally themselves and to understand intentions in others sooner than those who do not.

In summary, it appears that by 3 months infants are social creatures who, in addition to discriminating perceptually between contingent and non-contingent interactions, understand something about the social message parents deliver, because mothers that display positive affect to their infants have infants that display positive affect in return. These findings are a function of and evidence for primary inter-subjectivity; awareness that affective feelings can be shared, rather than the result of mimicking or contingency. This sharing of affect is founded on the infants' innate sense of emotional attunement (intra and interpersonal awareness) and facilitated through sensitive parenting. As detailed in chapters 2 and 4, if caretakers are attuned to the emotions of infants then infants identify with them, and through this conceptualization develop shared representations. As discussed above, sensitive parenting minimizes the overlapping of shared representations which results in an awareness of a unique self, and the development of social and cognitive independence.

8 Affect attunement and pre-linguistic communication

Maternal affectivity promotes infant socio-cognitive abilities

The studies reviewed so far suggest that young infants are social creatures at birth that have particular expectations about their interactions with caretakers. If these expectations are violated, infants get upset. In the study just discussed in chapter 7, Legerstee and Varghese (2001) revealed that mothers who produced high levels of affective attunement (HAM group) had infants who smiled, vocalized, and gazed longer at them than infants of mothers who were less sensitive. These HAM infants distinguished between video-taped natural interactions and replays of these interactions, regardless of the order in which the natural and replay conditions were presented. Infants of low ranking affective mothers (LAM group) also discriminated between the natural and replay conditions, in that they reduced their smiles and gazes during replay. However, if the "replay" versions were presented *before* the natural interactions, infants got so upset that they did not recuperate during the subsequent natural interactions with their mothers. Thus, infants in the HAM group did not become disturbed if the interaction with their mothers was somewhat "off." They happily adjusted their communicative attempts when mothers resumed natural interactions. In contrast, infants of less sensitive mothers lacked such efficacy or resilience. The lack of responsiveness of their mothers was so unsettling to these babies that they remained disturbed during subsequent natural interactions.

These types of responses of the 3-month-olds are actually reminiscent of the behavior of 12-month-old infants during the attachment episodes of the strange situation (Ainsworth, Blehar, Waters, and Wall, 1978). During these episodes, the securely attached infants forgave their mothers for leaving them alone temporarily with a stranger. They wanted to be hugged by her during reunion. In contrast, the less securely attached infants either ignored their mothers or could not be consoled when she returned. These findings suggest that maternal attunement

143

may have enduring effects on the behavior of infants. The data I am going to present in the present chapter will show that mothers who ranked low on affect attunement at 3 months remained that way until 10 months. Their infants were not only less sociable than the infants of mothers who ranked high on affect attunement, but they seemed delayed on important socio-cognitive abilities such as the development of their ability to *coordinate attention* between people and objects.

The development of pre-linguistic communication

As discussed in the previous chapters, soon after birth, infants communicate with eye contact, emotions, pre-linguistic vocalizations, and gestures, while adapting the rhythm of their interactions to that of their caretakers (Trevarthen, 1979). As infants mature, they become increasingly sophisticated in their interaction skills. They express their intentions through coordinating their eye contact with various gestures and vocalizations to request help from people in obtaining objects, or to direct people's attention to interesting events (Bakeman and Adamson, 1984; Legerstee and Weintraub, 1997; Bruner, 1999). Around 6 months, infants achieve a major developmental milestone in pre-linguistic development because they begin to coordinate their attention between people and things. Coordinated attention is one of the mechanisms that allows for sharing of meaning before language sets in. As such, coordinated attention is considered an intention to communicate and to play a central role in the infants' communicative and subsequent language development (Schaffer, Collins, and Parsons, 1977; Bruner, 1999).

Theoreticians have proposed different developmental paths for the acquisition of language in infants. For instance, Chomsky (1965) posits that because the language that children hear does not provide enough information for them to learn the abstract structures of generative grammar, they must have an innate language acquisition device. Social interactionists, on the other hand, argue that language acquisition is not the work of the child alone, but that language is socially and cognitively constructed, and consequently language development should be considered in relation to the social and cognitive abilities of the infants. As a consequence they focus on the richly structured socio-cultural environment in which children live, and argue that it is this structure that enables human infants to learn language. Thus, language is seen as a cultural skill and is similarly acquired; namely in dyadic and triadic interactions under the auspices of supportive parents (e.g. Vygostky, 1978; Bruner, 1999).

Effects of maternal affect attunement on pre-linguistic communication

For instance Bruner (1999) proposes that early parent–infant interactions occur within common "formats" or "routines" where infants and caregiver are jointly attending to the same object or event, such as picture book reading or object play. During these routines infants maintain a common focus of attention with their partners. They readily perceive what the object of attention is for the adult, which makes the task of determining reference easier for the children. Even after infants acquire words, they continue to benefit from such joint attentional abilities (Markus et al., 2000).

There is a substantial amount of developmental literature that has associated maternal attunement with pre-linguistic and linguistic development. Maternal responsiveness *in the first six months* of life has been found to predict the size of speaking vocabulary at 12 months (Ruddy and Bornstein, 1982), language comprehension at 13 months (Tamis-LeMonda and Bornstein, 1989), and performance of intelligence based on the mental scale of the Bayley at 21 months (Crockenberg, 1983). Maternal sensitivity is also positively correlated with attention span and symbolic play at 13 months (Bornstein and Tamis-LeMonda, 1997). Maternal responsiveness in the *second half* of the first year is related to language comprehension at 9 months, and accounts for 15 percent of the variance in language comprehension at 13 months (Baumwell, Tamis-LeMonda, and Bornstein, 1997).

The relationship between sharing attention and language development

Thus, as argued above, infants progress from pre-linguistic communication to linguistic communication through active scaffolding of their parents. Bruner calls this scaffolding "narrative structuring" where caretakers treat the infant as if they have things in mind. Trevarthen (1979) argues that infants are capable of these behaviors because they are progressing from primary inter-subjectivity (the ability to share emotions with others) to secondary inter-subjectivity (the ability to share with others things that they perceive in the environment). Secondary inter-subjectivity eventually promotes language learning in infants. Thus social interactionists believe that inter-subjectivity facilitates language learning just as much as the actual structure of maternal language does, and emphasizes that the interactive strategies of parents can facilitate or interfere with pre-linguistic as well as linguistic behavior in infants and children.

For instance, Legerstee et al. (2002) revealed that mothers who maintained their infants' foci of attention while naming objects had children who increased their referential communication more than mothers who did not. This indicates that specific maternal strategies such as maintaining infant attention while naming objects influences pre-linguistic communication in infants. The quality of this scaffolding varies among dyads. Depressed mothers spend less time engaged in joint focus than non-depressed mothers (Goldsmith and Rogoff, 1997), and highly sensitive mothers spend significantly more time focused on the object their infants are focused on than do low sensitive mothers (Raver and Leadbeater, 1995). These studies clearly indicate a connection between maternal behavior and children's early communicative attempts.

As discussed in chapter 6, infant attentional skills during the first year of life progresses from monitoring the gazes of people, to following their gazes to interesting sights between 5 and 6 months of age (Butterworth, 1994; Legerstee et al., 1987), to coordinating attention (CA) between people and objects between 5.5 and 7.5 months. Although by 9 months the use of CA is well established in infants, Carpenter et al. (1998) found in their longitudinal study of 9 to 15-month-old infants that whereas the number of CA episodes increased significantly from 9–14 months of age, there were large individual differences in this development among the infants. That is, infants could be classified into four categories: *early* (approximately 30 sec. of CA at 9 months), *middle* (very little CA at 9 to 10 months, but significant CA at 11 and 12 months), *late* (no CA until 13 or 14 months), *never* (no CA until 15 months). It is possible that these individual differences were the result of maternal support of the attentional abilities of their infants.

This hypothesis would find support in the longitudinal study by Bakeman and Adamson (1984). The authors showed that, when interacting with their mothers, infants produced more coordinated attention than when interacting with same-aged peers, although by the end of the study even quite unskilled peers became appropriate partners for the exercise of these capacities (Bakeman and Adamson, 1984, p. 1278). These results strongly suggest that the social environment plays an important role in the development of these skills. In a more recent study, Legerstee and Weintraub (1997) (see also Legerstee et al., 2002) replicated and expanded the Bakeman and Adamson study to include infants with Down syndrome (see figure 8.1). Results showed that both groups of infants displayed significantly less CA when they played with peers than when interacting with adults and that infants without Down syndrome displayed more CA when they played with their mothers than with the peer's mother. Thus parental guidance seems an important mechanism in the development of CA for typical and atypical children.

Figure 8.1 Infants with Down syndrome engage in (a) object play, (b) person play, (c) passive joint, and (d) coordinated attention.

Maternal affectivity and enduring changes in infant behavior

The particular structure of maternal interactive style is recognized early by infants, because 4-month-olds are more contingently responsive with strangers whose level of contingent responsiveness resembles those of their parents (Bigelow, 1998). Other research found that although infants do not differ in their total number of gazes, smiles, and vocalizations to mother and stranger, starting from 4 months the overall rhythms of mother–infant and stranger–infant interaction could be differentiated. Infants' turn and pause durations were shorter and infants had a more coordinated speech with strangers than with their mothers. Jaffe et al. (2001) argued that the behavior in the novel context with the stranger gives more realistic information about the infant's cognitive abilities than the familiar context with the mother. The authors found that stranger interaction at 4 months had eight times more power in predicting infants' 12-month Bayley scores than did mother–infant interaction.

In addition, it could be argued that infants are primarily reacting to what their mother does "on line" rather than causing an enduring change in the infant attention pattern. If maternal interactions affect the pattern of CA development then infants in the LAM group should remain there even if they interacted with High attuned strangers. To control for this possibility, infants should be observed with their mothers as well as female strangers.

Longitudinal study with 3, 5, 7, and 10-month-olds

To date little systematic investigation of the relationship between maternal attunement and CA has been pursued. To examine the precursors to CA and the effects of the interactive strategies on the development of CA, a longitudinal study was conducted. Through examining variations in maternal affect attunement with variations in infant gaze monitoring at 3 months, and the production of CA at 5, 7, and 10 months, we hoped to clarify the precursors to CA and the mechanism that promoted its development. These analyses would reveal the influence of maternal affective behavior and the relationship between dyadic and triadic attention skills at these ages. In order to examine whether mothers' attunement is of an enduring nature rather than simply an "online" effect, infants were also observed in interaction with female strangers. In particular we hypothesized that infants of low attuned mothers should produce less CA than infants of highly attuned mothers, and should exhibit low gaze monitoring and CA even when interacting with strangers who are highly attuned.

In summary, there were three main predictions. First, we hypothesized that infants of mothers exhibiting high affect attunement (HAM group) would monitor the gazes of the adults longer at 3 months and would produce more coordinated gazes at 5, 7, and 10 months than infants whose mothers exhibited low affect attunement (LAM group). Second, if this effect is long lasting, then during interactions with a highly attuned stranger, this difference in gaze monitoring and coordinated attention between HAM and LAM infants should persist. That is, infants who display less CA with their LAM mothers will remain less competent in this area with a stranger, even when this partner is highly attuned. Thirdly, we expect that infants belonging to the HAM group would enjoy their interactions more with these adults and display more smiles and vocalizations than infants of the LAM group, and that this difference should endure with a highly attuned stranger.

To shed light on these issues, 3, 5, 7, and 10-month-old infants were observed during free-play with mothers and female strangers (Legerstee, Fisher, and Markova, 2005). We studied three-month-old infants because the ability to engage in CA is considered to be the result of a developmental sequence that begins with face-to-face interaction (Adamson and Bakeman, 1982; Bruner, 1999). Testing infants during the dyadic and triadic period may therefore yield important information about the relationship between these two periods and the effects of maternal scaffolding as an important mechanism that promotes the development of attention.

Fifty infants participated in the study. All families belonged to lower and middle class. Because maternal depression is a factor that affects mothers' interactive styles (Field et al., 1998; Legerstee and Varghese, 2001), mothers were asked to fill out the Beck Depression Inventory (BDI; Beck, Ward, Mendelson, March, and Erbaugh, 1961) at 3 and 5 months. None of the mothers fell into the depressed range. Mothers were given a small gift at the end of the study.

It is possible, of course, that mothers do not have the hypothesized influence on their children but that the capacities children bring to the interaction determine the outcome. It is therefore necessary that when evaluating the effects of maternal interactive skills the contribution of confounding variables such as IQ (Bayley, 1969) and temperament (Rothbart, 1981) of the infant is assessed.[1] Although the Bayley scales of infants' intelligence are excellent IQ measures during the early years, they rely much on social and motor skills of the infants. An assessment of intelligence should take into account information-processing skills in infancy in ways that are free of motor limitations. Consequently, we used a habituation paradigm (what Bornstein and Sigman, 1986, call "decrement and recovery of attention") to assess IQ, in addition to the Bayley. Attention has long been associated with intelligence and the study of cognitive development (Messer, Kagan, and McCall, 1970; Stankov, 1983). The "decrement of attention" is the amount that infants decrease their attention to something in their environment that is unchanging; the "recovery" is the attention they regain when there is a novel stimulus in their environment. The quicker infants are aware that they are being presented with recurring information, the quicker they process the information being presented to them, and the less long they look. To find out whether infants discriminated differently, they were presented with an abstract stimulus and their speed of habituation to the stimulus was measured.

Temperament has also been argued to influence mother and child interactions (van den Boom, 1994; Rothbart, 1981). In order to determine whether infants differed in temperament, mothers were asked to fill

---

[1] Portions of this section have been prepared by Amisha Vaish.

out the IBQ (Rothbart, 1981) at 7 months. The IBQ is administered through parent report by asking parents to rate the frequency of certain temperament-related behaviors that their infants have displayed over the past week or two weeks. Parents are asked to rate the frequency of these behaviors on a 7-point scale, going from "never" to "always."

Filming took place in a playroom at the Infancy Laboratory at the Max Planck Institute for Evolutionary Anthropology, Leipzig, when the children were 3, 5, 7, and 10 months old. The testing area was surrounded by white curtains to limit possible environmental distractions. Four digital cameras recorded the procedure: one focused on the infant's face, one on the adult's face, two on the interaction. Images were then combined into one picture with a split-screen generator.

Procedure at 3-month visits. Infants sat in an infant seat approximately 30 cm from the adult. The study consisted of two different interactions; infants interacted with their mothers and with a female stranger as they normally would at home for three minutes. There were no toys present, because at that age infants do not coordinate their gazes between two objects (Legerstee et al., 1987; Adamson and Bakeman, 1982).

Procedure at 5, 7, and 10-month visits. Infants sat on a red plastic mat facing either their mothers or a stranger and were gently supported by their backs by one of the adults. (The person who held the baby did not play with the infant and toys.) Infants played with a rattle mirror, a transparent plastic toy with little popping colored balls inside, a soft picture book, and a dumbbell rattle during the interactions at 5, 7, and 10 months. These joint play activities have shown to provide a rich set of conditions for infants for shifting the attentional focus from the mother to a toy and back to the mother (Bakeman and Adamson, 1984; Landry et al., 1998; Legerstee and Weintraub, 1997; Legerstee et al., 2002; Leyendecker, Lamb, Schölmerich, and Fricke, 1997).

Infants played with their mother and toys during one condition and with the stranger and toys during another condition. The adults were asked to play with the children as they usually would. Order of sessions were counterbalanced.

Maternal attunement during 3, 5, 7, and 10 months was assessed from the 3-minute play situation for each age group separately. Maternal attunement was operationalized as maintaining attention, redirecting attention, and warm sensitivity (Landry et al., 1998). *Maintaining attention* was coded when the mother followed the infant's attentional focus by making comments, suggestions, or requests either verbally or nonverbally (Legerstee et al., 2002). For example, if the infant is looking at a rattle and the mother says, "Would you like to play with that rattle?" maintaining was coded from the moment that the mother looks at the rattle until the focus of attention is changed by any of the play partners. *Warm sensitivity* is the degree of sensitivity that a mother displays to her infant's cues. Mother's warm sensitivity was rated by a 5-point rating scale. Three ratings were made for the behaviors – positive affect, warm concern, and social responsiveness – once every minute of each 3-minute interaction. The final composite score was then calculated by the average of the ratings of each behavior (Legerstee and Varghese, 2001; Landry et al., 1998). Positive affect included the tone of voice, the intensity and duration of affective behaviors (e.g. smiles), and the use of affective words (e.g. "Are you happy?"). Warm concern is the mother's acceptance of the baby's activities, her concern for safety and comfort (e.g. "Are you okay?"), and her gentleness when the baby played. Social responsiveness was the mother's contingent and imitative responses to her infant's smiles and positive vocalizations, and her modulation of any negative expressions of infant affect (Legerstee and Varghese, 2001). Depending on the scores mothers got for maintaining attention, redirecting attention, and warm sensitivity, mothers and infants were divided into two groups, high-attuned (HAM) and low-attuned (LAM) groups. Stranger attunement was assessed in the same way as for the mother.

Infant social measures during 3, 5, and 7 months were coded to find out whether infants of high attuned mothers engaged in more gazes and social behaviors throughout the period of the study. Consequently, their social behaviors at 3, 5, and 7 months were coded for smiles, gazes, and vocalizations (Legerstee et al., 1987). Because infants' social behaviors decreased rapidly between 3 and 10 months, the social behaviors at 10 months were not included in the analysis.

Coding of coordinated attention at 5, 7, and 10 months was done from videotapes. The videotape of each interaction was first coded for episodes of CA. Coordinated attention was coded when infants looked from an object to the adult's face and back to the same object (Carpenter et al., 1998).

To divide mothers into high and low attuned groups, their scores on maintaining and warm sensitivity were rank ordered for each age group. A natural split was observed in these scores such that 52 percent of mothers were in the high maintaining group and 48 percent were in the low maintaining group. Score percentages for maintaining attention for the high maintaining group ranged from 50.08 percent to 77.91 percent. Score percentages for maintaining attention for the low maintaining group ranged from 17.87 percent to 48.41 percent. Scores for warm sensitivity for the high maintaining group ranged from 3.44 to 4.56. Scores for warm sensitivity for the low maintaining group ranged from 2.44 to 3.33 for all ages.

To determine the relationship between maintaining attention and warm sensitivity a correlational analysis was performed between scores on maintaining and warm sensitivity for all ages combined. The analysis showed that there was a significant correlation between maintaining attention and warm sensitivity. Mothers who ranked high on maintaining also ranked high on warm sensitivity at all ages. None of the mothers changed their attunement style from 3 to 10 months. Those mothers who ranked high on maintaining and warm sensitivity were labeled the HAM group and those that ranked low on these variables were labeled the LAM group.

Twenty-five percent of each stranger's interaction was coded for attunement. Scores for maintaining attention ranged from 72.78 percent to 100 percent. Scores for warm sensitivity ranged from 3.50 to 5 for all ages. The correlational analysis between scores on maintaining and warm sensitivity showed that there was a significant correlation between maintaining attention and warm sensitivity. Strangers ranked high both on maintaining and warm sensitivity.

Overall, the results showed that there were no significant differences between the High and Low affect groups of infants as a function of IQ at 3 months, speed of Habituation at 5 months, and IBQ at 7 months. The effects of maternal interactive style on infants' prosocial behavior, (1) gazes at mother, (2) smiles, (3) positive vocalizations, and (4) negative vocalizations at 3, 5, 7, and 10 months, and on CA at 5, 7, and 10 months, revealed the following.

Effects of maternal affect attunement on infant prosocial behaviors[2]

At 3 months, HAM babies gazed and smiled more at their mothers than did LAM babies. These results support the research by Legerstee and Varghese (2001). Infants whose mothers ranked high on maintaining attention and warm sensitivity appeared to "reflect back" maternal affect by gazing and smiling more at their mothers than infants whose mothers ranked low on these behaviors. Thus, during free-play interactions, infants in the HAM group participated more in interpersonal communication and appeared to enjoy the interaction more.

Overall HAM babies' and LAM babies' social behaviors decreased drastically with age from the dyadic to the triadic interactions. However, rather than attributing this to a change in the quality of the relationship infants have with their caretakers, the decrease in the production of social behaviors in infants can be attributed to a decline in

---

[2] All reported results were significant at the $p > .05$ level.

face-to-face interactions and an increase in attention to objects (Adamson and Bakeman, 1982; Legerstee et al., 1987; Legerstee and Weintraub, 1997). Even though HAM babies continued to engage in more social behavior than the LAM babies, the low level of responsiveness in general made it hard to detect the difference between HAM and LAM babies during the subsequent months. It should also be noted that at 5, 7, and 10 months, toys had been added to the interactions. These toys were attractive to the maturing infants and, except for sharing their excitement about the toys through CA, infants did not communicate dyadically with their social partners.

Effect of maternal and stranger affect attunement on CA at 5, 7, and 10 months There was a significant interaction between maternal affect attunement and age, indicating that HAM infants increased their ability to coordinate attention with age, as opposed to LAM infants. HAM infants showed an elevated level of CA as compared to LAM infants at both 5 and 10 months. There was no difference between the two groups of infants at 7 months.

In free-play interactions with a highly attuned stranger, CA was found to increase with age for both HAM and LAM groups. However, HAM infants engaged in more CA with the stranger than LAM infants at all ages studied. This finding exemplified the fact that LAM infants did not change their CA abilities according to the person with whom they were engaging.

Maternal attunement was found to be stable from 3 to 10 months. Thus, mothers kept their level of maintaining attention, and warm sensitivity providing infants with stable consensual frames (Fogel, 1993). Such continuity in maternal affectivity has also been confirmed in other longitudinal studies (Nicely et al., 1999; Seifer, Schiller, Sameroff, Resnick, and Riordan, 1996). The effect of maternal affect mirroring was not simply due to online scaffolding of skilled partners, but rather was the result of a consistently stable pattern of interaction that supported infants in their play. If online scaffolding had been the most important determinant in producing changes, then *both* HAM and LAM babies should get high CA scores during stranger interaction, because the strangers were highly attuned. However, the strangers did not affect the CA scores of LAM babies. That is, LAM babies remained low even though they played with high maintaining and sensitive strangers. This result suggests that rather than the skill level of the play partner, it is the continued level of maternal attunement (as measured in this study) that affects the sociocognitive ability of the child.

The results further showed that although the ability to engage in CA increased with development for both groups, it increased significantly more for HAM than for LAM infants. The finding that infants monitored their caretakers' gazes and increased smiles and vocalizations when they were sensitively being responded to at 3 months, and increased coordinated attention at 5 and 10 months with responsive caretakers, supports the idea that infants develop their communication skills with the support of sensitive adults during the first year of life.

Although HAM infants engaged in more CA than LAM infants at 5 and 10 months, there was no significant difference between groups at 7 months. Rather than proposing that a lack of significant differences may suggest that maternal affect attunement does not influence CA at 7 months, there are several explanations that more adequately explain this lack of production of CA at that age. Variation in responsiveness may be linked to periods of rapid change during the first year of life. What we noticed was that the 7-month-old infants often wanted to stand up during the social interactions, which could be the result of their increased motor abilities rather than as a function of a regression period. The most common assumption holds that three periods centered on the ages of 2, 7, and 12 months exist (see Fischer et al., 1990). During these periods infants temporarily lose stability due to intrinsic reorganization. They become difficult to handle and are not as easily motivated to participate in parent–infant interactive games than at the other periods. Of course, when infants practice standing, they do not engage in games with toys with caretakers, which in turn might affect the production of CA.

Relation between gaze monitoring and CA A regression analysis was conducted between gaze monitoring and CA. Because gaze monitoring had not yet begun to decline at 3 months, gazes at this age were used to predict mean CA at 5, 7, and 10 months. Results revealed that the early gaze monitoring of HAM infants significantly predicted their subsequent CA with mothers. No such relationship was found for LAM infants.

Continuity in innate motivation to engage psychologically with others

This study was conducted to assess the hypothesis that attuned caretakers promote the development of pre-linguistic abilities (Vygotsky, 1978; Bruner, 1999; Bakeman and Adamson, 1984). Previous studies had shown that interactive strategies such as maintaining attention and maternal sensitivity increased referential communication in language-using infants (Carpenter et al., 1998). This hypothesis was based on the idea that joint focus of attention is important for the acquisition of conventional linguistic forms in infants, and that the progress of children depends on the establishment of a shared world of events. We hypothesized that before infants are able independently to coordinate their attention between caregiver and referent, adults need to scaffold infant gazes through maintaining infant attention and following their gaze to objects and events.

Consequently, it was predicted that mothers who displayed high levels of support (maintaining attention and sensitivity) would have infants who monitored maternal gazes more at 3 months, and produced more CA when playing with adults than infants of mothers who displayed low levels of support. We predicted that HAM infants would also enjoy the interactions more as expressed through more smiles and longer gazes than LAM infants. These hypotheses were supported.

The present findings further showed that maternal affect mirroring is a stable exogenous mechanism that consistently promoted the socio-cognitive skills in infants during the period tested. Those mothers who ranked high on affect attunement at 3 months remained highly attuned during the subsequent months. Maternal affect attunement also had an enduring effect on the behavior of the children. Already by 3 months, infants of sensitive mothers monitored the faces of strangers and mothers more than infants of less sensitive mothers. They engaged in communication with mothers and reflected back their emotional messages with gazing and smiles. This increased responsivity of infants continued in the following months. By 5 months, infants of highly attuned mothers were able to communicate through more advanced socio-cognitive means with their social partners because they coordinated their gazes in order to share attention with their communicative partners over objects of mutual interest.

We further predicted that maternal attuned strategies have an enduring rather than "on-line" effect on the socio-cognitive abilities of their infants. This hypothesis was also confirmed, because infants of LAM mothers continued to lag behind infants of HAM mothers when interacting with highly attuned female strangers. Thus, based on the available empirical evidence in the literature and our own findings, it can be concluded that maternal interactive style exerts an important influence on infant communicative competence.

As discussed previously, within the social-interaction view point, there are two theoretical orientations that are pertinent to the studies discussed in this chapter. Namely, some researchers believe that all JA skills are manifestations of a unitary social cognitive ability to understand people as intentional agents (e.g. Carpenter et al., 1998; Charman et al., 2000). Their evidence comes from the limited finding that the different emerging JA skills such as CA, symbolic gestures, and imitation are synchronized, interrelated behaviors that have their onset within a brief developmental period, namely between 9 and 15 months.

On the other hand, there are those who claim that coordinated attention during the triadic period has its roots in gaze monitoring during the dyadic period. As discussed in chapter 5, infants during the dyadic state do not appear to engage in reflexive types of communication. Rather, there is sufficient theoretical and empirical support for the idea that at 3 months "there is something particular at the focus of infant attention that they wish to bring to the attention of others" (Bruner, 1999, p. 336). However, instead of a third object, as in triadic communication, during dyadic communication the infant is directing attention to the self. Bruner (1999, p. 337) calls this type of intentional behavior epistemic intention. Both epistemic and instrumental acts of intentions are acts of indicating "that provide the means for extending individual human attention to an interpersonal, intersubjective level." As the results of the present research show, these processes are supported and fostered through sensitive scaffolding. Reddy (2003) argued that infants are aware that they are the object of attention during the first months of life. They react with intense emotions when being looked at, and as demonstrated here, they increase their responsiveness when they are treated sensitively as subjects with feelings rather than as material objects. As indicated in chapter 5, communication with others should not only be studied in terms of categories (i.e. whether it is intentional or not), but also in terms of motivational salience of information creation for the participants. This is the primary source of stability, change, and diversity of consensual frames. Affectively attuned mothers provide relationships to their infants that are more supportive and creative than less affectively attuned mothers.

These findings support Fogel's (1993) theory of relationships. He argues that each relationship with each participant is different because of the process of interaction infants engage in. Relationships infants create with affectively attuned mothers lead to continued co-regulation and creativity. "As long as the relationship pattern is creative, negotiated and mutually maintained, stability is a dynamic and mutually engaging process that embodies the seed of change" (1993, p. 114). These relationships develop a history of consensual frames that are maintained by continued co-regulation, characterized by inventiveness. In some cases, such as the interactions infants have with less sensitive mothers, the actions of the partners are not mutually creative. The partners seem to act in ways that curtail avenues for negations. They are marked by lack of creativity, rigidity, sameness, and by lack of pleasure. Although this different interaction pattern may co-exist in all relationships, they become dominant in relationships where the quality of the relationship is either positive or disruptive. Mothers who tune in to their babies' emotions, and actions at 3 months create stable consensual frames of co-regulated action that persist over time. Highly attuned mothers remain supportive and, when infants begin showing an interest in object play, guide the infant's attention and object manipulation during their highly attuned co-regulated interactions. During attuned maternal interactions, infants develop a sense of "personal effectance" which strengthens the motivation to continue to interact with people and to act on the environment in order to acquire information (Bornstein and Tamis-LeMonda, 1997; Legerstee and Varghese, 2001). The present findings show that affect attunement is a mechanism that promotes gaze monitoring at 3 months, and coordinated attention at 5, 7, and 10 months. Thus the development of these communicative exchanges is the result of (1) innate motivations to psychologically engage with others (Bruner, 1999; Fogel, 1993; Trevarthen, 1979; Tronick, 2004) and (2) successful scaffolding of infant attentional abilities by parents (Bruner, 1999; Stern, 1985). The present study has provided support for social interaction theories that emphasize the importance of parental input as an integral component of socio-cognitive development.

9 The quality of social interaction affects infants' primitive desire reasoning

The importance of optimal interpersonal relationships

As indicated in chapter 8, the quality of caretaker–infant relationships is not only important for infants' social and emotional growth, but also for cognitive development which has traditionally been regarded as a separate domain (Bruner, 1990; Stern, 1985; Vygotsky, 1978; Trevarthen, 1979). Recent well-controlled studies are beginning to show that infants who consistently take part in optimal interpersonal interactions are better able to learn about the rich social and cognitive world in which they live, than infants who do not. As Jaffe et al. (2001) showed, the quality of mother–infant rhythmic coupling and bidirectional coordination at 4 months predicted attachment and performance on the Bayley at 12 months. The authors argued that coordination in communicative interactions between partners permits "prediction and anticipation of the pattern of accented elements, facilitating efficient information processing, memory, and the representation of interpersonal events" (p. 1). The authors defined the bidirectional approach they employed to imply that the partners are adjusting their behavior to each other.

The finding that mother–infant coordination in preverbal interactions promotes early social–cognitive understanding is both theoretically interesting and important, because it sheds light on the mechanisms that influence social cognitive development. Although quite a lot is known about when various aspects of social cognitive development emerge, there is less empirical evidence about the factors that contribute to its emergence. As indicated, several authors have proposed that infants come to know other minds through interacting with people (Fogel, 1993; Trevarthen, 1991; Tronick, 1989). According to them, intentionality is fundamentally an interpersonal phenomenon, and consequently, in providing a developmental account of the concept of intention, one must focus on the inter-subjective nature of intention attribution and see its foundation in inter-personal interaction.

The idea that maternal affect influences socio-cognitive skills is actually predictable for the following reasons. Toward the end of the first year, infants who have continuously engaged in optimal social interactions with their mothers have stronger attachment bonds (Ainsworth, Blehar, Waters, and Wall, 1978; van den Boom, 1994). These infants are more secure of themselves, which expresses itself in both proximity seeking behaviors (Ainsworth et al., 1978), and social initiating (Landry et al., 1998). Thus mothers who are highly responsive and who maintain infants' focus of attention have children who want to interact with them. As a result, infants become increasingly sophisticated in their interaction skills. These children are more likely to monitor their parents' gazes during the first three months of life and begin to express their intentions through coordinating eye contact with various gestures and vocalizations to request help from people in obtaining objects and in directing others' attention to interesting events during subsequent months (see chapter 8). Such a major advance in socio-cognitive development propels infants to engage in more advanced areas of functioning, such as imitative learning (Legerstee and Markova, 2005) and symbolic communication (Legerstee, Van Beek, and Varghese, 2002; Legerstee and Barillas, 2003). In addition, as discussed in chapter 6, infants have been shown to seek and use information from people in order to understand how to act in the world, but also in order to understand the actions of others. When confronted with ambiguous objects or unfamiliar events infants will look at their parents' facial expressions in order to gain information about the situation and then determine whether to approach the object or not (Feinman, 1982; Hornick et al., 1987; Moses et al., 2001; Walden and Ogan, 1988). Similarly, 12-month-old infants who are confronted with other people who emote positively while gazing at objects do not simply focus on the movements of the eyes and face; rather they infer that these emotions are *about* things, and that people's actions are *about* objects (Phillips, Wellman, and Spelke, 2002).

In this chapter, I will discuss research that was inspired by a recent study by Phillips et al. (2002) and by some earlier work I conducted with a graduate student Joanne Barna (Barna and Legerstee, 2005). The present study was developed under an SSHRC grant, and started in my laboratory (Centre for Research on Infancy, York University), but finished during a sabbatical at the Infancy laboratory of the MPI in Leipzig. The purpose of this study was to investigate whether infants whose mothers ranked high on affect attunement at 9 and 14 months would be better able to attribute intentionality to people's actions than infants who participated in less optimal interactions. Intentionality was defined as the infant's appreciation that a person's expression of pleasure when gazing toward an object is consistent with that person's subsequent handling of the object.

Precursors to desire reasoning

During day-to-day activities, infants spend quite some time observing people act and react to their immediate environment. They watch their mothers smile and look at them while saying "Oh what a nice baby you are" and then experience that they are being picked up. Or infants may observe their mothers while emoting disgustingly saying "Yak, don't put that in your mouth!" removing the object. In these situations, it is quite easy for infants to determine to what and to whom the mother is referring because she subsequently performs actions on the things she looks and emotes about. Infants also begin to understand the valence of her emotions; she will pick up and hold things she likes, but not things she finds disgusting. Thus, infants during these situations understand that they are the object of attention (cf. Reddy, 2003). However, as infants mature, they observe increasingly that maternal behaviors are directed at others, that others are the object of her attention and emotion. In order to predict accurately to what and to whom the mother is referring, infants should not only interpret the meaning of her emotions correctly, but also where mother's attention is directed. Through observing their mothers in these events, infants come to understand not only the referential nature of her emotions and attention (see chapter 6), but infants also learn to predict her subsequent actions.

Research on desire reasoning

Current research that has focused on an awareness of beliefs and desires in infants has revealed that infants as young as 3–4 years of age understand that people have things in mind (Wellman and Estes, 1986), and that mental states such as beliefs (Perner, 1991) and desires (Wellman and Estes, 1986) compel humans to act. In fact, it appears that by 3 years of age infants have a well developed understanding of desire. They can reason about what people want (Moses, 1993; Wellman and Banerjee, 1995) and they use mental terms such as "want" and "like" to express this understanding (Bartsch and Wellman, 1995; Legerstee et al., 2004).

Although younger children may not solve complex verbal laboratory tasks that inquire into their understanding of cognitive mental states such as beliefs, there is ample evidence that infants are able to solve tasks that involve an awareness of simple mental states such as emotions and desires (Bartsch and Wellman, 1995; Wellman and Woolley, 1990), and that these states may lead to actions (Wellman, 1990). Wellman (1990, p. 16) has argued that "before becoming belief-desire psychologists young children are simple desire psychologists." For instance, when watching people who direct their attention and emotions toward objects in the environment, infants with primitive mental states understand that these cues may signal the person's intention to act on objects, but they do not understand that people may have mental representations about the objects. Although much work has been done to investigate the child's understanding of beliefs and desires (Bartsch and Wellman, 1995; Flavell, Green, and Flavell, 1986; Flavell, Flavell, Green, and Moses, 1990; Wimmer and Perner, 1983), little is known about the origins of these abilities.

Primitive desire reasoning in 18-month-olds

Recently, Repacholi and Gopnik (1997) showed that by 18 months, infants have developed some aspect of the concept of desire. In that study, an experimenter tasted either crackers or broccoli and facially and vocally expressed either disgust or happiness. Following the displays of emotions the experimenter made a verbal and manual request gesture for the food by moving the tray in front of the infant and then putting her hand between the bowls in which the food was presented with the palm of her hand turned upward. The experimenter asked the infant, "Can you give me some?" Whereas the 18-month-old infants responded correctly to the experimenter's request, the 14-month-olds commonly gave the experimenter the food that they liked themselves. The authors concluded that only the 18-month-olds understood the subjective nature of the request and the relation between emotional expressions and desires.

If 18-month-old infants demonstrate an appreciation of a person's desires and intentions, then the origins probably can be traced to early infancy. Infant research consistently points to a transition in the infants' awareness of people's actions between 8 and 12 months. During this time infants demonstrate a robust awareness that people's actions are directed to external objects. Although the 14-month-olds in the Repacholi and Gopnik (1997) study responded egocentrically, they did appear to understand that the experimenter desired something. In order to determine how younger preverbal infants reason about such actions, nonverbal tasks rather than verbal tasks should be used and infant looking behavior rather than active (manual) participation should be recorded as dependent variables. Infants tend to look less long at familiar events that confirm expectations and longer at events that are novel or violate expectations (Spelke, Breinlinger, Macomber, and Jacobson, 1992).

Primitive desire reasoning in 12 and 14-month-olds, but not in 8-month-olds

In order to find out whether the quality of infant–mother relationships influences infants' appreciation that a person's expression of pleasure when gazing toward an object is consistent with that person's subsequent handling of the object, the present study elaborated and expanded on the work by Phillips et al. (2002) and Barna and Legerstee (2005). These authors had investigated whether toward the end of the first year infants begin to appreciate that a person who emotes positively while gazing toward an object may subsequently want to reach and grasp it. Phillips et al. (2002) found that 12 but not 8-month-old infants are aware that people are likely to obtain objects that they regard with positive affect. In a habituation paradigm, infants were first shown an actor who looked at one of two similar objects with a positive facial expression. A curtain then blocked the infants' view of this display. When the curtain opened, the infants saw the actor holding the object she had been looking at earlier. After habituation, the infants were presented with two test events. In the test event that was consistent with their hypothesis, the actor was shown holding the object she had looked at during habituation. In the inconsistent test event, the actor was shown holding the *other* object. Twelve-month-olds, but not 8-month-olds, looked longer at the inconsistent event. The authors suggested that one of the reasons the 8-month-old infants failed the tasks was because they had difficulty following the actor's gaze when *two* objects were presented at the same time. Three additional studies employing small variations and controls further supported the earlier findings. Phillips et al. interpreted their findings to suggest that 12-month-olds use information about direction of gaze and emotional expression to predict action. However, in order to provide information about the cues infants use in solving this task, these cues need to be controlled. Furthermore, it is likely that infants younger than 12 months may succeed in the tasks if only one object is used.

Barna and Legerstee (2005) investigated these questions. The authors randomly assigned 9–12-month-old infants to an experimental and control condition. In the experimental condition, infants were presented with a pretrial in which happy and unhappy actors alternately looked and emoted at an abstract object while vocalizing. To control for learning during testing, the actors did not emote positively and then pick up the objects during habituation. Rather, to facilitate an understanding of the tasks, infants were given a cue during habituation; namely, they were shown an actor holding an object but the emotional expression (e.g. happy or unhappy) was concealed. Consequently, infants' looking time during the test trials could not reflect the acquisition of a simple association. To prevent that infants may expect people to pick up the toy because they associated particular behavioral patterns with it (e.g. in the Phillips et al. study the toy was a cute kitty), an abstract object was used. Finally, because young infants have trouble following the gazes of people to more than one object (Spelke, Phillips, and Woodward, 1995), we presented the infants with only one stimulus at a time. In the control group, infants received the same three-phase procedure, except that no object was present during the pre- and habituation trials. Analyses comparing the between-subject variables revealed that infants in the experimental group looked significantly longer at the unhappy actor than infants in the control group but less long at the happy actor. This study was the first to compare positive and negative emotions and to show that infants as young as 9 months use these emotions to make inferences about people's subsequent actions on objects.

However, the findings do not clarify what the mechanisms are that may influence an understanding of such primitive awareness of the concept of desire. In particular whether the quality of the interactive relationship infants have with their caretakers might influence this development. Consequently, we divided 9 and 12-month-old infants into high and low attuned interactive groups. We then submitted infants to two studies, one where they were provided with an action cue during habituation, the other, where they were presented with pretrials before being administered the post-test events. During the pretrials infants were familiarized with actors who emoted either positively or disgustedly until infants looked away. In the test trials, infants were presented alternately with either the happy or the disgusted actors holding the objects.

It was predicted that infants who have developed a positive relationship with their mothers as assessed during natural interactions in the laboratory will develop sooner than infants who do not, an understanding that people's emotions are about things and predictive of intentional action.

General method[1]

Infants were recruited from hospitals on two continents. A total of 121 infants were recruited for the study, $N = 49$ from North America and $N = 72$ from Europe. Data from 108 infants were included in the final sample. There were 56 nine-month-olds ($M = 292$ days, sd $= 14.24$;

[1] This study was funded by a Social Sciences and Humanities Research grant 410–2001–0197 from Canada. We acknowledge Tricia Striano for conducting the statistical analyses.

35 males and 21 females) and 52 twelve-month-olds ($M = 388$ days, sd $= 9.45$; 27 males and 25 females). An additional 13 infants were tested but excluded from the analysis because they failed to achieve a quiet state ($N = 7$) (Wolff, 1966), or because of experimental error ($N = 6$). Infants from both samples came from lower to middle class families based on parental education. Infants received a small gift for participating.

Infants were observed in an infancy room that was 4×5 meters. Four white walls surrounded the infants to limit possible environmental distractions. Infants were placed in an infant seat facing a table, on which the abstract stimulus was placed, and behind which the actor stood. The table was positioned 60 cm in front of the infants. The infants sat on their mother's lap. Mothers wore headphones, and were asked to look to the side, so that they could not see the experimental paradigm and mimic the facial expressions of the actors. Consequently, infants could not receive cues from their mothers when trying to look at them. Thus mothers were naive to the experimental paradigm and were asked to refrain from communicating with their infants. One camera and zoom lens focused on the infant's face from a distance of 1.8 m. The camera was positioned at eye level of the infant and was placed above and behind a curtain. Another video camera and zoom lens focused on the stimuli presented to the infants. This camera was situated behind and to the left of the infant.

To ensure that infants were not responding to the task with a situation-action script (infants may associate a particular behavioral pattern with familiar targets, cf. Wellman, Harris, Banerjee, and Sinclair, 1995), two different unfamiliar stimuli were used throughout the study. Mothers reported that none of the infants had played with such objects.

Infants were shown two different actors. In one display the "happy" actor stood behind the table facing the object and in the other display the "disgusted" actor stood behind the table facing the object. Both actors were similar in appearance to control for confounding variables (i.e. both actors were female, dressed in the same black sweaters or white blouses, and bandanas, and were matched for hair and eye color). Four actors were used to ensure that infant looking was a function of the affective message and not specific to one actor's attractiveness over another.

An assistant watched the infants' looking behavior on a television behind a curtain. This television displayed the infant's upper torso, arms, and head. A television and VCR were situated in the control room. The VCR was employed to videotape the sessions of each infant. A date–time generator recorded the length of each session in seconds, for later coding purposes. A computer was used to code infant responses using a computer habituation program (Schmuckler, 1981) which kept track of the infants' looks and determined when trials are finished and when infants look away for longer than 2 s.

In Experiments 1 and 2, infants were presented with two procedures. One to obtain information about maternal interactive styles and the infants' pro-social behaviors, and the other to assess the effect maternal interactive style may have on the infants' recognition that people's emotions and perception may relate to action.

Mother–infant interactions. To obtain information about the social interactions of the dyad, maternal interactive behaviors and infants' pro-social behaviors were coded during a 3-minute interaction period, during which mother and infant played with toys on the floor. Toys were used that had previously been shown to elicit stimulating exchanges between mother and child. These were: two books, a rattle with mirror, a puzzle (train), a hand puppet, stacking cubes, musical toys, an Elmo on a bicycle, a ball filled with water and swimming ducks, and push toys.

Maternal behaviors. Affect attunement was composed of three maternal behavioral categories: (1) maternal maintaining, (2) warm sensitivity, and (3) social responsiveness. The definitions of these maternal behaviors were provided in chapter 8.

Infant pro-social measures. To assess infants' level of pro-social behavior, three infant measures were coded during the natural interaction condition: (1) referential behaviors, (2) smiles, and (3) vocalizations, and words. *Referential behaviors* consisted of points, offers/shows, and meaningful gestures (e.g. bye-bye, no/yes [head shake]). *Smiles* were defined as raised eyebrows and raised corners of the mouth, with the mouth either open or closed. *Vocalizations* were defined as relatively long vocal sounds with varied pitch contours and oral resonance. These sounds are defined as discrete, voiced sounds occurring within one aspiration. Wheezes, sneezes, coughs, and cries were not included in the vocalization count.

Interrater reliability. Two coders coded the frequencies and duration of infants' and mothers' behaviors. Coding began when infants and mothers looked at each other and discontinued when three minutes were finished. Coding was done separately for each behavior and in real time. On and offset times of the variables were indicated by a video recorder with an internal time generator. The time generator imposed a clock directly onto the tapes to aid in determining the length (in seconds and minutes) of conditions and behaviors. One observer coded all the sessions whereas the second observer coded 20 percent of the sessions to assess reliability. The second observer was trained to 90 percent reliability with an experienced trainer and was unaware of the hypotheses and the mothers' affective state. Kappas for infant behaviors were 0.82 for gazes, 0.88 for smiles, and 0.88 for referential behaviors. Kappas for maternal behaviors were 0.83 for maintaining attention, 0.80 for warm sensitivity, and 0.80 for social responsiveness.

High and low attuned mothers. To divide mothers into high and low attuned, their scores on maintaining were rank ordered. A natural split was observed which allowed the division of mothers in such a way that 54.5 percent of them were in HAM (high maintaining) and 45.5 percent in LAM (low maintaining). The range of duration of scores for HAM was from 160–178, and for LAM was from 39 to 156 for the 3-minute interaction.

Relation between maintaining, warm sensitivity, and social responsiveness. To determine whether the three maternal scores correlated, Pearson Rs were conducted. Significant correlations were found between maintaining and social responsiveness: $r = 0.381$, $p = 0.05$; between maintaining and warm sensitivity: $r = 0.474$, $p < 0.01$; and between warm sensitivity and social responsiveness: $r = 0.563$, $p < 0.001$.

Thus mothers who ranked high on maintaining attention also ranked high on warm sensitivity and social responsiveness. We labeled those mothers who ranked high on maintaining, warm sensitivity, and social responsiveness the high affect attunement group (HAM) and those who ranked low on these variables, the low affect attunement group (LAM).

Pro-social infant behavior. To determine whether the infants of HAM mothers scored higher on pro-social behaviors than infants of LAM mothers, one-way ANOVAs were performed with maternal interactive styles as the independent factor for each of the following infant behaviors: (1) referential gestures at mother, (2) smiles, and (3) vocalizations. The first test showed that infants whose mothers ranked higher on affect attunement produced more referential communicative gestures, such as pointing, in the presence of their mothers than infants whose mothers ranked lower on affect attunement, $F (1, 107) = 5.33$, $p = 0.023$ (M = 0.13 for LAM and M = 0.61 for HAM). The second test revealed that infants whose mothers ranked high on affect attunement smiled significantly more than infants whose mothers ranked low on affect attunement, $F (1, 107) = 10.74$, $p = 0.001$ (M = 2.43 for LAM and M = 6.05 for HAM). The third test showed that infants of high affect attunement mothers produced more vocalizations than infants of low affect attunement mothers, $F (1, 107) = 9.02$, $p = 0.003$ (M = 1.75 for LAM and M = 4.03 for HAM) (see table 9.1).

In summary, mothers and infants could be divided into two distinct groups in terms of their interactive styles. High affectively attuned (HAM) mothers had infants who ranked high on pro-social behaviors; they produced more pointing gestures, smiles, and vocalizations to their mothers than infants of the low affectively attuned group (LAM).

Table 9.1. *Means and standard deviations for mother and infant social behavior as a function of age and high and low dyad*

	Low interactive dyad		High interactive dyad	
	9 months	12 months	9 months	12 months
Mother behaviors				
Maintaining	99.75 (32.58)	109.14 (37.35)	123.04 (30.65)	154.30 (26.58)
Warm sensitivity	2.88 (.53)	2.80 (.56)	3.45 (.30)	3.77 (.60)
Infant behaviors				
Referential behaviors	0.00 (0.00)	0.22 (1.00)	0.18 (.38)	0.98 (1.72)
Smiles	1.13 (2.45)	1.19 (2.47)	6.76 (6.53)	7.52 (7.28)
Vocalizations	1.18 (2.03)	1.91 (2.35)	2.75 (2.50)	5.40 (6.14)

(Legerstee and Barillas, 2003, Experiment 2, subsequently used the HAM group to examine the amount of declarative pointing in these infants; see chapter 5.)

To evaluate the effects of maternal interactive styles on infant abilities to relate adult emotions to actions on objects, the HAM and LAM infants were randomly assigned to the cued habituation study and the familiarization study. The method of the two studies will be described successively. However, because there were no significant differences in the way the infants responded in the test events as a result of the different methods, the results for the test events for the two studies have been collapsed and will be described together.

Experiment 1 – cued habituation study In order to find out whether an action cue would facilitate an understanding of the tasks, and to prevent infants from learning a simple association during habituation (e.g. smile and pick up), we showed infants during a pretest either a happy or disgusted actor emoting while looking at an object. Infants were then habituated to an actor holding an object but obscured the face of the actor behind a screen, thereby concealing the emotional expressions (e.g. happiness or disgust) (see figure 9.1).

It was hypothesized that if infants understood that people who emote happily toward an object want to grab it, then they should infer during this habituation sequence that the "happy" actor is holding the object and not the "disgusted" actor.

Participants. Seventy-eight infants participated in Study 1 ($N = 41$ males). Four babies were eliminated due to fussiness, and four due to experimenter error. Seventy infants were included in the final analysis.

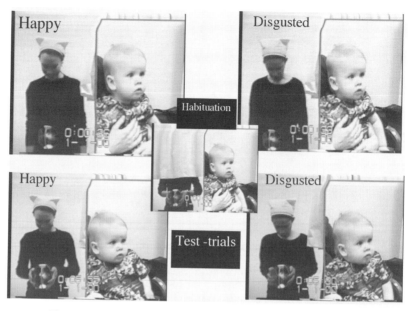

Figure 9.1 Cued experiment: pretrials, habituation, and test trials.

The mean age of the remaining 9-month-olds was 290 days. The mean age of the remaining 12-month-olds was 387 days.

Habituation event. When infants were in an alert and quiet state (Wolff, 1966), they were shown the two different events twice alternately. In the happy trial, the actor would say "Oh a wassagossi" twice (total of 12 s), and then leave. Multimodal (facial/vocal) happy or unhappy affective states were used to facilitate the perception of this affect (Walker-Andrews, 1997). Then the other actor appeared, looked at the abstract objects, and said "Yak, a wassagossi" twice (total of 12 s). A screen then closed (1 s). When the screen opened (1 s) the infants saw one of the actors holding the object, but a curtain blocked the actor from the shoulders to the head. Thus, the identity of the actor (happy or disgusted) was unknown to the infants. Looking times were recorded for attention to this second phase. Infants had to look at the event for at least 0.5 s. The trial ended when infants looked away for longer than 2 s. The criterion for habituation consisted of infants producing two successive gazes at the stimulus, for a total of less than 50 percent of the total duration of their first two consecutive gazes. The first two gazes had to sum to at least 12 s. The minimum number of habituation trials was 4, and the maximum number of trials was 14. The observer signaled silently to the actor when the habituation trial had ended. Order of presentation was counterbalanced.

Test trials. After reaching the criterion for habituation, the curtain closed (1 s) and then opened (1 s) to show the infants two different types of test trials twice alternately. In one test trial, the happy actor was holding the object. In the other, the disgusted actor was holding the object (see figure 9.1).

A look began when the infants looked at the stimulus for more than 0.5 s. A look ended when infants looked away from the display for longer than 2 s. Inter stimulus intervals were 2 seconds. These two sessions were repeated three times each. Order of presentation was counterbalanced among infants.

Experiment 2 – infant controlled study

Participants. Forty-three infants participated in Study 2 ($N = 21$ males). Three were eliminated due to fussiness, two to experimenter error. The mean age of the 38 remaining infants was 294 days (9-month-olds) and 388 days (12-month-olds).

Familiarization. When infants were in an alert and quiet state (Wolff, 1966), they were presented with either a happy or a disgusted actor twice alternately. In each condition, the actor stood in front of the table while looking at the object. In the happy actor condition, the actor said with a happy facial expression, "Oh! A wassagossi," as soon as the infant looked at the event, and for as long as the infant looked at the stimulus for more than 2 seconds. A session ended when the infant looked away for longer than 2 seconds. In the other condition, the actor said, "Yak, a wassagossi," while displaying a disgusted facial expression, until the infant looked away for longer than 2 s. The same number of syllables was contained within each expression. Each utterance was 6 s long, and the utterances were divided by 1 s pauses. Each condition was repeated twice. After the four familiarization trials had ended the experimenter closed the curtain (1 s). Order of presentation was counterbalanced among infants.

Test trials. The test trials began when the curtain opened (1 s) to show the infants two different types of test trials twice alternately. In one test trial, the curtain was raised to reveal that the happy actor was holding the object. In the other, the curtain was raised to reveal that the disgusted actor was holding the object. A look began when the infants looked at the stimulus for more than 0.5 s. A look ended when infants looked away from the display for longer than 2 s. Inter stimulus intervals were 2 seconds. These two sessions were repeated three times each. The order of the test trials was counterbalanced among infants.

Coding and inter-rater reliability. Each coder underwent a rigorous training period with a practiced coder to attain an inter-observer reliability of 90 percent or above. Gazes were coded as duration. Two research assistants coded the infants' gazes during the habituation trials and the test trials. Reliability between the two coders was $r = 0.962$, $p = 0.001$. Normal speed was used in coding the data. The assistants who recorded the infants' looking behavior during the experiment were blind to the group of the infants. The second assistant coded the videotaped recordings of the infants without sound. As such she was also blind to the order of the test trials.

Results of the habituation trials during the *cued habituation* study showed that nine-month-old HAM infants took 8.9 trials and LAM infants took 9.3 trials to reach habituation. On the last two habituation trials the 9-month-old HAM infants looked for an average of 4.3 seconds and the LAM infants 4.9 seconds. The 12-month-old HAM infants reached habituation on an average of 7.1 trials and the LAM infants on an average of 7.9 trials. On the last habituation trial, 12-month-old HAM infants looked for an average of 3.8 seconds and the LAM infants for an average of 3.9 seconds. The number of trials for all infants fell within 4 and 14 trials.

Results of the infant *controlled familiarization* study showed that 9-month-old HAM infants looked at the happy actor for an average of 36.89 s (SD = 27.13) and at the disgusted actor for an average of 30.62 s (SD = 18.84). The 9-month-old LAM infants looked for an average of 49.84 s (SD = 34.55) at the happy actor and an average of 41.19 s (SD = 34.55) at the disgusted actor. Twelve-month-old HAM infants looked at the happy actor for an average of 44.93 s (SD = 27.84) and at the disgusted actor for an average of 32.27 s (SD = 15.96). The 12-month-old LAM infants looked for an average of 29.69 s (SD = 15.13) at the happy actor and an average of 18.62 s (SD = 9.92) at the disgusted actor.

Test events. Infants in studies 1 and 2 had been presented with the same test events. To determine whether there was a significant difference between the test events as a function of the cue infants were given in study 1, the gazes for the 9-month-old infants and the 12-month-old infants were submitted separately to a mixed model ANOVA, with group (2, high and low affect attunement) and experiment (2, familiarization, habituation) as the between-subjects factor, and condition (2, happy versus disgust) as the within-subjects factor. There was no significant effect of experiment for either the 9-month-olds ($p = 0.78$) or the 12-month-olds ($p = 0.94$). Consequently, infant gazes produced during the test events of studies 1 and 2 were collapsed.

The gazes of the younger and older group are reported separately because these infants do not always perform alike in looking-time events (Phillips et al., 2002). The data of the 9-month-olds and the 12-month-olds are reported below.

Nine-month-old infants. If infants, during the familiarization and habituation trials, develop an expectation when viewing the happy actor emoting to the object that this actor wants the object, then during the test trials they should look less long at the happy actor where the expectancy is confirmed (familiarity effect) and longer at test trials where the expectancy is violated (novelty effect). Consequently, infant gazes during the test trials were submitted to a mixed model design. Because there were no effects of sex and order, the data were re-analyzed without these variables, but with group (2, HAM, LAM) as the between subjects factor, and test event (2, happy versus disgust) as the within subjects factor.

The 9-month-old infants in the LAM group looked significantly longer at the happy than the disgusted actor, F (1, 29) $= 4.75$, $p = 0.038$. In contrast, the 9-month-old infants of HAM mothers looked longer at the disgusted versus happy actor during the test trials, F (1, 25) $= 5.39$, $p = 0.029$. This suggests that the HAM infants had developed an expectation during the pre-trials that people who emote positively toward objects may want to pick them up. When this expectation was violated during the test events, the infants looked longer at this novel event, but less long at the familiar event that supported this expectation.

Twelve-month-old infants. Infant gazes during the test trials were submitted to a mixed model design. Again, because no effects of sex and order were found the data were re-analyzed without these variables, but with group (2, HAM, LAM) as the between subjects factor and test event (2, happy versus disgust) as the within subjects factor.

The results showed that the 12-month-old LAM infants did not discriminate between the happy and disgusted actor, F (1, 25) $= 0.001$, $p = 0.918$. In contrast, the 12-month-old HAM infants showed a significant preference for the disgusted actor over the happy actor, F (1, 25) $= 30.00$, $p < 0.001$.

In summary, the results of studies 1 and 2 showed that infants of HAM mothers appreciate that when people emote positively toward an abstract object they tend to act on it; whereas, infants of LAM mothers do not. This suggests that the LAM infants did not see the test events as a violation of expectancy. Whereas the 9-month-old LAM infants looked longer at the happy versus the disgusted actors, the 12-month-olds did not differentiate between the two stimuli. In contrast, infants of the HAM group, regardless of age, looked significantly longer at the disgusted than the happy actors. Thus by 9 months, infants use the emotional valence of the positive and negative expressions of people to predict what actions the experimenter will engage in. The finding that infants of HAM mothers performed better than infants of LAM mothers indicates that affect attunement plays an important role in the development of this ability.

Experiment 3 – incongruent focus study

Studies 1 and 2 indicated that infants in the HAM group are not only skilled at decoding emotional information, but also have expectations about the actions of people who express emotions to objects. Namely, they expected people who emoted positively to act on these objects, and not those who emoted negatively. Thus it appears that infants understand that emotions are referential, that they are about things. However, these studies did not clarify whether infants understood that the actor's emotions were referring to a *specific* object, namely the one she *looked at*. One of the cues adults use to infer what people are emoting about is gaze direction. If infants do not inquire about the gaze of the adult, then they may make mistakes about what the person is emoting to. It is not clear whether infants in the previous studies used gaze as a cue because we did not control for attentional focus *of the infant* (see also Barna and Legerstee, 2005; Legerstee and Barillas, Experiment 1; 2003; and Phillips et al., 2002 for similar problems). Thus, instead of demonstrating that infants use referential understanding to infer what people will do, a reliance on temporal contiguity between the infant's focus of attention and the actor's emotional expression may lead infants to associate the emotions of others with actions on objects.

To determine whether infants in this study relied on attentional cues to interpret what the actor wanted, study 3 was conducted. This study has been inspired by the discrepant-focus scenario used in social referencing studies by Moses et al. (2001). In that social referencing study, 12-month-old infants relied on the presence of referential cues to determine which object the actor emoted about. They tracked an object gazed at by an emoter (in focus condition), and modified their responses to that object as a result of positive or negative emotions directed at the object. However, when the actor did not look at the object while emoting (out of focus condition), the infants did not attribute the valence of a particular emotion to that object. This incongruent focus scenario has not been used with infants whose mothers varied on affect attunement, and thus it remains unclear whether emotionally sensitive mothers promote the development of referential understanding of attention and affect in infants. In fact, this scenario has only been used to test what *infants* will do after reading the emotions of adults (e.g. whether they will either pick up the object or not) and not what infants expect *others* to do (e.g. whether others will pick up the object or not). Consequently, study 3 examined this ability in 11–14-month-old infants. The sample included 23 infants from studies 1 and 2, nine from the original 9-month-olds in the HAM group, and fourteen of the original 12-month-old infants from the LAM group seen approximately one month later. We predicted that because the original 9-month-old sample had successfully completed the tasks in studies 1 and 2, they would provide information about the cues they were using during the task. Given the further demands of the task, we expected that the LAM infants would not succeed. In addition to this sample, we tested a new group of 38 infants of the same mean age. These infants engaged with their mother in a three minute interaction exactly matching that of studies 1 and 2. One-way ANOVAs with group (original sample vs. new sample) performed on maternal maintaining, warm sensitivity, and responsiveness for the HAM and LAM groups revealed no significant main effects or interactions. Furthermore, a one-way ANOVA with group (original sample vs. new sample) as the factor was performed on mean looking during the test trials. This analysis also revealed no main effects or interactions. These samples were therefore collapsed for all analyses. All relations between maternal sensitivity and infant prosocial behaviors matched those reported in studies 1 and 2. Thus, the focus is specifically on whether infants will use the attentional cues of the experimenter to determine which object she is emoting about and will act upon next. We hypothesized that infants of HAM mothers would acquire this ability sooner than infants of LAM mothers.

Participants. Infants were recruited from hospitals and birth announcements. Data from 61 infants were included in the final sample (35 males and 26 females). The mean age of infants was 369 days (SD = 26). The sample included 39 HAM infants ($M = 368$ days, SD = 19) and 22 LAM infants ($M = 370$ days, SD = 35). An additional four infants were tested but excluded from the final sample due to fussiness ($N = 2$), or experimental error ($N = 2$). The sample came from lower to middle class families based on parental education. Infants received a small gift for participating.

Stimuli. Infants were shown two toy remote-controlled white fluffy dogs. One of the dogs had a scarf on and the other wore shorts. Different clothes were selected to make the toys distinguishable from each other. Experimenter 2 sat on the floor behind the table and activated the toy dogs via a remote control. She watched the infant's looking behavior on a TV monitor out of sight from infant and mother. Different clothes and their opposite locations made it less likely that infants would mistake which dog the experimenter directed her affective display toward.

Equipment. Infants were filmed in the same environment as studies 1 and 2, and with the same video equipment. Consequently, a video record was obtained with time in seconds digitally recorded on it, providing information about the continuous flow of events.

Procedure. Infants were placed in front of a table (67 × 117 cm) on their mother's lap and facing a female experimenter. The two toys were placed on the left and right side of the table, at a 60 cm distance from each other, and at 60 cm from the infants. The infants were seated in such a way that they could see both toys and the experimenter when looking straight ahead. Parents listened to music and were asked to look in the opposite direction from the toy the infant had to focus on.

A standard procedure was followed across the congruent and incongruent conditions. The experimenter sat down in front of the infant, and gently called the infant's name. When the infant looked at her, she slowly turned her head toward the in-focus dog until the infant followed her head turn. She would look at the in-focus dog for 5 s.

Congruent condition. As soon as the infant followed the head turn of experimenter 1 toward the in-focus dog, experimenter 2 would activate the in-focus dog that began to move and bark. At that time both experimenter and infant would be looking at the in-focus dog, and experimenter 1 would say, "Oh isn't that beautiful?" for 5 seconds in an infant controlled pretrial period. If the infant shifted gaze toward the out-of-focus dog, experimenter 1 would stop emoting (facially and vocally, so that the infants would not develop expectations about the incongruent events), but resume again when the infant looked at the in-focus dog. This sequence continued until the infants had looked for a total of 5 seconds at the in-focus dog. This session was repeated twice (see figure 9.2).

Incongruent condition. This condition was similar to the congruent condition except that experimenter 1 now emoted only when the infant looked at the out-of-focus dog. As before, the infant followed the head turn of experimenter 1. By continuing to gaze at the in-focus dog until 5 s had elapsed, the infants had ample time to notice what the experimenter was looking at. After 5 s were completed, experimenter 2 activated the out-of-focus dog opposite experimenter 1. When the infant looked toward the out-of-focus dog, experimenter 1, while continuing to look at the in-focus dog, said "Oh isn't that beautiful?" If the infants looked at the in-focus dog, the experimenter would stop emoting (facially and vocally), so that the infants could not develop any expectations about a congruent event during the incongruent condition. The experimenter would continue to emote until the infants had looked for 5 seconds at the out-of-focus dog. Experimenter 1 was able to follow the gazes of the

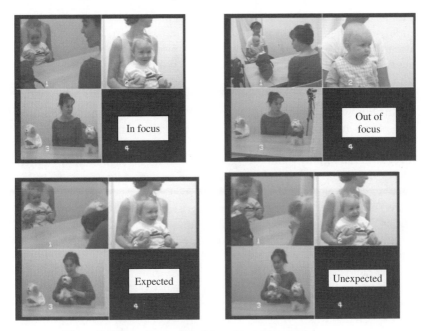

Figure 9.2 Experiment 3: habituation and test trials.

infants because a TV monitor was placed behind the in-focus dog. This TV monitor showed the face of the infant, and consequently, experimenter 1 could follow the gazes of the infant while she herself was looking at the in-focus dog. The session was again repeated twice.

Test events. As soon as the familiarization periods were finished, a curtain was drawn that prevented the infants from seeing the displays. When the curtain opened the test phase began with the experimenter holding either the in- or out-of-focus dog. Looking was coded when infants looked longer than 2 s at the experimenter, and looked away from her for longer than 2 s. Thereafter the curtain closed (1 s) and then opened (1 s) and the sessions were repeated twice for the in-focus (congruent) and out-of-focus (incongruent) conditions.

Coding and inter-rater reliability. As in studies 1 and 2, the video close-up provided an accurate view of the infant's face and eyes. This allowed us to check the infant's understanding of the experimenter's referential intent (see also Moses et al., 2001). The duration of infant gazes were coded as before. Two research assistants coded the infant's gazes during the test trials. These coders were naive to the experimental hypotheses and could not influence the results one way or another. Normal speed was used in coding the data. One coder coded the videotapes without sound. Each coder underwent a rigorous training period with a practiced coder to attain an inter-observer reliability of 90 percent or above. Reliability between the two coders was $r = 0.967$, $p < 0.001$. Results of Experiment 3 showed that infants use emotions and attention to infer people's subsequent actions.

Test events. Gazes during the test event would reveal what expectations the infants had developed during the pre-trials. Thus during the test events, infants who understood that gazes and emotions are important for referential intent, would be surprised if the actor picked up the object *she* had not looked at and emoted about. Consequently, the gazes of the infants were submitted to a two way ANOVA, where group (HAM, LAM) and condition (congruent, incongruent) were the between subject variables. The results showed that infants in the HAM group looked significantly longer when the experimenter picked up the object she had not been looking at, $F (1, 37) = 23.45$, $p < 0.0001$. Thus, these infants had developed an expectation during the pre-trials that the experimenter would pick up the object she emoted and gazed at, and looked longer when this expectation was violated. However, they looked less long when the expectancy was confirmed (familiarity effect). No significant differences were found for the LAM group, $F (1, 19) = 0.153$, $p = 0.700$.

Summary. Results of infant gazes in study 3 indicated that HAM infants and not LAM infants looked longer when the experimenter held the out-of-focus dog than at the in-focus dog. These HAM infants paid attention to both gaze and affect when relating emotions to actions. They must have noticed during the familiarization period what the experimenter was looking at, and consequently expected her to pick up that object. These findings provide strong evidence that affect attunement of mothers promotes an awareness of these abilities, because only infants of HAM mothers succeeded on these tasks.

General discussion

The research I have discussed here investigated some of the earliest ways in which infants reason about the behavior of people. Specifically, it asked whether infants would use information about affect and perception to predict action. In chapter 5, I discussed how previous studies aimed at identifying the origins of psychological understanding in dyadic (mother–child) interactions. In the present chapter, we continued this investigation in triadic (person–object–infant) interactions. In particular, we wanted to find out whether 9–14-month-old infants of attuned mothers are better able to infer the referential nature of her emotions and attention, than infants who have less optimal interactions with their mothers, and whether infants use these cues to infer subsequent action. Previous research (Phillips et al., 2002) had shown that from as early as 12 months, infants begin to understand that people are likely to obtain objects to which they regard with positive affect. The ability to infer that people who emote positively toward things may want to handle them is important because it is evidence of a primitive concept of desire in infants (Bartsch and Wellman, 1995) which can be said to be a foundation of a mature concept of desire and a Theory of Mind (Wellman, 1990). In the Phillips et al. (2002) study such awareness was demonstrated in paradigms where infants were habituated to a person who emoted happily to one of two objects. In the test events, infants looked longer when actors picked up objects they had not emoted toward. The authors suggested that 12-month-old infants use information about direction of gaze and emotional expression in combination to predict action in others. However, in that study the emotional expressions of the actors and the attentional focus of the infants had not been controlled, and consequently no direct information about the use of these cues in infants was available.

Barna and Legerstee (2005) replicated and extended the Phillips et al. (2002) study with 9-month-old infants, in order to examine whether this ability develops prior to 12 months of age. They further presented infants with two emotional (facial/vocal) displays, namely a happy and unhappy actor who emoted toward an object. The authors argued that if infants understand that positive emotions directed at things are related to subsequent handling, then during the test events infants should look less long at the happy actor holding the object (congruent test event) but longer at the unhappy actor (incongruent test event). The incongruent test event should have been seen as novel and elicit greater recovery from looking than the congruent test event. Infants showed during the experimental and control pretrials that they preferred happy over unhappy actors. This preference disappeared in the experimental posttests, but not in the control posttests. These findings indicate that only infants in the experimental group had developed expectations during habituation that people who emote positively toward objects may want to act on the object and increased looking from pre- to test trials for the unhappy actor (novel event). Thus 9-month-old infants understood that people's behavior such as emotions are cues to people's intentions, such as the subsequent actions on objects.

Mechanisms that promote socio-cognitive development

The present study focused on the mechanisms that promote an awareness of intentional behavior in infants. As I have argued throughout this book, intentions are fundamentally interpersonal phenomena and develop within an interpersonal context. I agree with others who argue that interpersonal relationships are the most germane feature to foster intentional understanding in infants (Stern, 1995; Fogel, 1993). Consequently, in providing a developmental account of the concept of intention one must focus on the inter-subjective nature of intention attribution and see its foundation in interpersonal interaction. Thus, infants who engage in affective relationships with their mothers must be better able to detect intentional behavior in others than infants who do not. Affect sharing promotes inter-intentionality (Trevarthen, 1979). Consequently, we divided mothers and infants into high and low attuned dyads, and submitted them to tasks in which the infants' abilities to infer the intentions of people who emote happily and disgustingly at objects were assessed. The results showed that 9-month-old infants of highly affective dyads understand the valence of emotional expressions sooner than infants of low affective dyads. They seem to be aware that different types of emotions are related to different kinds of actions. Such awareness is quite impressive. It enables infants not only to rely on others for more sophisticated information about the social world (Moses et al., 2001; Baldwin and Moses, 1994), but it also allows infants to begin to predict how others will act in certain situations.

The importance of the ability that infants have manifested in studies 1 and 2 depends on the scope of this knowledge. In order to examine whether this ability involves an understanding of primitive desire reasoning, infants need to show that they are aware that people emote about objects to which they attend and want to act upon. Study 3 was conducted to investigate the development of this referential awareness in 11–14-month-old infants, and whether the HAM group would be superior in performance than the LAM group. The results showed that infants in the highly affective group were aware which object the actor emoted about and subsequently wanted to pick up. They used the direction of her gaze to make these predictions (see also Legerstee and Barillas, 2003, Experiment 2). Thus, only the HAM infants had developed the appropriate skills to connect attention and emotion to subsequent action. These infants consequently expected the experimenter to pick up the object *she* had looked at. When she picked up the object she had not looked at, infants increased attention, presumably because they found the behavior unusual. The present study is the first to point out that the quality of interpersonal relationships influences an awareness of the referential nature of attention and emotions.

How does the development of primitive desire reasoning develop in infants? If one takes a developmental approach, then one needs to take into consideration how infants come to understand (1) the valence of emotions expressed by others, (2) that people's focus of attention is referential, and (3) how these two abilities coordinate in infants and begin to relate to an understanding of people's actions.

As discussed in the earlier chapters, infants in the first months of life discriminate among happy and negative facial expressions (Field et al., 1982; LaBarbera, Izard, Vietze, and Parisi, 1976) in particular if these facial expressions are presented by mothers (Barrera and Maurer, 1981), and if these mothers provide sensitive interactions that enhance the infant's exploration and attention to her face (Kuchuk, Vibbert, and Bornstein, 1986). By 3 months infants are also sensitive to the feelings expressed in these facial expressions because mothers who mirror the infant's actions have infants who are more socially responsive than mothers who do not (Legerstee and Varghese, 2001). Between 2 and 6 months infants recognize emotional expressions of happiness and anger, because they produce appropriate responses to them (Walker-Andrews, 1997; Soken and Pick, 1992). Thus, infants, from very early on, understand the meaning or feelings of others by the expression of their faces (Darwin, 1877). Infants are not only sensitive to the facial expressions of people, but also to their eyes (Haith, Bergman, and Moore, 1977; Johnson and Morton, 1991). Infants' own actions on objects and an awareness of others' object-directed actions mature during the first 6 months of life. Sensitive mothers support object-directed actions during co-regulated interactions (Fogel, 1993; Hsu and Fogel, 2003). At this age, infants clearly show that they have specific expectations about the behavior of people and understand that the actions of people are directed at things (Legerstee et al., 2000).

The increasing sophistication of an understanding of the meaning of emotion, direction of gaze, and action during the first 6 months of life prepares the way to understanding the referential nature of these behaviors during triadic episodes. Between 6 and 12 months, infants begin to show that they recognize that actions are not only directed at objects, but that they form part of, and are situated within, a rich context of other domains. By 12 months, infants use the emotional valence and attention of people to make decisions about their own movements on objects (Moses et al., 2001). As the results of the present study show, 9-month-old infants of highly sensitive mothers also use the emotions and gazes of other people to make predictions about what actions *other* people will engage in. We hypothesized that because an important element in the development of this ability is that sensitive mothers treat their infants as mental agents, whose behaviors are intentional (Bruner, 1990) we expected infants of HAM mothers to develop this awareness earlier than infants of LAM mothers. These hypotheses were confirmed in the present study.

Theoretical interpretations of the data

There are various ways that these findings can be interpreted. One theoretical explanation would argue that infants have learned to associate people's positive emotions with actions on objects. Thus rather than knowing that people's actions are about things, e.g. are intentional, infants have developed perceptions about the behavior of people who look and smile at things. Toward the end of the second year, these perceptions turn into conceptions of wanting or desire and an understanding of intentional behavior in others (Baldwin and Moses, 1996; Perner, 1991). Perner (1991) argues that the reason infants respond appropriately to emotional signals is because they have a simple behavioral rule that allows them to use emotional signals as a guide for action, but not as a cue to another's internal state. Thus, when the infant sees a novel object and someone is looking at it with fearful expressions, the rule dictates to avoid that object.

Similarly, Corkum and Moore (1995; 1998) suggest that infants know which object actors emote about because they follow the direction of their heads. Infants follow people's head-turns because they have learned in the past that interesting objects can be found when the head stops in a certain direction (Corkum and Moore, 1995; 1998). This mechanistic interpretation does not require an understanding of mental states of people.

It is true that head-turning may not in itself indicate that infants engage in intentional behavior at 12 months, but that does not mean that 12-month-old infants do not understand intentions in others. As discussed in chapter 5, Legerstee and Barillas (2003) found that infants as young as 12 months of age can be conditioned to follow head turns/gazes of people and inanimate agents, but they use declarative points when facing people *only* and not when presented with inanimate agents (Legerstee and Barillas, 2003). Thus gaze following *by itself* is not the right test to assess an awareness of intentionality in infants. In fact, no single experiment *alone* can rule out a particular interpretation; rather, various studies addressing a similar concept should be considered.

There are two experiments that provide evidence for a rich interpretation: Experiment 3 of the present study and Experiment 2 of the Legerstee and Barillas (2003) study. I described the Legerstee and Barillas (2003) study in detail in chapter 5. However, I would like to return to this study for a moment because Experiment 3 of the present (primitive desire) study provided the impetus and paradigm for Experiment 2 of the Legerstee and Barillas (2003) study. In the present primitive desire study infants in the HAM group produced significantly more communicative gestures (such as points) during the natural play conditions than infants of LAM mothers (see table 9.1).[2] Thus we knew that these infants were "pointers," which is important information if one wants to know whether infants point discriminatively (e.g. whether they are able to use imperative and declarative points; see also Camaioni et al., 2004). More importantly, however, only the HAM infants in the present study expected the experimenter to pick up the object *she* had looked at and not the one she had not looked at. Thus, only the HAM infants were aware of the attentional focus of the adult and the LAM infants were not. Thus the HAM group of the present primitive desire study provided a wonderful sample to test whether infants would ***point*** in order to direct the *attention* of the experimenter to an object she was not looking at.

The results of Experiment 2 of the Legerstee and Barillas (2003) study showed that infants produced more points to the dog the experimenter was not looking at (out-of-focus dog) versus the one she was looking at (in-focus dog). Declarative points are aimed at ***redirecting*** the attention of a person to something she is not looking at, and hence involve recognition of mental states. Thus the declarative points the infants produced revealed that the infants knew something about the mental, e.g. psychological state of people. Together the results of Experiment 3 of the present primitive desire study and those of Experiment 2 of the Legerstee and Barillas (2003) study provide converging evidence that infants are aware of the attentional state of the person.

If one can reject a lean interpretation then one must accept the rich interpretation. The rich interpretation explains this early behavior in terms of the infants' understanding of intentions in others. The evidence that infants of highly sensitive mothers develop this ability before infants of less sensitive mothers suggests that variation in social support interacts with conceptual abilities to affect referential understanding and psychological causality (Bruner, 1990; Tomasello, 1999). The results of this research can be taken to support the idea that inter-subjective exchanges promote conceptual development in infants during the first year of life. Infants perceive people to be intentional entities, whose actions are motivated by internal states. Infants expect people who emote and regard objects with positive affect to act on these things because they interpret the person as wanting or desiring that object. Infants expect people to act in accord with such mental states; if they do not, infants show surprise (Wellman, 1993; Phillips et al., 2002; Premack, 1990).

[2] Prepared by Tricia Striano, MPI, Leipzig.

Both theoretical orientations provide important insights into the development of behavior and thought in infants. Concepts of people are acquired through perceptual associations, but also through inferential processes. The fact that infants in everyday life may have become familiar with sequences where people pick up things toward which they express positive affect does not preclude that infants also conceptually process these events. Indeed, authors of various theoretical backgrounds emphasize that it would be difficult to postulate how infants could make inferential attributions later if totally incapable of something similar to it earlier (Flavell, 1999; Fodor, 1992). Familiarity of behavioral sequences is an important factor in violation-of-expectation studies, because it allows infants to pick out the conceptually consistent (familiar event) from the conceptually inconsistent, and hence unfamiliar event (Munakata, 2000).

The infants in our studies were able to use gaze direction and emotional expression to predict behavior. Infants evaluated the actor's behavior in accord with the actor's expressed affect, and whether or not the actor attended to the object. Moses et al. (2001) provide a powerful argument that the 12-month-old infants in their study evidenced intentional understandings in their social referencing behaviors because they inferred from the actor's attention referential intentions. Our infants demonstrated an awareness that emotions inform about things to which the emoter attends. This finding suggests that maternal interactive skills affect emerging appreciations of an internal state of others, such as desire, in infants. Social interaction theorists such as Vygotsky (1978), Fogel (1993), and Valsiner (1997) have argued for the dialogic nature of cognition. The authors propose that mental functions develop through the dialogic processes infants engage in with their caretakers. Thus, mental functions develop through the progressive internalization of semiotically manifested perspectives on reality that are negotiated within the mother–infant dyad. Cognition is thus embodied and relational, a reflection of our participation in a dynamic system. Cognition is the history of the experiences in which our bodies have engaged, rather than a record of objective represented contents of "reality" (Fogel, 1993). The results of this research have provided powerful empirical support for the idea that inter-subjective exchanges promote conceptual development in infants during the first year of life.

10 Social cognition – affect attunement, imitation, and contingency

Concluding speculations

In this book, I have focused on the way infants get to know people. A constraint constructivist view has been contrasted against the traditional Piagetian theories; associationist theories, the modular theories, the bio-social and social cognitive theories that postulate some type of prepared-ness in their models for social interaction. When choosing particular authors to represent these views, I have focused on those who provided specific theoretical analyses of the way infants become linked with the environment after birth. The particular predictions of these theories have been presented recurrently at specific points and in various chapters throughout the book in order to clarify the hypotheses being tested when reporting a particular study, and to further develop topics in later chapters.

My own belief is that infants are born with a special sense of people. This sense of people is the result of their biological propensity to perceive others as analogous to the self. This ability to perceive others "like me" allows infants to identify with others. This identification occurs first on an emotional level where infants recognize their own emotional state and compare these states to those of their conspecifics. Only caretakers who tune into their infants' affective states facilitate the sharing of emotions in their infants. Parents who do not engage in affect sharing with their infants, either because their infants have emotional difficulties, or because of their own psychological pre-occupations (see chapter 7), have infants who show delays in their social and cognitive development (Legerstee and Varghese, 2001; Legerstee et al., 2004). Thus, if the affective relationship is congruent, then infants develop a feeling of effi-cacy which will promote social and cognitive competence (Legerstee and Varghese, 2001). If the affective exchanges are not congruent or if there is no mutual sharing of affect, then infants display a generalized lack of efficacy which may result in a delay in the acquisition of certain cognitive milestones. Because emotional states are mental states, it is crucial that emotional sharing takes place from the beginning, so that infants may perceive primitive mental states of self and others which leads to the infants' identification with conspecifics.

Thus, my brand of constraint constructivism incorporates an affect sharing device that gives infants a leg up in learning about people. I have detailed this view throughout the chapters of this book, in particular in the first five chapters, while providing strong empirical evidence to support this view in the subsequent chapters.

Prepared learning theorists

Throughout this book, I have contrasted my own view with pertinent and very informative accounts of others. These theorists identified important aspects of how infants come to know people. Many of them proposed that infants are biologically prepared for social interaction. The content of this preparedness ranged from innate modules to perceive intentions without social interaction (Baron-Cohen, 1991), to perceive intentions in movement (Premack, 1991; Rakison and Poulin-Dubois, 2000; Gergely and Watson, 1999), and to have a special attraction for social stimuli (Barresi and Moore, 1996; Moore, 1996). However, I propose that these theories have various shortcomings. They either do not believe that people are important for ToM development (Baron-Cohen, 1991), or they do not believe that people are important early enough (Barresi and Moore, 1996; Piaget, 1954). Others have not explained *why* it would be adaptive that infants initially identify people through biological motion; nor have they put into place a mechanism that allows infants eventually to shift from their attraction to biological motion to the identification with social stimuli (e.g. Premack, 1991; Rakison and Poulin-Dubois, 2000).

"Like me" theorists

Although some theorists have put forth a simulation (e.g. Barresi and Moore, 1996) or "like me" view (e.g. Gergely and Watson, 1996; Tomasello, 1995) to explain the infant's awareness of people, they use this mechanism initially to explain the infant's identification with the physical aspects of people, and only much later with the psychological. For these authors infants are not inter-subjective organisms at birth who through sharing emotions with their partners are able to perceive others as "like me." These simulation theorists do not acknowledge the well-documented finding that infants use different means to achieve a goal during the dyadic period, such as when the 3-month-old infant uses her smiles as a means to re-engage a passive face person into communication, and when this attempt fails, uses another means such as crying before withdrawing from the interaction (Legerstee et al., 1987; Tronick, 2003). These simulation theorists, like the prepared learning theorists, propose a discontinuous development in the awareness of mental states in people, and fail to introduce a mechanism that can account for the conversion from one level to the next.

My account of how "like me" works has been inspired by Meltzoff and his colleagues (Meltzoff and Gopnik, 1993; Meltzoff and Moore, 1977; Meltzoff and Brooks, 2001) and by various bio-social and social interactionist theorists (e.g. Fogel, 1993; Trevarthen, 1991; Tronick, 2003; Stern, 1985; Bruner, 1990). Meltzoff postulates that infants have a perceptual mechanism, namely cross-modal matching, that allows them to perceive actions seen and produced as equivalent (see Meltzoff and Brooks, 2001). The reciprocal nature of the matching process is depicted by a proprioceptive feedback loop, which enables infants to evaluate their own motor performance against the seen target act. Perceived and produced behavior is processed within a supramodal framework which allows infants to notice equivalences between them. Developmentally, infants progress from sharing acts to sharing minds, thus there is a time where infants are *acting* rather than *thinking* creatures.

In contrast, I propose that rather than beginning life as a behavioral organism, infants are psychological creatures right from birth. As the above mentioned bio-social and relational theorists have documented, infants have an innate ability to communicate their emotions and to evaluate whether their emotions are reciprocated. This emotion sharing ability is the starting point to perceive people as similar to self. Extensive interaction with people is the catalyst for further growth (Legerstee and Varghese, 2001; Fogel, 2001; Murray and Trevarthen, 1985; Stern, 1995; Tronick, 2003. That infants have a special sense of people, a sense that is emotion based and that allows infants to perceive others as analogous to the self, is supported by the finding that infants do not have to learn everything about human characteristics.

Throughout the book, extensive evidence has been provided that infants come prepared to interact and communicate with the social environment. Neonates show a preference for human stimuli (e.g. Reddy et al., 1997). They prefer face-like arrangements (Goren, Sarty, and Wu, 1975; Johnson et al., 1991) and quickly favor their mothers' faces over other faces (Field et al., 1985). Infants also attend preferentially to human speech over other sounds, and recognize voices of their mothers over those of a female stranger (DeCasper and Fifer, 1980). Together these studies suggest that already at birth, infants are sensitive to some aspects of humans that are important for sharing of emotions with conspecifics. In particular, these attention biases suggest that infants have domain specific predispositions that direct them to people. These predispositions facilitate the "like me" correspondence infants make, and support the building of representations that are the precursors to the development of a Theory of Mind. However, infants do not have to work alone in their subsequent discovery of the social aspects of their conspecifics. Caretakers who are attuned to their infants' affective states promote infants' tendencies to match the adult's behavior and emotional expressions and feelings.

Affect sharing and development

In 1963, Spitz emphasized that mother–infant sharing was fundamental to an understanding of the self and the development of an identity. He introduced the concept of mother–infant dialogue. He proposed that reciprocal action exchanges and coordination of responses between mother and infant were crucial to the development of a sense of self and efficacy. Within the interaction, infants learned that they were affecting their partners, and that they had some control over the environment. Cohn and Tronick (1989) defined the term bi-directional coordination and Fogel (2001) called these interactions co-regulations. Thus, early mother–child interactions provide an important foundation for the infants' social awareness and subsequent socio-cognitive functioning.

Comparison of CDM, AIM, and AFS models at 1.5 and 3.5 months of age

As pointed out above, there are several theoretical models that have addressed how infants become connected to the social world. Some of the most pertinent are the social biofeedback model of Gergely and Watson (1999), the active intermodal mapping theory of Meltzoff and Moore (1997), and the social interactionist theories of Fogel (1993); Stern (1985); Trevarthen (1991); Tronick (1989); and others. Although these theories have been discussed in the earlier chapters, I will summarize briefly the important points here, because they are tested in a study that follows and that I developed under a SSHRC grant and filmed in the Infancy laboratory of the MPI at Leipzig, but which I completed with my PhD student Gabriela Markova in the Centre for Research in Infancy at York University in Toronto (Markova and Legerstee, 2004; Markova and Legerstee, in press).

The CDM

The Contingency Detection Module and the Social Biofeedback model of Gergely and Watson (1999) focus on social mirroring as an explanatory tool for the infant's developing social understanding. However, initially this type of social mirroring does not involve the infant mirroring the caretaker. The authors do not believe that there is mutuality in the response pattern of infant and adult; rather, it involves the caretaker matching the infant's responses in an intermittent contingent way. The infants' contingency detection module (CDM) will then allow infants to recognize other people as similar, but not until 3 months of age.

Before 3 months of age, the infants' CDM draws infants to *perfect contingencies*, which in a sense identifies the self to the baby (e.g. by touching the crib, or sucking the breast, I become aware of myself). After 3 months, the CDM becomes receptive to imperfect contingencies and infants begin to prefer intermittent responses which are provided primarily by people. That is, unlike mirror reflections, people smile and talk in response to infant responses, but not always to every response. Thus, by 3 months, infants become aware of people and begin to tune into their emotions.

Another function mediated by CDM is the development of emotional self-awareness and control. In the beginning infants have no differential awareness of their own emotional states; parental affect mirroring establishes this awareness in infants. But because infants begin to orient to people only after 3 months, affect mirroring can only be effective after that age. Parental affect mirroring also establishes secondary representations which leads to attributing emotions to self. From these intermittently contingent experiences, and through the infants' potent capacity for contingency analysis, infants begin to perceive others to be "like me."

The finding that infants are sensitive to perfect contingent responding by 2 months has been supported by Watson (1972); and that they are sensitive to intermittent contingent responding by 3 months has been confirmed by Bahrick and Watson (1985), and Field (1992). In addition, Tarabulsy and colleagues (Tarabulsy, Tessier, and Kappas, 1996) reviewed evidence indicating that the detection of a contingency is associated with positive affect, whereas Bigelow (1998) points out that contingency levels experienced during early mother–infant interactions are responsible for the quality of the child's later social relations.

That infants are not oriented toward the social environment until 3 months is not supported by empirical evidence. As argued throughout the book (and in particular in chapters 3, 4, and 5), infants before 3 months reveal that they have particular expectations about the communicative interactions they engage in with their social partners and are sensitive to maternal affect attunement at that age (Legerstee and Varghese, 2001).

The AIM

The Active Intermodal Mapping model (AIM) by Meltzoff and Gopnik (1993) (see also Meltzoff and Brooks, 2001) proposes that infants are born with an intermodal mapping device which enables them to imitate, and to perceive when they are being imitated. The device operates from birth, and enables infants to recreate acts with their own bodies. This way the acts get special meaning (Meltzoff and Brooks, 2001, p. 173). Infants that are being imitated by others find that person very attractive (attention getter). They pay more attention to that person, because the person is perceived as "like me." Thus infants begin to separate people from inanimate objects because people imitate actions and inanimate objects do not.

When infants see others reacting in return (imitating their actions) they attribute the same mental experiences to them (interpersonal inference). Meltzoff argues that a process of cross-modal perception allows infants to imitate actions of others, and consequently to perceive them to be "like me." "The cross-modal knowledge of what it feels like to perform observed acts provides a privileged access to people not afforded by things. This sends the child down the pathway of ascribing psychological properties to people" (Meltzoff and Brooks, 2001, p. 174). Furthermore, Meltzoff argues that together with the ability to perceive actions as similar, infants have intra-personal experience and interpersonal inference that allow them to perceive the emotions of self and others as equivalent. Because emotions are mental states, this awareness gives infants insight into the primitive mental states of others soon after birth (e.g. the first months or so). Thus, sharing emotions allows infants to progress from sharing behavior to sharing mental states.

There is empirical support for the process of intermodal matching in early infancy (e.g. Bahrick, 1988; Legerstee, 1990; Legerstee et al., 1998; Spelke, 1981). Meltzoff (1990) has further provided support for part of his model by showing that as early as 6 weeks, infants are more attentive to a perfect match and thus look longer at an imitative model as opposed to a temporally contingent, but spatially dissimilar, model. He argued that this finding provides evidence that infants prefer when people are acting "just like me" and not "just when I act." Additionally, Field, Guy, and Umbel (1985) found that 3½-month-old infants vocalized and smiled more often after being imitated than after non-imitative, spontaneous maternal behavior.

Although infants may seem captivated by people who imitate their actions, imitation would seem limiting for sharing experiences due to its emphasis on overt behavior. As revealed in chapter 7, Stern (1985) defined the term "affect attunement" as expressing the "quality of a shared affect state but without imitating the exact behavioral expression of the inner state" (p. 6). Instead of matching the exact behaviors of the child, the adult attunes to some specific aspects of the emotion state, such as intensity, timing, or shape. Through such attunement, the adult provides the infant with a sense of goodness of fit which is vital for social awareness in infants (Stern, 1985) and an awareness of self.

The AFS

The Affect Sharing model (AFS) predicts that affect sharing between a communicative partner who tunes into the emotional state and other vocal and nonverbal actions of a responsive infant creates dialogues and attuned interactions that are necessary mechanisms to promote the development of an understanding of people's minds. Fogel (1993) argues that there are preferential pathways and receptivities in the newborn which form the core of later development and which facilitate infants' interactions with conspecifics. These interactions or relationships are creative processes during which the two interlocutors observe and regulate each other's behavior. It is through these affective exchanges that infants learn about people's mental states and psychological processes. According to Piaget (1981) development should be considered as an affective/cognitive relationship. He argued that affect is the fuel (motivation), and cognition the chassis; without either one, there is no development. Other authors also have argued that it makes little sense to argue for a separation between the cognitive and affective or socio-emotional (Reddy, 2003; Stern, 1995).

With their work, Field et al. (1982) have supported the hypothesis that infants at birth are sensitive to human emotions, because they discriminate and *imitate* happy, sad, and surprise emotional expressions. Izard (1971) argues persuasively that when infants behaviorally produce or express emotions, the corresponding physiological emotion state in the infant is activated through pre-wired connections (see Izard, 1971 for discussions of innate expression-to-feeling concordance in the young infant). Izard proposes that these emotions serve the foundation of a social relationship. In support, Fogel (2001) writes that emotions are experienced with respect to the body's encounter with a relational dynamic, although they are felt within individual bodies.

Trevarthen (1991) maintains that infants have an innate sense of intersubjectivity which is activated through sensitive and compassionate interactions. Tronick (2004) argued that meaning can only be created when connection with the other is successful, when the partners are "attuned." It is essential that initially parents are affective communicators who sensitively tune into and elaborate the infants' feelings in order for the infants to perceive that they are understood. Caregivers thereby establish an optimum reciprocal exchange and coordination of responses with their infants so that infants develop a sense of self and a feeling of efficacy (Legerstee and Varghese, 2001). Thus according to the AFS model, infants not only perceive emotions at birth, they are able to evaluate their affective quality. If the quality is optimal, if it matches or elaborates on the infant's affective states, e.g. if the partner's affective state is child centered, then it enables affective sharing and mental state awareness.

In summary, the three developmental models, CDM, AIM, and AFS, have different predictions about infants' social awareness. According to CDM theory, infants during the first three months are not attentive to the social world, because they prefer perfect over intermittent contingencies. However, by 3 months, infants begin to prefer imperfect, intermittent contingencies, and become sensitive to the quality of maternal responding. According to AIM theory, from birth infants identify with people in specific human ways, and this is evident in neonatal imitation. Through such imitation, infants comprehend that others are "like me." Thus, social interaction allows infants to "interpret interpersonal exchanges in special ways" (Meltzoff and Brooks, 2001, p. 178). Consequently, during the first 3 months of life, infants prefer imitative over natural interactions. According to AFS theories, infants have an innate sense of people, which is activated through sympathetic emotions. Infants learn about themselves and other people through ongoing relationships. Through these dyadic relationships infants progress toward an increasing consensus about shared meaning. These theorists argue that infants do not characterize others as providers of certain levels of temporal contingencies or of structurally similar responses to their actions, but as beings with whom they can exchange inter-subjective experiences and establish social attunement.

The above models have important implications for an understanding of the process by which infants become aware of social agents. To assess their validity we conducted a study where infant responses toward perfect and imperfect contingencies were contrasted before and after 3 months of age, and where the effect of the quality of affect mirroring styles on the responses of the infants in these situations was being measured.

Testing the concluding speculations

Seventy-seven mother–infant dyads participated in the study. They were seen during four visits in the infancy laboratory at 4 and 5 weeks (1.5 m), 12, and 13 weeks (3.5 m). Mothers were administered a variety of tests to examine the extent to which they felt confident about the arrival of a new baby (Lukesch and Lukesch, 1976). At 1.5 and 3.5 months, mothers were given the post-partum depression tests (BDI; Beck et al., 1961) in order to determine whether they suffered from depression. Because we were interested in deviations in behavior of normal pairs, mothers who were depressed were not included in the study. We further assessed mothers on their affect mirroring during three minutes of informal inter-actions at 4 and 12 weeks. Maternal behavior was coded for maintaining attention, warm sensitivity, and contingent responding (see Legerstee and Varghese, 2001 and chapters 8 and 9 for a detailed description of the coding schemes). To determine whether infants enjoyed their mothers' interactions, infants' smiles, vocalizations, negative face, and gazes were coded. This allowed us to assess "goodness of fit" of the interaction.

Mothers and infants were divided into High and Low affective groups based on these measures. At 1.5 months, the two groups of mothers were randomly assigned to three conditions: (1) natural interactions, during which mothers were asked to interact with their infants as they usually would, (2) an imitative condition, where mothers imitated all oral, vocal, facial, and gestural behaviors of infants, and (3) a non-imitative (yoked) interaction. The yoked interaction was one minute long and was prepared from the 3-minute natural interaction taken the previous week. Mothers listened to the interaction that was played over a portable cassette recor-der and repeated what they had said to the baby a week before, thereby also repeating the same emotions expressed earlier. This interaction consequently had the same amount of stimulation as the previous normal interaction, but was not contingent, nor imitative, because it was not in response to the infants' signals.

During the third visit, at 12 weeks, mother–child dyads were again assessed for a 3-minute natural interaction and the infants were also tested with the Bayley Scales of Infant Development (Bayley, 1969) to make sure that the infants were of similar developmental backgrounds. During the fourth visit at 13 weeks (3.5 m), the infants again received randomly: (1) natural interaction, (2) imitative interaction, and (3) yoked interactions (1-minute tape from the earlier interaction at 12 weeks) (see figure 10.1).

To determine whether mothers produced the same amount of stimula-tion during the normal and the yoked conditions, mothers' smiles, voca-lizations, and gazes were coded. No significant differences in amount of

Figure 10.1 Mother and infant in normal, imitative, and yoked interactions.

stimulation was observed between the two conditions. Thus, if infants discriminated between the natural and yoked conditions, it had to be the result of changes in temporal contingency of the two interactions.

This design allowed us to test the following hypotheses. According to Gergely and Watson's CDM theory (1999), it is expected that at 1.5 m infants of high- and low-quality mothers prefer the imitative interactions due to a high level of contingency (immediate responsiveness by the mother). However, at 3.5 m infants of high-quality mothers would be expected to switch their preference to the natural interaction (intermittent, imperfect contingency), and should get upset when presented with the yoked condition, due to its diminished contingency (i.e. temporal delay). On the contrary, infants of low-quality mothers should continue to prefer imitative interactions, because the natural interactions of low affective mothers lack in responsiveness.

According to Meltzoff and Moore's (1997; 1999) AIM hypothesis, it is expected that at both 1.5 m and 3.5 m, infants of high- and low-quality mothers prefer imitative interactions, because they represent the best matching situation, over the natural or yoked conditions. Both groups would be expected to decrease their responsiveness during the yoked interactions at both ages, because the yoked conditions match least with their own behaviors.

According to theories of affect sharing, it would be expected that, at both 1.5 m and 3.5 m of age, infants of mothers who display high quality affective sharing prefer natural interactions as they provide more sensitive and responsive exchanges of affect than the imitative and yoked interactions. Infants of mothers who display low quality affect sharing would be expected to evaluate normal and yoked conditions similarly at 1.5 m and 3.5 m of age. Their mothers' behavior is neither responsive to their infants' communicative bids, nor sensitive to the infant's emotional behavior in the two situations, and thus infants do not experience mutual affective sharing. It is possible that infants increase looking at the imitative mother because of a violation of her expected (e.g. usual) behavior.

Results showed a significant correlation between maternal maintaining attention and warm sensitivity and social responsiveness. Mothers who ranked high on maintaining, warm sensitivity, and social responsiveness were labeled HAM, the others were labeled LAM. None of the mothers was classified as depressed. At both 5 and 13 weeks no significant difference was found between the two groups as a function of the other tests, except that LAM mothers showed significantly elevated scores on the subscale "open disapproval of pregnancy," on the SSG test (Lukesch and Lukesch, 1976), indicating that these

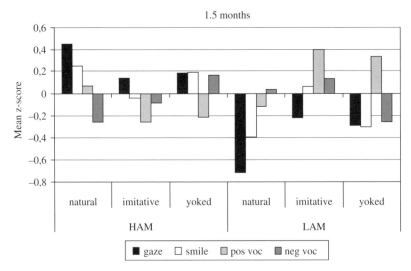

Figure 10.2 1.5-month-old infant gazes, smiles, and positive and negative vocalizations during normal, imitative, and yoked interactions.

mothers had a more negative attitude towards pregnancy and the developing child. Similarly, LAM mothers were more overcautious and anxious toward their child, as revealed by their significantly different scores on the subscale "fear of injury of the child" and showed a more disapproving and shameful attitude toward sexuality than the HAM mothers. Thus different maternal attitudes contributed to the qualitative difference in interaction between LAM and HAM mothers. We further found that there was no significant difference for maternal smiles and vocalizations at both ages across the yoked and natural conditions. Hence differences in infant responsiveness must be due to temporal delays.

Overall, the results showed that at 1.5 months infants of HAM mothers gazed, smiled, and vocalized positively more during the natural interactions with their mother than during the yoked and imitative interactions, between which there was no difference on these measures. However, these infants vocalized negatively more during the yoked than during the other conditions. Overall, infants of LAM mothers did not react differently to the three conditions (see figure 10.2).

Similarly to 1.5 months, at 3.5 months infants of HAM mothers gazed, smiled, and vocalized positively more during the natural interaction, as opposed to imitative or yoked, and increased negative vocalizations during the yoked interactions. Although infants of LAM mothers

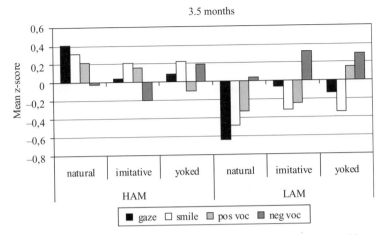

Figure 10.3 3.5-month-old infant gazes, smiles, and positive and negative vocalizations during normal, imitative, and yoked interactions.

gazed significantly more at their mothers' imitative behaviors, they did not discriminate with their smiles and positive and negative vocalizations. Together, the longer looks and lack of social responsiveness during the imitative condition suggests that the infants found this situation somewhat unnatural (see figure 10.3).

Experimental support for affective sharing

How do the findings support the predictions of the three theories? According to Gergely and Watson, at 1.5 months of age, infants when facing their mothers in natural interactions (intermittent responsiveness) and imitative interactions (highly contingent responsiveness) prefer imitative interactions between the two, because the imitative interactions are perfectly contingent on the infant's responses. The data of the present study do not support this. In fact, the data argue against the idea that in the beginning infants have no access to their emotions and those of others because already at 1.5 months infants of HAM mothers discriminate the normal from the yoked and imitative groups, whereas the LAM infants do not. This finding also argues against the idea that it is not until 3 months that parental affect mirroring makes infants aware of their affective states.

The AIM hypothesis suggests that at 1.5 and 3.5 months both HAM and LAM infants prefer imitative behaviors of their mothers over natural and yoked responses. These assumptions are not upheld either. Infants of

HAM mothers preferred imitative interactions more than infants of LAM mothers, which argues against the proposition that imitative matching is primarily responsible for an understanding that others are like the self (Meltzoff and Brooks, 2001). The difference in responsiveness to the three conditions by the HAM and LAM groups reveals that maternal attunement, rather than imitative games or very high levels of contingent responding, lay the foundation for the infant's awareness of the social world.

Theories of affect sharing emphasize the social origins of infants, such as self and other emotional awareness. These theories predict that infants in the HAM group favor natural interactions with their mothers at both ages, because she tunes into the infant's attention and provides high levels of warm sensitivity and responsiveness.

The findings revealed that at both ages, HAM infants preferred natural over imitative and yoked interactions. Because this was only true for the infants in the HAM group, it suggests that the infants' innate predisposition for inferential awareness of emotions of self and others provide a goodness of fit only for those dyads where mothers accurately and sensitively interpret their infants' emotions. LAM mothers rank lower on affect attunement and responsiveness and consequently their normal interactions are similar to their yoked interactions. The difference in responsiveness between the two groups of infants indicates that their predispositions for awareness of own and others' emotions, which allows for affective sharing, is an important mechanism for understanding the social world.

The findings of the above study provide support for the argument that knowledge about people and their mental states can not occur purely endogenously via maturation. Infants who receive high quality emotional interactions with their mothers show a continued preference for natural interactions over imitative or yoked interactions. In contrast, infants who are faced with lower quality emotional interactions show an overall much diminished response to social interactions. The results support the theoretical writings and empirical studies of those who have argued for the importance of affect sharing as a mechanism that connects infants with the social world (e.g. Izard, 1978; Fogel, 1993; Reddy et al., 1997; Stern, 1985; Trevarthen, 1991; Tronick, 1989). Stern (1985) suggests that affect attunement, the ability to know what the other is experiencing subjectively, underlies not only empathic understanding, but is the basis for early communication and, most importantly, provides a way for mutual appreciation of the other's mental state.

Taken together, the evidence supports the hypotheses that infants construct knowledge of self and others through an interaction of domain specific representations and social exchanges. Studies discussed in this book investigating the effect of maternal responsiveness on infant development

(Bornstein and Tamis-LeMonda, 1989a, b; Brazelton, Koslowkski, and Main, 1974; Landry et al., 1998; Fogel, 1993; Stern, 1985; Trevarthen 1991; Tronick, 2004) have shown that mothers who act sensitively to infants' signals influence the infants' social and cognitive competencies. Recent work conducted with my students and discussed in chapters 7, 8, 9, and 10, on the effects of affect mirroring on social expectations in 2–3-month-old babies (Legerstee and Varghese, 2001; Markova and Legerstee, in press), on the development of self (Legerstee et al., 2004), on gaze monitoring and coordinated attention in 3, 5, 7, and 10-month-old infants (Legerstee et al., 2004), on the development of referential communication in typical and atypical populations aged between 6 and 18 months (Legerstee et al., 2002; Legerstee and Weintraub, 1997), on precursors to desire reasoning in 9, 12, and 14-month-old infants (chapter 9), and finally on the production of symbolic gestures at 15 months, and the production of internal state words at 30 months (Legerstee, Fahy, Blake, Fisher, and Markova, 2004), all demonstrate the powerful effect of attuned social interaction on the development of infant socio-cognitive development. It seems natural to infer that social partners who provide more information about their own internal states are not only more likely to be reciprocated, but also further the development of internal state awareness in their children.

Although it would seem that the pathways toward emotional understanding is quite a sophisticated process, it should not be inferred that the infant's understanding of emotions is similar to that of adults. Rather than reflecting upon their own emotional states (which does not occur until children are about 3 to 4 years of age) (Bartsch and Wellman, 1995), young infants are "in" an emotion state, the realization of which makes them willing and prepared to share their feelings with their environment (as if the infant would say: "Look what I have discovered about me!"). Although not as complex as the older child's awareness of emotions, they do involve an awareness of simple mental states of self and others.

Sharing emotions between partners engenders understanding and comfort while lack of emotional sharing and co-regulation has devastating effects on the infant's well being (e.g. Field, 1984; Field et al., 1998; Fogel, 1993; Rogers and Pennington, 1991). The studies I have discussed in this book provide support for the idea that the development of a Theory of Mind is a gradual and continuous process. Its domain specific precursors are activated and become refined through affective sharing.

Social cognition and affect sharing: interpreting the data

In this chapter, I have discussed how the infant's awareness of people's mental states develops during the first year of life. I have examined this development from various developmental perspectives and have used the available empirical evidence to evaluate the predictions of these frameworks, in order to come to a balanced view about the ontogeny of mental state awareness. Although I have tried to be objective in presenting these views, I must admit that I am strongly committed to one theoretical perspective and this may have colored the interpretations I have given to the available empirical data. In doing that, of course, I am not alone. Most, if not all, developmental psychologists are driven by their own personal and academic views when presenting the so called "status quo" of infant social cognitive development. It is these convictions that drive research, that advance science, and that change the prevailing Zeitgeist into a different one, usually one that a few decades ago was in fashion, but under a different name perhaps.

As students of the social sciences we were told very early that the study of people's behavior is, unlike the study of material things, much less of an exact science, and many of us have come to accept this. There are, however, a few truths that remain. New methodologies have shown that infants are social organisms from birth with primitive mental capacities that have prepared them to interact adaptively with conspecifics, and to learn rapidly from them. The idea that infants are mechanical creatures seems unwarranted at the moment. Not only because of an overwhelming amount of empirical data that suggests otherwise, but also because there seems no inherent or intuitive rationale for why this should be so. The idea that infants are mindless at birth (and for some continue to be for a long time) is a leftover of the Behaviorist Zeitgeist. Skinner's learning theory heavily influenced the ideas on how to educate children. Fortunately, as the result of some clever experiments, it became known that warm affective social interaction, rather than training infants to obey senseless rules (e.g. 4-hour feeding schedules, infants should be seen not heard, not picking up babies when they cry, etc.), made infants socially competent. Infants who were fed and cuddled when they appeared to need it seemed more relaxed and capable than infants who were trained on schedules (Rheingold, 1961). Infants who received lots of caretaker attention and warm responsiveness were found to be more socially skilled than infants who were ignored (Legerstee and Varghese, 2001). Behaviorism may have had a long lasting effect on layman psychology but also on developmental psychologists. Some still believe that the social smiles of 3-month-old infants are the result of physiological processes rather than an intent to communicate.

Somewhat less unsettling is the idea that nonhuman primates have a behaviorist rather than a mentalist conception of others' actions. In a survey of the available data on imitation, self-recognition, social relationships, and joint attention (the concept seeing) Heyes (1998) concluded that chimps do not reveal evidence of using mentalist processes. Their success on many of the tasks could have been explained "through processes such as associative learning or inferences based on non-mental categories."

In the introduction of this chapter, I compared the ball playing abilities of my golden Labrador retriever Aquarius to those of our Canadian Wayne Gretzky. Both seem innately prepared to play ball and to anticipate where the ball could land, except when it came to deception. It is clear from the performance of Aquarius on dog experiments (not infant experiments tested on dogs!) I have put him in that he uses perceptual (smell) and behavioral (head turn, arm direction) cues, rather than mental states, when tested on the concept of seeing. Why do I appear to be so parsimonious when interpreting the behaviors of canine puppies, and rich when interpreting those of human infants? The first reason is empirical; if I can rule out a lean interpretation of a well designed experiment, then the outcome deserves a "rich" interpretation. Secondly, when it comes to the human infants I see in my laboratory, whose parents all display evidence of representational abilities, it is reasonable to assume that some precursory ability of mental state attribution resides in the infants of those parents (Flavell, 1999; Bjorklund, 2005). In this book, I have provided ample evidence for the mental activities of infants throughout the first year of life. This converging evidence attests to the idea that infants are aware of the mental states of others (albeit very primitive ones) from birth (see Bruner, 1999; Reddy, 2003; Tronick, 2003). As indicated in chapter 5, infants do a variety of things during the dyadic period that reflect their awareness of being the object of people's attention (Bruner, 1999; Reddy, 2003), and of being the aboutness of people's communication. I showed that infants progress from an awareness of being the object of attention during the dyadic state, to an awareness that a third object had become the focus of attention of their communicative partner. During this triadic state, infants through coordinating their attention between people and things signal their intent to share interesting aspects of the object at which they look together. Somewhat later, infants will look, point, and vocalize at an object that is out of focus of the adult's attention, intending to make her aware of it. Infants will check, vocalize, and point again if their attempts have been unsuccessful (Legerstee and Barillas, 2003). Furthermore, as described in chapter 9, infants between 9 and 12 months of age have developed a primitive type of desire reasoning (Barna and Legerstee, 2005). Infants are aware that if people look at objects while vocalizing positively, they may want to handle the object. All these findings reveal the infant's understanding from the beginning, that it is the emoter's attentional focus which provides cues to the person's referential intent (Bruner, 1999; Flavell, 1999; Reddy, 2003).

However rich or lean the interpretations may be, I agree with Flavell (1999, p. 33) that "all of us who labor in this area – rich or lean interpreters alike – would happily trade all our arguments for better empirical evidence on the matter. The truth is that we really do not know what infants actually input to themselves and others in the way of mental state and subjective experiences."

Another truth prevails, however. There is a wealth of knowledge that has been accumulated within the last two decades. There is detailed empirical evidence about infants' precocious social cognitive capacities at birth that support the idea that infants come prepared to interact with the social and cognitive world. There are also some fine-tuned theoretical frameworks from which these studies have originated. My own theory has been heavily influenced by the works of some great past (Piaget, 1954; Baldwin, 1902) and present thinkers. Those of the present generation who read this compilation of essays will recognize their contribution. I dedicate this book to my mentors, my children, their father, and my students.

References

Adamson, L. B. and Bakeman, R. (1982). Affectivity and reference: Concepts, methods, and techniques in the study of communication development of 6- to 18-month-old infants. In T. M. Field and A. Fogel (eds.), *Emotion and early interaction*. Hillsdale, NJ: Erlbaum.

Ainsworth, M. D. S., Blehar, M. C., Waters, E., and Wall, S. (1978). *Patterns of attachment: A psychological study of the strange situation*. Hillsdale, NJ: Erlbaum.

Astington, J. W. (2001). The paradox of intention: Assessing children's metarepresentational understanding. In B. F. Malle, L. J. Moses, and D. A. Baldwin (eds.), *Intentions and intentionality: Foundations of social cognition* (pp. 85–103). Cambridge, MA: MIT Press.

Bahrick, L. R. (1988) Intermodal learning in infancy: Learning on the basis of two kinds of invariant relations in audible and visible events. *Child Development*, *59*, 197–209.

Bahrick, L. R., Moss, L., and Fadil, C. (1996). Development of visual self-recognition in infancy. *Ecological Psychology*, *8*, 189–208.

Bahrick, L. R., and Watson, J. S. (1985). Detection of intermodal proprioceptive-visual contingency as a potential basis of self-perception in infancy. *Developmental Psychology*, *21*, 963–973.

Baillargeon, R. (1986). Representing the existence and the location of hidden objects: Object permanence in 6–8-month-old infants. *Cognition*, *23*, 21–41.

(1993). The object concept revisited: New directions in the investigation of infants' physical knowledge. In C. Granrud (ed.), *Visual perception and cognition in infancy* (pp. 265–315). Hillsdale, NJ: Erlbaum.

Bakeman, R., and Adamson, L. (1984). Coordinating attention to people and objects in mother–infant and peer–infant interaction. *Child Development*, *55*, 1278–1289.

Baldwin, D. A., and Moses, L. J. (1994). The mindreading engine: Evaluating evidence for modularity. *Cahiers der Psychologie*, *13*, 553–560.

(1996). Early understanding of referential intent and attentional focus: Evidence from language and emotion. In C. Lewis and P. Mitchell (eds.), *Children's early understanding of mind: Origins and development* (pp. 133–156). Hillsdale, NJ: Erlbaum.

Baldwin, J. M. (1902). *Social and ethical interpretations in mental development*. New York: Macmillan.

Ball, A. W. (1973). *The perception of causality in the infant.* Presented at the Meeting of the Society for Research in Child Development, Philadelphia, PA.

Ball, A. W., and Tronick, E. (1971). Infant responses to impending collision: Optical and real. *Science, 171*, 818–820.

Bandura, A. (1962). Social cognitive theory of social referencing. In S. Feinman (ed.), *Social learning through imitation.* University of Nebraska Press: Lincoln, NE.

Banks, M. S., and Salapatek, P. (1983). Infant visual perception. In M. M. Haith and J. J. Campos (eds.), *Infancy and developmental psychobiology* (vol. II of P. H. Mussen [ed.], *Handbook of Child Psychology*), 4th edn. New York: Wiley.

Barna, J., and Legerstee, M. (2005). Nine and 12-month-old infants relate emotions to people's actions. *Cognition and Emotion, 19*, 53–67.

Baron-Cohen, S. (1989). Are autistic children "behaviorists"? An examination of their mental–physical and appearance–reality distinctions. *Journal of Autism and Developmental Disorders, 19*, 579–600.

(1991). Precursors to a theory of mind: Understanding attention in others. In A. Whiten (ed.), *Natural theories of mind: Evolution, development and simulation of everyday mindreading.* Cambridge, MA: Basil Blackwell.

(1993). From attentional-goal psychology to belief-desire psychology. The development of theory of mind and its dysfunction. In S. Baron-Cohen, H. Tager-Flusberg, and D. J. Cohen (eds.), *Understanding other minds: Perspectives from autism* (pp. 59–82). Oxford: Oxford University Press.

(1995). *Mindblindness: An essay on autism and theory of mind.* Cambridge, MA: MIT Press.

Baron-Cohen, S., Campbell, R., Karmiloff-Smith, A., Grant, J., and Walker, S. (1995). Are children with autism blind to the mentalistic significance of the eyes? *British Journal of Developmental Psychology, 13*, 379–398.

Barrera, M. E., and Maurer, D. (1981). Recognition of mother's photographed face by the three-month-old infant. *Child Development, 52*, 714–716.

Barresi, J. (1984). Knowledge and representation: Transparent and opaque. *Contemporary Psychology, 29*, 160–161.

Barresi, J., and Moore, C. (1996). Intentional relations and social understanding. *Behavioral and Brain Sciences, 19*, 107–154.

Barrett, M. D. (1989). Early language development. In A. Slater and J. G. Bremner (eds.), *Infant development* (pp. 211–241). London: Erlbaum.

Bartsch, K., and Wellman, H. M. (1995). *Children talk about the mind.* Oxford: Oxford University Press.

Baumwell, L., Tamis-LeMonda, C. S., and Borstein, M. H. (1997). Maternal verbal sensitivity and child language comprehension. *Infant Behavior and Development, 20*, 247–258.

Bayley, N. (1969). *Bayley scales of infant development.* New York: Psychological Corporation.

Beck, A. T., Ward, C. H., Mendelson, M., March, J. E., and Erbaugh, J. (1961). An inventory for measuring depression. *Archives of General Psychiatry, 4*, 561–571.

Beebe, B., Stern, D., and Jaffe, J. (1979). The kinesic rhythm of mother-infant interactions. In A. W. Siegman & S. Feldstein (eds.), *Of speech and time: Temporal patterns in interpersonal contexts.* Hillsdale, NJ: Erlbaum.

Bellagamba, F. and Tomasello, M. (1999). Re-enacting intended acts: comparing 12- and 18-month-olds. *Infant Behavior and Development*, 22, 277–282.

Berthenthal, B. I., and Bai, D. L. (1989). Infants' sensitivity to optical flow for controlling posture. *Developmental Psychology*, 25, 936–45.

Berkley, G. (1975). *Philosophical works*. Edited by M. R. Ayers. London: Dent.

Bigelow, A. E. (1998). Infants' sensitivity to familiar imperfect contingencies in social interaction. *Infant Behavior and Development*, 21, 149–161.

Bjorklund, D. F. (2005). *Children's thinking. Cognitive development and individual differences*. Belmont, CA: Wadsworth/Thomson.

Bornstein, M. H., and Lamb, M. E. (1992). *Development in infancy: An introduction* (3rd edn, xiv, pp. 560). New York, NY, England: Mcgraw-Hill Book Company.

Bornstein, M. H., and Sigman, M. D. (1986). Continuity in mental development from infancy. *Child Development*, 57, 251–274.

Bornstein, M. H., and Tamis-LeMonda, C. S. (1989a). Maternal responsiveness and cognitive development in children. In M. H. Bornstein (ed.), *Maternal responsiveness: Characteristics and consequences* (pp. 49–61). San Francisco: Jossey-Bass.

(1989b). Habituation and maternal encouragement of attention in infancy as predictors of toddler language, play, and representational competence. *Child Development*, 60, 738–751.

(1997). Maternal responsiveness and infant mental abilities: Specific predictive relations. *Infant Behavior and Development*, 20, 283–296.

Bowlby, J. (1951). *Maternal care and mental health*. London: HMSO; New York: Columbia University.

(1969). *Attachment and loss. Vol. I: Attachment*. Pelican Books, Penguin.

(1979). On knowing what you are not supposed to know and feeling what you are not supposed to feel. *Canadian Journal of Psychiatry*, 24, 403–408.

Brazelton, T. B., Koslowski, B., and Main, M. (1974). The origins of reciprocity: The early mother–infant interaction. In M. Lewis and L. Rosenblum (eds.), *The effect of the infant on its caregiver* (pp. 49–76). New York: Wiley.

Bremner, J. G. (1988). *Infancy*. Cambridge, MA: Basil Blackwell.

(1998). From perception to action: The early development of knowledge. In F. Simion and G. Butterworth (eds.), *The development of sensory, motor and cognitive capacities in early infancy: From perception to cognition* (pp. 239–255). Hove, England: Psychology Press/Erlbaum.

Brentano, F. (1874/1973). *Psychology from an empirical standpoint*. Trans. A. C. Rancurello, D. B. Terrel, and L. L. McAlister. London: Routledge and Kegan Paul.

Bretherton, I. and Beeghly, M. (1982). Talking about internal states: The acquisition of an explicit theory of mind. *Developmental Psychology*, 18, 906–921.

Bronfenbrenner, U. (1974). *A report on longitudinal evaluations of pre-school programs*, Vol. 2, *Is early intervention effective?* Washington, DC: D. H. W. Publications No. (OHD) 74-25.

Bruner, J. S. (1973). Organization of early skilled action. *Child Development*, 44, 11.

(1975). From communication to language: A psychological perspective. *Cognition*, 3, 255–287.

(1983). *Child's talk: Learning to use language*. New York: Norton.

(1990). *Acts of meaning*. Cambridge, MA: Harvard University Press.

(1999). The intentionality of referring. In P. Zelazo and J. W. Astington (eds.), *Developing theories of intention: Social understanding and self-control* (pp. 329–339). Mahwah, NJ: Erlbaum.

Bruner, J. S., and Koslowski, B. (1972). Visually preadapted constituents of manipulatory action. *Perception*, *1*, 3–14.

Bushnell, I. W. R., Sai, F., and Mullin, J. T. (1989). Neonatal recognition of the mother's face. *British Journal of Developmental Psychology*, *7*, 3–15.

Butterworth, G. (1990). On reconceptualizing sensorimotor development in dynamic systems theory. In H. Bloch and B. J. Berthenthal (eds.), *Sensorimotor organizations and development in infancy and early childhood* (pp. 57–73). Dordrecht: Kluwer.

(1991). The ontogeny and phylogeny of joint visual attention. In A. Whiten (ed.), *National theories of mind: Evolution, development, and simulation of everyday mind reading* (pp. 223–232). Cambridge, MA: Basil Blackwell.

(1994). Theories of mind and the facts of embodiment. In C. Lewis and P. Mitchell (eds.), *Children's early understanding of mind: Origins and development* (pp. 115–132). Sussex, England: Erlbaum.

(1995). Factors in visual attention eliciting manual pointing in human infancy. In H. L. Raiblat and J. Meyer (eds.), *Comparative approaches to cognitive science* (pp. 329–338). Cambridge, MA: MIT Press.

Butterworth, G., and Hicks, L. (1977). Visual proprioception and postural stability in infancy: A developmental study. *Perception*, *6*, 255–262.

Butterworth, G., and Hopkins, B. (1988). Hand–mouth coordination in the newborn baby. *British Journal of Developmental Psychology*, *6*, 303–314.

Butterworth, G., and Jarrett, N. (1991). What minds have in common in space: Spatial mechanisms serving joint visual attention in infancy. *British Journal of Developmental Psychology*, *9*, 55–72.

Camaioni, L., Perucchini, P., Bellagamba, F., and Colonnesi, R. (2004), The role of declarative pointing in developing a Theory of Mind. *Infancy*, *5*, 291–308.

Camaioni, L., Perucchini, P., Muratori, F., and Milone, A. (1997). Brief report: A longitudinal examination of the communicative gestures deficit in young children with autism. *Journal of Autism and Developmental Disorders*, *27*, 715–725.

Campbell, S. B., Cohn, J., and Myers, T. (1995). Depression in first-time mothers: Mother–infant interaction and depression chronicity. *Developmental Psychology*, *31*, 349–357.

Campos, J., and Sternberg, C. (1981). Perception, appraisal, and emotion: The onset of social referencing. In M. Lamb and L. Sherrod (eds.), *Infant social cognition: Empirical and theoretical considerations* (pp. 273–314). Hillsdale, NJ: Erlbaum.

Carey, S. (1985). *Conceptual Change in Childhood*. Cambridge, MA: MIT Press.

Caron, A., Carfon, R., Mustelin, C., and Roberts, J. (1992). Infant responding to aberrant social stimuli. *Infant Behavior and Development*, *15*, 335 (Special ICIS Conference Issue).

Carpenter, M., Nagell, L., and Tomasello, M. (1998). Social cognition, joint attention, and communicative competence from 9 to 15 months of age. *Monographs of the Society for Research in Child Development, 63* (4, serial no. 255).

Chada, S. W. (1996). A comparison of mother–infant, father–infant and stranger–infant affect attunement: Characteristics and consequences of discrete parenting roles in infant affective development. *Dissertation Abstracts International, 52* (12-B), 7060.

Chapman, M. (1992). Equilibration and the dialectic of organization. In H. Beiling and P. Putfall (eds.), *Piaget's theory: Prospects and possibilities* (pp. 39–59). Hillsdale, NJ: Erlbaum.

Charman, T., Baron-Cohen, S., Swettenham, J., Baird, G., Cox, A., and Drew, A. (2000). Testing joint attention, imitation, and play as infancy precursors to language and theory of mind. *Cognitive Development, 15,* 481–498.

Charman, T., Swettenham, J., Baron-Cohen, S., Cox, A., Baird, G., and Drew, A. (1997). Infants with autism: An investigation of empathy, pretend play, joint attention, and imitation. *Developmental Psychology, 33,* 781–789.

Chi, M. T. H. (1988). Children's lack of access and knowledge reorganization: An example from the concept of animacy. In F. E. Weinert and M. Perlmuter (eds.), *Memory development: Universal changes and individual differences* (pp. 169–194). Hillsdale, NJ: Lawrence Erlbaum Associates.

Chomsky, N. (1965). *Aspects of the theory of syntax.* Cambridge, MA: MIT Press.

Churchland, P. M. (1991). Folk-psychology and the explanation of human behavior. In J. D. Greenwood (ed.), *The future of folk psychology: Intentionality and cognitive science.* Cambridge: Cambridge University Press.

Cicchetti, D., and Schneider-Rosen, K. (1984). Toward a transactional model of childhood depression. *New Directions for Child Development, 26,* 5–27.

Cohn, J. F., and Tronick, E. Z. (1989). Specificity of infants' response to mothers' affective behavior. *Journal of the American Academy of Child and Adolescent Psychiatry, 28,* 242–248.

Corkum, V., and Moore, C. (1995). Development of joint visual attention in infants. In C. Moore and P. J. Dunham (eds.), *Joint attention: its origins and role in development* (pp. 61–83). Hillsdale, NJ: Erlbaum.

(1998). The origin of joint visual attention in infants. *Developmental Psychology, 34,* 28–38.

Coster, W. J., Gersten, M. S., Beegly, M., and Cicchetti, D. (1989). Communicative functioning in maltreated toddlers. *Developmental Psychology, 25,* 1020–1029.

Crockenberg, S. (1983). Early mother and infant antecedents of Bayley Scale performance at 21 months. *Developmental Psychology, 19,* 727–730.

Csibra, G., Gergely, G., Biro, S., Koos, O., and Brockbank, M. (1999). Social attribution without agency cues: The perception of "pure reason" in infancy. *Cognition, 72,* 237–267.

Darwin, C. (1877). A biographical sketch of an infant. *Mind, 2,* 285–294.

Davis, K. (1947). Final note on a case of extreme isolation. *American Journal of Sociology, 52,* 432–437.

DeCasper, A. J., and Carstens, A. A. (1981). Contingencies of stimulation: Effects on learning and emotion in neonates. *Infant Behavior and Development, 4,* 19–35.

DeCasper, A. J., and Fifer, W. P. (1980). Of human bonding: Newborns prefer their mother's voice. *Science, 208*, 1174–1176.

DeCasper, A. J., Lecanuet, J. P., Busnell, M. C., Granier-Deferre, C., and Maugeais, R. (1994). Fetal reactions to recurrent maternal speech sounds. *Infant Behavior and Development, 9*, 133–150.

DeCharmes, R. (1968). *Personal Causation: The Internal Affective Determinants of behavior.* New York: Academic Press.

Descartes, R. (1641/1985). *The philosophical writings of Descartes* (Vols. 1 and 2). Trans. J. Cottingham et al. Cambridge: Cambridge University Press.

Desrochers, S., Morrissette, P., and Ricard, M. (1995). Two perspectives on pointing in infancy. In C. Moore and P. J. Dunham (eds.), *Joint attention: Its origins and role in development* (pp. 85–101). Hillsdale, NJ: Erlbaum.

Dodd, B. (1979). Lip reading in infants: Attention to speech present in- and out-of-synchrony. *Cognitive psychology, 11*, 478–484.

Dondi, M., Simion, F., and Caltran, G. (1999). Can newborns discriminate between their own cry and the cry of another newborn infant? *Developmental Psychology, 35*, 418–426.

Dunham, P., and Dunham, F. (1990). Effects of mother–infant social interactions on infants' subsequent contingency task performance. *Child Development, 61*, 785–793.

Dunham, P., Dunham, F., Hurshman, A., and Alexander, T. (1989). Social contingency effects on subsequent perceptual-cognitive tasks in young infants. *Child Development, 60*, 1486–1496.

Emde, R. N. (1989). Early emotional development: New modes of thinking for research and intervention. In J. G. Warhol (ed.), *New perspectives in early emotional development* (pp. 29–45). Johnson and Johnson Pediatric Institute.

Eimas, P. D., Siqueland, E. R., Juscyk, P., and Vigorito, J. (1971). Speech perception in infants. *Science, 171*, 303–306.

Ekman, P., and Friesen, W. V. (1975). *Unmasking the face: A guide to recognizing emotions from facial clues.* New York: Prentice-Hall.

Ellsworth, C. P., Muir, D., and Hains, S. (1993). Social competence and person–object differentiation: An analysis of the still-face effect. *Developmental Psychology, 39*, 63–73.

Fagan, J. F. (1972). Infants' recognition memory for faces. *Journal of Experimental Child Psychology, 14*, 453–476.

Feinman, S. (1982). Social referencing in infancy. *Merrill-Palmer Quarterly, 28*, 445–470.

Feinman, S., and Lewis, M. (1983). Social referencing at 10-months. A second order effect on infants' responses to strangers. *Child Development, 54*, 878–887.

Field, T. (1984). Early interactions between infants and their postpartum depressed mothers. *Infant Behaviour and Development, 7*, 527–532.

(1990). Neonatal stress and coping in intensive care. *Infant Mental Health Journal, 11*, 57–65.

(1992). Psychobiological attunement in close relationships. In R. Lerner, D. L. Featherman, and M. Perlmutter (eds.), *Life-span development and behavior* (pp. 2–22). Hillsdale, NJ: Erlbaum.

(1994). The effects of mother's physical and emotional unavailability on emotion regulation. *Monographs of the Society for Research in Child Development*, 59 (23).

(1995). Infant of depressed mothers (Presidential address). *Infant Behavior and Development*, 18, 1–13.

Field, T., Cohen, D., Garcia, and Greenberg, R. (1985). Mother–stranger face discrimination by the newborn. *Annual Progress in Child Psychiatry and Child Development*, 3–10.

Field, T., Guy, L., and Umbel, V. (1985). Infants' responses to mothers' imitative behaviors. *Infant Mental Health Journal*, 6, 40–44.

Field, T., Healy, B., Goldstein, S., Perry, S., Berry, D., Schanberg, S., Zimmerman, E. A., and Kuhn, C. (1998). Infants of depressed mothers show "depressed" behavior even with nondepressed adults. *Child Development*, 59, 1569–1579.

Field, T., Woodson, R., Greenberg, R., and Cohen, D. (1982). Discrimination and imitation of facial expressions of neonates. *Science*, 218, 179–181.

Finkelstein, N. W., and Ramey, C. T. (1977). Learning to control the environment in infancy. *Child Development*, 48, 806–819.

Fischer, K. W., Shaver, P. R., and Carnochan, P. (1990). How emotions develop and how they organize development. *Cognition and Emotion*, 4, 81–127.

Fisher, L., Ames, E. W., Chisholm, K., and Savoie, L. (1997). Problems reported by parents of Romanians orphans adopted to British Columbia. *International Journal of Behavioral Development*, 20, 67–82.

Flavell, J. H. (1988). The development of the children's knowledge about the mind: From cognitive connections to mental representations. In J. W. Astington and P. L. Harris (eds.), *Developing theories of mind*. New York: Cambridge University Press.

(1999). Cognitive development: Children's knowledge about the mind. *Annual Review of Psychology*, 50, 21–45.

Flavell, J. H., Flavell, E. R., Green, F. L., and Moses, L. J. (1990). Young children's understanding of false beliefs versus value beliefs. *Child Development*, 61, 915–928.

Flavell, J. H., Green, F. L., and Flavell, E. R. (1986). Development of knowledge about the appearance–reality distinction. *Monographs of the Society for Research in Child Development*, 51, 1–68.

Fodor, J. A. (1983). *The modularity of the mind*. Cambridge, MA: MIT Press.

(1992). A theory of the child's theory of mind. *Cognition*, 44, 283–296.

Fogel, A. (1977). Temporal organization in mother–infant face-to-face interaction. In H. Rudolph Schaffer (ed.), *Studies in mother–infant interaction* (pp. 5–56). Hillsdale, NJ: Erlbaum.

(1993). *Developing through relationships: Origins of communication, self and culture*. Chicago, IL: University of Chicago Press.

(2001). *The history (and future) of infancy. Blackwell handbook of infant development. Handbooks of developmental psychology* (pp. 726–757). Malden, MA: Blackwell Publishers.

Fogel, A., and Hannan, T. E. (1985). Manual actions of nine to fifteen-week-old human infants during face-to-face interaction with their mothers. *Child Development*, 56, 1271–1279.

Fogel, A., and Thelen, E. (1987). Development of early expressive and communicative action: Reinterpreting the evidence from a dynamic systems perspective. *Developmental Psychology*, *23*, 747–761.

Franco, F., and Butterworth, G. (1996). Pointing and social awareness: Declaring
and requesting in the second year. *Journal of Child Language*, *23*, 307–336.

Freeman, W. J. (2000). Emotion is essential to all intentional behaviors. In
I. Granic and M. Lewis (eds.), *Emotion, development, and self-organization:
Dynamic systems approaches to emotional development* (pp. 209–235). New
York: Cambridge University Press.

Freud, S. (1949). *An outline of psychoanalysis* (rev. edn, Strachey). New York:
Norton (original work published 1940).

(1961). *The ego and the id.* New York: W. W. Norton and Co.

Frye, D. (1981). Developmental changes in strategies of social interaction.
In M. Lamb and L. Sherrod (eds.), *Infant social cognition*. Hillsdale, NJ:
Erlbaum.

Gallagher, S. (1996). The moral significance of primitive self-consciousness: The
response to Bermúdez. *Ethics*, *107*, 129–140.

Gallup, G. G. (1982). Self-awareness and the emergence of mind in primates.
American Journal of Primatology, *2*, 237–248.

Gekoski, M. J., and Fagen, J. W. (1984). Noncontingent stimulation, stimulus
familiarization, and subsequent learning in young infants. *Child Development*,
55, 2226–2233.

Gelman, R., and Spelke, E. (1981). The development of thoughts about animate and inanimate objects: Implications for research on social cognition.
In J. H. Flavell and L. Ross (eds.), *Social cognition development: Frontiers and
possible futures*. New York: Cambridge University Press.

Gelman, S. A., and Coley, J. D. (1990). The importance of knowing a dodo is a
bird: Categories and inferences in 2-year-old children. *Developmental
Psychology*, *26*, 796–804.

Gelman, S. A., Durgin, F., and Kaufman, L. (1995). Distinguishing between animates and inanimates: Not by notion alone. In D. Sperber and D. Premack
(eds.), *Causal cognition: A multidisciplinary debate* (pp. 150–184). Oxford:
Clarendon Press.

Gelman, S. A., and Markman, E. M. (1986). Categories and induction in young
children. *Cognition*, *23*, 183–209.

Gergely, G. (2001). Is early differentiation of human behavior a precursor to the
1-year-old's understanding of intentional action? Comment on Legerstee,
Barna, and DiAdamo (2000). *Developmental Psychology*, *37*, 579–582.

(2002). The development of understanding self and agency. In Usha
Goswamia (ed.), *Blackwell's Handbook of Childhood Cognitive Development*.
Malden, MA: Blackwell.

Gergely, G., and Watson, J. (1996). The social biofeedback theory of
parental affect-mirroring: The development of emotional self-awareness
and self-control in infancy. *International Journal of Psycho-Analysis*, *77*,
1181–1212.

(1999). Early socio-emotional development: Contingency perception and the
social biofeedback model. In P. Rochat (ed.), *Early social cognition:*

Understanding others in the first months of life (pp. 101–136). Mahwah, NJ: Erlbaum.

Gergely, G., Nadasdy, Z., Csibry, G., and Biro, S. (1995). Taking the intentional stance at 12 months of age. *Cognition, 56,* 165–193.

Gibson, E. J. (1969). *Principles of perceptual learning and development.* East Norwalk, US: Appleton Century Crofts.

(1993). Ontogenesis of the perceived self. In U. Neisser (ed.), *The perceived self: Ecological and interpersonal sources of self-knowledge* (pp. 25–42). New York: Cambridge University Press.

(1995). Are we automata? In P. Rochat (ed.), *The self in infancy: Theory and research. Advances in psychology* (pp. 13–15). Amsterdam: Elsevier.

Glick, J. (1978). Cognition and social cognition: an introduction. In J. L. Glick and K. A. Clarke-Stewart (eds.), *The development of social understanding,* (pp. 1–9). New York: Cambridge University Press.

Glick, J., and Clarke-Stewart, K. A. (eds.) (1978). *The development of social understanding.* New York: Cambridge University Press.

Goldberg, S., Lojkasek, M., Gartner, G., and Corter, C. (1989). Maternal responsiveness and social development in pre-term infants. In M. H. Bornstein (ed.), *Maternal responsiveness: Characteristics and consequences* (pp. 89–103). San Francisco: Jossey-Bass.

Goldfarb, W. (1943). Infant rearing and problem behavior. *American Journal of Orthopsychiatry, 13,* 249–265.

Goldsmith, D. F., and Rogoff, B. (1997). Mothers' and toddlers' coordinated joint focus of attention: Variations with maternal dysphoric symptoms. *Developmental Psychology, 33,* 113–119.

Gopnik, A. (1995). How to understand beliefs. *Behavioral and Brain Sciences, 18,* 398–400.

Gopnik, A., and Meltzoff, A. N. (1997). *Words, thoughts, and theories.* Cambridge, MA: MIT Press.

Gopnik, A., and Wellman, H. M. (1992). Why the child's theory of mind really is a theory. *Mind and Language, 7,* 145–171.

Goren, C. C., Sarty, M., and Wu, P. Y. K. (1975). Visual following and pattern discrimination of face-like stimuli by newborn infants. *Pediatrics, 56,* 544–549.

Gotlieb, S. J. (1991). Visual memory in neonates. *Dissertation Abstracts International, 51* (10-B), 5049–5050.

Granic, I. (2000) Emotion, development, and self-organization: dynamic systems approaches to emotional development. In M. D. Lewis and I. Granic (eds.), *The self-organization of parent–child relations: Beyond bidirectional models* (pp. 267–297). Cambridge: Cambridge University Press.

Grant, K. W., Ardell, L. H., Kuhl, P. K., and Sparks, D. W. (1986). The transmission of prosodic information via an electrotactile speedreading aid. *Ear and Hearing, 7,* 243–251.

Hains, S. M., and Muir, D. W. (1996). Effects of stimulus contingency in infant–adult interactions. *Infant Behavior and Development, 19,* 49–61.

Haith, M. M. (1966). The response of the human newborn to visual movement. *Journal of Experimental Psychology, Child Psychology, 3,* 243–253.

Haith, M. M., Bergman, T., and Moore, M. J. (1977). Eye contact and face scanning in early infancy. *Science*, *198*, 853–855.

Harding, C. G. (1982). Development of the intention to communicate. *Human Development*, *25*, 140–151.

Harlow, H. F. (1958). The nature of love. *American Psychologist*, *13*, 673–685.

(1961). The development of affectional patterns in infant monkeys. In B. M. Foss (ed.), *Determinants of infant behaviour* (Vol. I). London: Methuen.

Harlow, H. F. and Harlow, M. K. (1965). The affectional systems. In A. M. Schrier, H. F. Harlow, and F. Stollnitz (eds.), *Behavior of nonhuman primates* (Vol. II, pp. 287–334). New York: Academic Press.

Harlow, H. F., and Zimmermann, R. R. (1959). Affectional responses in the infant monkey. *Science*, *130*, 421–432.

Harris, P. L. (1989). *Children and emotion: The development of psychological understanding*. Oxford, England: Basil Blackwell.

(1992). From simulation to folk psychology: The case for development. *Mind Language*, *7*, 120–144.

Haviland, J. M., and Lewica, M. (1987). The induced affect response: 10-week-old infants' responses to three emotion expressions. *Developmental Psychology*, *23*, 97–104.

Heyes, C. M. (1998). Theory of mind in nonhuman primates. *Behavioral and Brain Sciences*, bbsonline.org.

Hobson, R. P. (1989). Beyond cognition: A theory of autism. In G. Dawson (ed.), *Autism, Nature, diagnosis and treatment* (pp. 48–). New York, Guilford.

(1989). On sharing experiences. *Development and Psychopathology*, *1*, 197–203.

(1990). On the origins of self and the case of autism. *Development and Psychopathology*, *2*, 163–181.

(1993). *Autism and the development of mind*. Hove: Erlbaum.

(1998). The intersubjective foundations of thought. In S. Braten (ed.), *Intersubjective communication and emotion in early ontogeny: Studies in emotion and social interaction* (2nd series, pp. 283–296). New York: Cambridge University Press.

(2002). *The cradle of thought: Exploring the origins of thinking*. Oxford: Oxford University Press.

Hoffman, M. (1981). Perspectives on the difference between understanding people and understanding things: the role of affect. In H. Flavell and L. Ross (eds.), *Social cognitive development: Frontiers and possible futures*, pp. 67–81. New York: Cambridge University Press.

Hofsten, C. von (1980). Predictive reaching for moving objects by human infants. *Journal of Experimental Child Psychology*, *30*, 369–382.

Hood, B. M., Willen, J. D., and Driver, J. (1998). Adults' eyes trigger shifts of visual attention in human infants. *Psychological Science*, *9*, 131–134.

Hornick, R., Risenhoover, N., and Gunnar, M. (1987). The effects of maternal positive, neutral, and negative affective communications on infant responses to new toys. *Child Development*, *58*, 937–944.

Hsu, H. C., and Fogel, A., (2003). Stability and transitions in mother–infant face-to-face communication during the first 6 months: A micro-historical approach. *Developmental Psychology*, *39*, 1061–1082.

Hsu, H. C., Fogel, A., and Messinger, D. S. (2001). Infant non-distress vocalization during mother–infant face-to-face interaction: Factors associated with quantitative and qualitative differences. *Infant Behavior and Development, 24,* 107–128.

Hume, D. (1739/1888). *A treatise of human nature.* Ed. L. A. Selby-Bigge. Oxford: Clarendon.

Izard, C. E. (1971). *The face of emotion.* East Norwalk: Appleton Century Crofts.
   (1978). Emotions as motivations: An evolutionary-developmental perspective. *Nebraska Symposium on Motivation, 26,* 163–200.

Jaffe, J., Beebe, B., Feldstein, S., Crown, C. L., and Jasnow, M. D. (2001). Rhythms of dialogue in infancy. *Monographs of the Society for Research in Child Development, 66,* 2001.

James, W. (1890). *Principles of psychology.* New York: Holt.

Johnson, M. H., Dziurawiec, S., Ellis, H. D., and Morton, J. (1991). Newborns' preferential tracking of face-like stimuli and its subsequent decline. *Cognition, 40,* 1–19.

Johnson, M. H., and Morton, J. (1991). *Biology and cognitive development: The case of face recognition.* Oxford: Basil Blackwell.

Johnson, S. C., Booth, A., and O'Hearn, L. (2001). Inferring the goals of a non-human agent. *Cognitive Development, 16,* 637–656.

Johnson, S., Slaughter, V., and Carey, S. (1998). Whose gaze will infants follow? The elicitation of gaze following in 12-month-olds. *Developmental Science, 1,* 233–238.

Juscyk, P. W., Kennedy, L. J., and Juscyk, A. (1995). Young infants' retention of information about syllables. *Infant Behavior and Development, 18,* 24–41.

Kagan, J. (1976). Resilience and continuity in psychological development. In A. M. Clarke and A. D. B. Clarke (eds.), *Early experience: Myth and evidence* (pp. 97–121). New York: The Free Press.

Kalins, I. V., and Bruner, J. S. (1973). The coordination of visual observation and instrumental behavior in early infancy. *Perception, 2,* 307–314.

Kant, I. (1781/1996). *Critique of pure reason.* Trans. W. S. Pluhar. Indianapolis: Hackett.

Karmiloff-Smith, A. (1992). *Beyond modularity: A developmental perspective on cognitive science.* Cambridge, MA: MIT Press.
   (1998). Is atypical development necessarily a window on the normal mind/brain? The case of Williams Syndrome. *Developmental-Science, 1,* 273–277.

Karmiloff-Smith, A., Klima, E., Bellugi, U., Grant, J., and Baron-Cohen, S. (1995). Is there a social module? Language, face processing, and theory of mind in individuals with Williams syndrome. *Journal of Cognitive Neuroscience, 7,* 196–208.

Kaye, K. (1982). Self-image formation in adopted children: The environment within. *Journal of Contemporary Psychotherapy, 13,* 175–181.

Kaye, K., and Fogel, A. (1980). The temporal structure of face-to-face communication between mothers and infants. *Developmental Psychology, 16,* 454–464.

Kaye, K., and Markus, J. (1981). Infant imitation: The sensory-motor agenda. *Developmental Psychology, 3,* 258–265.

Keil, C. K., Smith, W. C., Simons, D. J., and Levin, D. T. (1998). Two dogmas of conceptual empiricism: Implications for hybrid models of the structure of knowledge. *Cognition*, *65*, 103–135.

Kenny, J. (1988), *The self*. Marquette: Marquette University Press.

Killen, M., and Uzgiris, I. C. (1981). Imitation of action with objects: The role of social meaning. *Journal of Genetic Psychology*, *138*, 219–229.

Koluchova, J. (1972). Severe deprivation in twins: A case study. *Journal of Child Psychology and Psychiatry*, *13*, 107–114.

Kuchuk, A., Vibbert, N. M., and Bornstein, M. H. (1986). The perception of smiling and its experiential correlates in three-month-old infants. *Child Development*, *57*, 1054–1061.

Kuhl, P., and Meltzoff, A. N. (1982). The bimodal perception of speech in infancy. *Science*, *218*, 1138–1141.

LaBarbera, J. D., Izard, C. E., Vietze, P., and Parisi, S. A. (1976). Four- and six-month-old infants' visual responses to joy, anger, and neutral expressions. *Child Development*, *47*, 535–538.

Landry, S. H., Smith, K. E., Millar-Loncar, C. L., and Swank, P. R. (1998). The relation of change in maternal interactive styles to the developing social competence in full-term and pre-term children. *Child Development*, *69*, 105–123.

Legerstee, M. (1990). Infants use multimodal stimulation to imitate speech sounds. *Infant Behavior and Development*, *13*, 345–356.

  (1991a). Changes in the quality of infant sounds as a function of social and nonsocial stimulation. *First Language*, *11*, 327–343.

  (1991b). The role of people and objects in early imitation. *Journal of Experimental Child Psychology*, *51*, 423–433.

  (1992). A review of the animate/inanimate distinction in infancy: Implications for models of social and cognitive knowing. *Early Development and Parenting*, *1*, 59–67.

  (1994a). Patterns of 4-month-old infant responses to hidden silent and sounding people and objects. *Early Development and Parenting*, *3*, 71–80.

  (1994b). The role of familiarity and sound in the development of person and object permanence. *British Journal of Developmental Psychology*, *12*, 455–468.

  (1997a). Changes in social-conceptual development: domain specific structures, self-organization and indeterminism. In A. Fogel, M. C. D. P. Lyra, and J. Valsiner (eds.), *Dynamics and indeterminism in development and social processes* (pp. 245–260). Mahwah, NJ: Erlbaum.

  (1997b). Contingency effects of people and objects on subsequent cognitive functioning in three-month-old infants. *Social Development*, *6*, 307–321.

  (1998). Mental and bodily awareness in infancy: Consciousness of self-existence. *Journal of Consciousness*, *5*, 627–644.

  (2001a). Domain specificity and the epistemic triangle in the development of animism in infancy. In F. Lacerda, C. von Hofsten, and M. Heinemann (eds.), *Emerging cognitive abilities in early infancy* (pp. 193–212). Hillsdale, NJ: Erlbaum.

  (2001b). Six-month-old infants rely on explanatory inference when relating communication to people and manipulatory actions to inanimate objects: Reply to Gergely. *Developmental Psychology*, *5*, 583–586.

Legerstee, M., Anderson, D., and Schaffer, A. (1998). Five- and eight-month-old infants recognize their faces and voices as familiar and social stimuli. *Child Development*, 69, 37–50.

Legerstee, M., and Barillas, Y. (2003). Sharing attention and pointing to objects at 12 months: Is the intentional stance implied? *Cognitive Development*, 18, 91–110.

Legerstee, M., Barna, J., and DiAdamo, C. (2000). Precursors to the development of intention at 6 months: Understanding people and their actions. *Developmental Psychology*, 3, 627–634.

Legerstee, M., and Bowman, T. (1989). The development responses to people and a toy in infants with Down syndrome. *Infant Behaviour and Development*, 12, 462–473.

Legerstee, M., Bowman, T., and Fels, S. (1992). People and objects affect the quality of vocalizations in infants with Down syndrome. *Early Development and Parenting*, 1, 149–156.

Legerstee, M., Corter, C., and Kienapple, K. (1990). Hand, arm and facial actions of young infants to a social and nonsocial stimulus. *Child Development*, 61, 774–784.

Legerstee, M., Fahy, L., Blake, J., Fisher, T., and Markova, G. (May, 2004). *Maternal Factors Contributing to Toddlers' Early Development of Internal State Language: A Longitudinal Study*. Poster presented at 14th Biennial International Conference on Infant Studies (ICIS), Chicago, USA.

Legerstee, M., and Feider, H. (1986). The acquisition of person pronouns in French-speaking children. *International Journal of Psychology*, 21, 629–639.

Legerstee, M., Fisher, T., and Markova, G. (2005). *The development of attention during dyadic and triadic interactions: The role of affect attunement*. Paper presented at 35th Annual Meeting of the Jean Piaget Society, Vancouver, Canada, June, 2005.

Legerstee, M., and Markova, G. (2005). *Variation in imitation in 10-month-old infants: Awareness of intentional action*. Paper presented at 35th annual meeting of the Jean Piaget Society, Vancouver, Canada, June, 2005.

Legerstee, M., Pasic, N., Barillas, Y., and Fahy, L. (2004). Social emotional development: The basis for mentalism. In S. Gallagher, S. Watson, P. LeBrun, and P. Romanski. (eds.) *Ipseity and alterity: Interdisciplinary approaches to intersubjectivity* (pp. 33–46). Rouen, France: Publications de l'Université de Rouen.

Legerstee, M., Pomerlau, A., Malacuit, G., and Feider, H. (1987). The development of infants' responses to people and a doll: Implications for research in communication. *Infant Behavior and Development*, 10, 81–95.

Legerstee, M., Van Beek, Y., and Varghese, M. (2002). Effects of maintaining and redirecting infant attention on the production of referential communication in infants with and without Down syndrome. *Journal of Child Language*, 29, 23–48.

Legerstee, M., and Varghese, J. (2001). The role of affect mirroring on social expectancies in three-month-old infants. *Child Development*, 72, 1301–1313.

Legerstee, M., and Weintraub, J. (1997). The integration of person and object attention in infants with and without Down Syndrome. *Infant Behavior and Development*, 20, 71–82.

214   References

Leslie, A. M. (1984). Spatiotemporal continuity and the perception of causality in infants. *Perception*, *13*, 287–305.

Leung, E. H., and Rheingold, H. L. (1981). Development of pointing as a social gesture. *Developmental Psychology*, *17*, 215–220.

Lewis, M. and Brooks-Gunn, J. (1979). *Social cognition and the acquisition of self.*, New York, Plenum.

Lewis, M. D. (1997). Personality self-organization: Cascading constraints on cognition-emotion interaction. In Lyra, M. (ed.), et-al. Fogel, A. (ed.), *Dynamics and indeterminism in developmental and social processes* (pp. 193–216). Hillsdale, NJ: Lawrence Erlbaum Associates, Inc.

(2000). Emotional self-organization at three time scales, *The dynamics of emotion-related behaviors in infancy* (pp. 37–69). New York: Cambridge University Press.

Lewis, M. D., and Granic, I. (2000). *The dynamics of emotion-related behaviors in infancy*. New York: Cambridge University Press.

Leyendecker, B., Lamb, M. E., Schölmerich, A., and Fricke, D. M. (1997). Contexts as moderators of observed interactions: A study of Costa Rican mothers and infants from differing socioeconomic backgrounds. *International Journal of Behavioral Development*, *21*, 15–34.

Lillard, J., and Flavell, J. H. (1990). Young children's preference for mental state versus behavioral descriptions of human actions. *Child Development*, *61*, 731–741.

Locke, A. (1980). *The Guided Reinvention of Language*. London: Academic Press.

Locke, J. (1710/1975). *An essay concerning human understanding* (ed. with a foreword by P. H. Nidditsch). Oxford: Clarendon Press.

Lollis, S., and Kuczynski, L. (1997). Beyond one hand clapping: Seeing bidirectionality in parent–child relations. *Journal of Social and Personal Relationships*, *14*, 441–461.

Loveland, K. A. (1986). Discovering the affordances of a reflecting surface. *Developmental Review*, *6*, 1–24.

Lukesch, H., and Lukesch, M. (1976). *Fragebogen zur Messung von Einstellungen zu Schwangerschaft, Sexualität und Geburt (SSG)*. Göttingen: Hogrefe.

MacKain, K., Studder-Kennedy, M., Spieker, S., and Stern, D. (1983). Infant intermodal speech perception is a left-hemisphere function. *Science*, *218*, 1138–1141.

Mahler, M. S., Pine, F., and Bergman, A. (1975). Stages in the infant's separation from the mother. In G. Handel and G. G. Whitchurch (eds.), *The psychosocial interior of the family* (4th edn, pp. 419–448). Hawthorne, US: Aldine de Gruyter.

Malatesta, C. Z., and Izard, C. E. (1984). The ontogenesis of human social signals: From biological imperative to symbol utilization. In N. A. Fox and R. J. Davidson (eds.), *The Psychobiology of Affective Development* (pp. 161–206). Hillsdale, NJ: Erlbaum.

Mandler, J. M. (1992). How to build a baby: Conceptual primitives. *Psychological Review*, *99*, 587–604.

Maratos, O. (1973). The origin and development of imitation in the first six months of life. Unpublished doctoral dissertation. University of Geneva.

Markova, G. (Winter, 2004). PhD student participant in Graduate seminar, "Development of Affect, Consciousness and Social Cognition," (M. Legerstee). York University.

Markova, G., and Legerstee, M. (in press). Contingency, imitation or affect sharing? Foundations of infant's social awareness, *Developmental Psychology*.

(2004). Foundations of infant's social awareness. Paper presented at the Conference on Developmental relations between Executive Functioning, Social Understanding, and Social Interaction, September, Vancouver, BC).

Markus, J., Mundy, P., Morales, M., Delgado, C. E. F., and Yale, M. (2000). Individual differences in infant skills as predictors of child–caregiver joint attention and language. *Social Development*, *9*, 302–315.

Maurer, D., and Salapatek, P. (1976). Developmental changes in the scanning of faces by young infants. *Child Development*, *47*, 523–527.

McCall, R., and Kagan, J. (1970). Fixation time and tempo of play in infants. *Developmental Psychology*, *3* (3, pt. 1).

McGurk, H. and McDonald, J. (1976). Hearing lips and seeing voices. *Nature*, *264*, 746–748.

Meins, E., Fernyhough, C., Fradley, E., and Tuckey, M. (2001). Rethinking maternal sensitivity: Mothers' comments on infants' mental processes predict security attachment at 12 months. *Journal of Child Psychology and Psychiatry and Allied Sciences*, *42*, 637–648.

Meins, E., Fernyhough, C., Wainwright, R., Clark-Carter, D., Gupta, M. D., Fradley, E., and Tuckey, M. (2002). Maternal mind-mindedness and attachment security as predictors of theory of mind understanding. *Child Development*, *73*, 1715–1726.

(2003). Pathways to understanding mind: Construct validity and predictive validity of maternal mind-mindedness. *Child Development*, *74*, 1194–1211.

Meltzoff, A. N. (1985). Immediate and deferred imitation in fourteen- and twenty-four-month-old infants. *Child Development*, *56*, 62–72.

(1988). Infant imitation and memory: Nine-month-olds in immediate and deferred tests. *Child Development*, *59*, 217–225.

(1990). Foundations for developing a concept of self: The role of imitation in relating self to other and the value of social mirroring, social modelling, and self practice in infancy. In D. Cicchetti and M. Beeghly (eds.), *The self in transition: Infancy to childhood* (pp. 139–164). Chicago: The University of Chicago Press.

(1995). Understanding the intentions of others: Reenactment of intended acts by 18-month-old children. *Developmental Psychology*, *31*, 838–850.

Meltzoff, A. N., and Borton, R. (1979). Intermodal matching of human neonates. *Nature*, *282*, 403–404.

Meltzoff, A. N., and Brooks, R. (2001). "Like me" as a building block for understanding other minds: Bodily acts, attention, and intention. In B. F. Malle and L. J. Bertram (eds.), *Intentions and intentionality: Foundations of social cognition* (pp. 171–195). Cambridge, MA: The MIT Press.

Meltzoff, A. N., and Gopnik, A. (1993). The role of imitation in understanding persons and developing a theory of mind. In S. Baron-Cohen,

H. Tager-Flusberg, and D. J. Cohen (eds.), *Understanding Other Minds: Perspectives from Autism* (pp. 335–365). Oxford: Oxford University Press.

Meltzoff, A. N., and Moore, M. K. (1977). Imitation of facial and manual gestures of human neonates. *Science, 198,* 75–78.

(1983). The origins of imitation in infancy: Paradigm, phenomena, and theories. In L. P. Lipsitt and C. Rovee-Collier (eds.), *Advances in infancy research,* 2. Norwood: NJ, Ablex.

(1997). Explaining facial imitation: A theoretical model. *Early Development and Parenting, 6,* 179–192.

(1999). Persons and representation: Why infant imitation is important for theories of human development. In J. Nadel and G. Butterworth (eds.), *Imitation in infancy* (pp. 9–35). Cambridge: Cambridge University Press.

Merleau-Ponty, M. (1942/1963). *The structure of behavior.* Trans. A. L. Fisher. USA: Beacon Press.

Messer, D. (1997). Referential communication: Making sense of the social and physical worlds. In G. Bremner, A. Slater, and G. Butterworth (eds.), *Infant development: Recent advances* (pp. 291–309). Hove, UK: Psychology Press.

Messer, S. B., Kagan, J., and McCall, R. B. (1970). Fixation time and tempo of play in infants. *Developmental Psychology, 3,* 406.

Millar, W. S. (1972). A study of operant conditioning under delayed reinforcements in early infancy. *Monographs of the Society for Research in Child Development, 37,* 1–44.

Moerk, E. L. (1989). The fuzzy set called "imitation." In G. E. Speidel and K. E. Nelson (eds.), *The many faces of imitation in language learning* (pp. 277–303). New York: Springer.

Molina, M., Van de Walle, G. A., Condry, K., and Spelke, E. S. (in press). The animate/inanimate distinction in infancy: Developing sensitivity to constraints on human actions. *Journal of Cognition and Development.*

Montague, D. P. F., and Walker-Andrews, A. S. (2001). Peekaboo: A new look at infants' perception of emotion expression. *Developmental Psychology, 37,* 826–838.

Moore, C. (1996). Theories of mind in infancy. *British Journal of Developmental Psychology, 14,* 19–40. In C. Moore and P. J. Dunham (eds.), *Joint attention: Its origins and role in development* (pp. 251–271). Hillsdale: Erlbaum.

Moore, C., and Corkum, V. (1994). Social understanding at the end of the first year of life. *Developmental Review, 14,* 349–372.

Moore, C., and D' Entremont, B. (2001). Developmental changes in pointing as a function of attentional focus. *Journal of Cognition and Development, 2,* 109–129.

Moore, D. G., Hobson, R. P., Lee, A., and Anderson, M. (1992, September). *IQ-independent person perception: Evidence from developmental psychopathology.* Paper presented at the meeting of the 5th European Conference on Developmental Psychology, Seville, Spain.

Morrissette, P., Ricard, M., and Decarie, T. G. (1995). Joint visual attention and pointing in infancy: A longitudinal study of comprehension. *British Journal of Developmental Psychology, 13,* 163–175.

Moses, L. J. (1993). Young children's understanding of belief constraints on intention. *Cognitive Development, 8,* 1–25.

Moses, L. J., Baldwin, D. A., Rosicky, J. G., and Tidball, G. (2001). Evidence for referential understanding in the emotions domain at twelve and eighteen months. *Child Development*, *72*, 718–735.

Moses, L. J., and Flavell, J. H. (1990). Inferring false beliefs from actions and reactions. *Child Development*, *61*, 929–945.

Muir, D., Cao, Y., and Entremont, B. (1994, June). Infant social perception revealed during adult face-to-face interaction. *Infant Behavior and Development*, *17*, 86.

Muir, D., and Hains, S. (1999). Young infants' perception of adult intentionality: Adult contingency and eye direction. In P. Rochat (ed.), *Early social cognition: Understanding others in the first months of life* (pp. 155–187). Mahwah, NJ: Erlbaum.

Munakata, Y. (2000). Challenges to the violation-of-expectation paradigm: Throwing the conceptual baby out with the perceptual processing bathwater? *Infancy*, *1*, 471–477.

Mundy, P., and Sigman, M. (1989). The theoretical implications of joint-attention deficits in autism. *Development and Psychopathology*, *1*, 173–183.

Murphy, C. M., and Messer, D. J. (1977). Mothers, infants, and pointing: A study of gesture. In H. R. Schaffer (ed.), *Studies in mother–infant interaction* (pp. 325–354). London: Academic Press.

Murray, L., Fior-Cowley, A., Hooper, R., and Cooper, P. (1996). The impact of postnatal depression and associated adversity on early mother–infant interactions and later infant outcomes. *Child Development*, *67*, 2512–2526.

Murray, L., and Trevarthen, C. (1985). Emotional regulations of interactions between two-month-olds and their mothers. In T. M. Field and N. Fox (eds.), *Social perception in infants*. New Jersey: Ablex.

Nadel, J., Carchon, I., Kervella, C., Marcelli, D., and Reserbat-Plantey, D. (1999). Expectancies for social contingency in 2-month-olds. *Developmental Science*, *2*, 164–173.

Nakano, S. and Kanaya, Y. (1993). The effects of mothers' teasing: Do Japanese infants read their mothers' play intention in teasing? *Early Development and Parenting*, *2*, 7–17.

Neisser, U. (1993). The self perceived. In U. Neisser (ed.), *The perceived self: Ecological and interpersonal sources of self-knowledge*. Cambridge: Cambridge University Press.

(1995). Criteria for an ecological self. In P. Rochat (eds.), *The Self in Infancy: Theory and Research* (pp. 17–34). Amsterdam, Netherlands: North-Holland/Elsevier Science Publishers.

Nelson, L. A. (1987). The recognition of facial expression in the first two years of life: Mechanisms of development. *Child Development*, *58*, 889–909.

Nicely, P., Tamis-LeMonda, C. S., and Bornstein, M. H. (1999). Mothers' attuned responses to infant affect expressivity promote earlier achievement of language milestones. *Infant Behavior and Development*, *22*, 557–568.

Nicely, P., Tamis-LeMonda, C. S., and Grolnick, W. S. (1999). Maternal responses to infant affect: Stability and prediction. *Infant Behavior and Development*, *22*, 103–117.

Nishida, T. (1986). Local traditions and cultural transmission. In B. B. Smuts, D. L. Cheney, R. M. Seyfarth, R. W. Wrangham, and T. T. Struhsaker (eds.), *Primate Societies* (pp. 462–471).

Papousek, M., Papousek, H., and Symmes, D. (1991). The meanings of melodies in motherese in tone and stress languages. *Infant Behavior and Development*, *14*, 415–440.

Pascual-Leone, J., and Johnson, J. (1998). A dialectical constructivist view of representation: The role of mental attention, executives, and symbols. In I. E. Sigel (ed.), *The development of representational thought: Theoretical perspectives* (pp. 169–200). Mahwah, NJ: Erlbaum.

Perry, J. C., and Stern, D. N. (1976). Gaze duration frequency distributions during mother–infant interaction. *Journal of Genetic Psychology*, *129*, 45–55.

Perner, J. (1991). *Understanding the representational mind*. Cambridge, MA: The MIT Press.

Phillips, A. T., Wellman, H. M., and Spelke, E. (2002). Infant's ability to connect gaze and emotional expression to intentional action. *Cognition*, *85*, 53–78.

Phillips, W., Baron-Cohen, S., and Rutter, M. (1992). The role of eye contact in goal detection: Evidence from normal infants and children with autism or mental handicaps. *Development and Psychopathology*, *4*, 375–383.

Piaget, J. (1929). *The child's conception of the world*. Routledge and Kegan Paul.

(1952). *Play, dreams and imitation*. New York: W. W. Norton and Co. Inc.

(1954). *The origins of intelligence in children*. New York: Norton.

(1981). *Intelligence and affectivity: Their relationship during child development*. Oxford: Annual Reviews.

Poulin-Dubois, D. (1999). Infants' distinction between animate and inanimate objects: The origins of naïve psychology. In P. Rochat (ed.), *Early social cognition*. Hillsdale, NJ: Erlbaum.

Povinelli, D. J., and Eddy, T. J. (1996). What young chimpanzees know about seeing. *Monographs of the Society for Research in Child Development*, *61*, (3, Serial No. 247).

Premack, D. (1990). The infant's theory of self-propelled objects. *Cognition*, *36*, 1–16.

(1991). The infant's theory of self-propelled objects. In D. Frye and C. Moore (eds.), *Children's theories of mind: Mental states and social understanding* (pp. 39–48). Hillsdale, NJ: Erlbaum.

Rader, N., and Stern, J. D. (1982). Visually elicited reaching in neonates. *Child Development*, *53*, 1004–1007.

Rakison, D. H., and Poulin-Dubois, D. (2000). Developmental origin of the animate/inanimate distinction. *Psychological Bulletin*, *127*, 209–226.

Ramey, C. T., and Finkelstein, N. W. (1978). Contingent stimulation and infant competence. *Journal of Pediatric Psychology*, *3*, 89–96.

Raver, C. C., and Leadbeater, B. J. (1995). Factors influencing joint attention between socioeconomically disadvantaged adolescent mothers and their infants. In C. Moore and P. Dunham (eds.), *Joint attention: Its origin and role in development* (pp. 251–271). Hillsdale, NJ: Erlbaum.

Reddy, V. (1991). Playing with others' expectations: Teaching and mucking about in the first year. In A. Whitten (ed.), *Natural theories of mind:*

Evolution, development and simulation of everyday mindreading. Cambridge, MA: Basil Blackwell.

(1999). Prelinguistic communication. In M. Barrett (ed.), *The development of language. Studies in developmental psychology* (pp. 25–50). Philadelphia: Psychology Press.

(2003). On being the object of attention: Implications for self–other consciousness. *Trends in Cognitive Sciences, 7,* 397–402.

Reddy, V., Hay, D., Murray, L., and Trevarthen, C. (1997). Communication in infancy: Mutual regulation of affect and attention. In G. Bremner, A. Slater, and G. Butterworth (eds.), *Infant development: Recent advances* (pp. 247–273). Hove: Psychology Press.

Reed, E. S. (1995). Becoming a self. In P. Rochat (ed.), *The self in infancy: Theory and research.* Amsterdam, Netherlands: North-Holland/Elsevier Science Publishers.

Repacholi, B. M. (1998). Infants' use of attentional cues to identify the referent of another person's emotional expression. *Developmental Psychology, 34,* 1017–1025.

Repacholi, B. M., and Gopnik, A. (1997). Early reasoning about desires: Evidence from 14- and 18-month-olds. *Developmental Psychology, 33,* 12–21.

Rheingold, H. L. (1961). The effect of environmental stimulation upon social and exploratory behaviour in the human infant. In B. M. Foss (ed.), *Determinants of infant behavior* (pp. 143–171). Oxford, England: Wiley.

Ribble, M. (1944). Infant experience in relation to personality development. In M. V. Hunt (ed.), *Personality and the Behavior Disorders* (pp. 621–651). Ronald Press.

Rogers, S. J., and Pennington, B. F. (1991). A theoretical approach to the deficits in infantile autism. *Development and Psychopathology, 3,* 137–162.

Rothbart, M. K. (1981). IBQ. The Infant Behavior Questionnaire: Measurement of temperament in infancy. *Child Development, 52,* 569–578.

Rovee-Collier, C. K., and Fagan, J. W. (1981). The retrieval of memory in early infancy. *Advances in Infancy Research, 1,* 225–254.

Ruddy, M. G., and Bornstein, M. H. (1982). Cognitive correlates of infant attention and maternal stimulation over the first year of life. *Child Development, 53,* 183–188.

Rutter, M. (1971). Parent–child separation: Psychological effects on the children. *Journal of Child Psychology and Psychiatry, 12,* 233–260.

(1972). *Maternal deprivation reassessed.* Harmondsworth: Penguin.

Salapatek, P., and Kessen, W. (1966). Visual scanning of triangles by the human newborn. *Journal of Experimental Child Psychology, 3,* 155–167.

Saxon, T. F., Frick, J. E., and Colombo, J. (1997). A longitudinal study of maternal interactional styles and infant visual attention. *Merrill Palmer Quarterly, 43,* 48–66.

Scaife, M., and Bruner, J. S. (1975). The capacity for joint visual attention in the infant. *Nature, 253,* 265–266.

Schaffer, H. R. (1971). *The Growth of Sociability.* Harmondsworth: Penguin Books.

(1984). *The child's entry into a social world.* London: Academic Press.

Schaffer, H. R., Collins, G. M., and Parsons, G. (1977). Vocal interchange and visual regard in verbal and preverbal children. In H. R. Schaffer (ed.), *Studies in mother–infant interaction* (pp. 291–324). London: Academic Press.

Schmuckler, M. (1981). *Visual habituation programme.* Ontario: University of Toronto.

Schore, A. N. (2000). Emotion, development, and self-organization: Dynamic systems approaches to emotional development. In M. D. Lewis and I. Granic (eds.), *Neurobiological perspectives: The self-organization of the right brain and the neurobiology of emotional development.* Cambridge: Cambridge University Press.

Schultz, S., and Wellman, H. M. (1997). Explaining human movements and actions: Children's understanding of the limits of psychological explanation. *Cognition, 62*, 291–324.

Searle, J. R. (1983). *Intentionality: An essay in the philosophy of mind.* Cambridge: Cambridge University Press.

Seifer, R., Schiller, M., Sameroff, A. J., Resnick, S., and Riordan, K. (1996). Attachment, maternal sensitivity, and infant temperament during the first year of life. *Developmental Psychology, 32*, 12–25.

Seligman, M. E. P. (1975). *Helplessness: On depression, development and death.* San Francisco: Freeman.

Skinner, B. F. (1948). Concurrent operants. *American Psychologist, 3*, 359.

Smith, P. B., and Pederson, D. R. (1988). Maternal sensitivity and patterns of infant–mother attachment. *Child Development, 59*, 1097–1101.

Snow, C. (1977). The development of conversation between mothers and babies. *Child Language, 4*, 1–22.

Soken, N. H., and Pick, A. D. (1992). Intermodal perception of happy and angry expressive behaviors by seven-month-old infants. *Child Development, 63*, 787–795.

Spelke, E. S. (1981). The infant's acquisition of knowledge of bimodally specified events. *Journal of Experimental Child Psychology, 31*, 179–299.

    (1985). Preferential-looking methods as tools for the study of cognition in infancy. In G. Gotlieb and N. A. Krasnegor (eds.), *Measurement of audition and vision in the first year of postnatal life: A methodological overview.* Westport, US: Ablex Publishing.

    (1988). Where perceiving ends and thinking begins: The apprehension of objects in infancy. In A. Yonas (ed.), *Perceptual development in infancy. The Minnesota symposia on child psychology* (vol. 20, pp. 197–234). Hillsdale, NJ: Erlbaum.

Spelke, E. S., Breinlinger, K., Macomber, J., and Jacobson, K. (1992). Origins of knowledge. *Psychological Review, 99*, 605–632.

Spelke, E. S., and Cortelyou, A. (1981). Perceptual aspects of social knowing: Looking and listening in infancy. In M. E. Lamb and L. R. Sherrod (eds.), *Infant social cognition: Empirical and theoretical considerations.* Hillsdale, NJ: Erlbaum.

Spelke, E. S., Phillips, A. T., and Woodward, A. L. (1995). Infants, knowledge of object motion and human action. In D. Sperber, D. Premack, and A. J. Premack (eds.), *Causal cognition: A multi-disciplinary debate* (pp. 44–78). Oxford: Clarendon Press.

Sperber, D., Premack, D., and Premack, A. J. (1995). *Causal cognition: A multidisciplinary debate.* Oxford: Clarendon Press.

Spitz, R. (1963). Hospitalism: An inquiry into the genesis of psychiatric conditions in early childhood. *Psychoanalytic Study of Child, 1,* 53–74.

Stankov, L. (1983). Attention and intelligence. *Educational Psychology, 75,* 471–490.

Stern, D. N. (1977). *The first relationship: Infant and mother.* Cambridge, MA: Harvard University Press.

(1984). Affect attunement. In J. D. Call, E. Galenson, and R. T. Tyson (eds.), *Frontiers of infant psychiatry* (Vol. II, pp. 3–14). New York: Basic Books.

(1985). *The interpersonal world of the infant.* New York: Basic Books.

(1995). Self/other distinction in the domain of intimate socio-affective interaction: Some considerations. In P. Rochat (ed.), *The self in infancy: Theory and research. Advances in psychology.* Amsterdam: North Holland-Elsevier.

Sullivan, J. W., and Horowitz, F. D. (1983). Infant intermodal perception and maternal multimodal stimulation: Implications for language development. In L. P. Lipsitt and C. K. Rovee-Collier (eds.), *Advances in infancy research* (Vol. 2). Norwood, NJ: Ablex.

Summerfeld, Q. (1979). Use of visual information for phonetic perception. *Phonetica, 36,* 314–331.

Szajnberg, N. M., Skrinjaric, J., and Moore, A. (1989). Affect attunement, attachment, temperament and zygosity: A twin study. *Journal of the American Academy of Child and Adolescent Psychiatry, 28,* 249–253.

Tager-Flusberg, H. (1989). An analysis of discourse ability and internal state lexicons in a longitudinal study of autistic children. Paper presented at *Biennial Meeting of Society for Research in Child Development,* Kansas City.

Tamis-LeMonda, C. S., and Bornstein, M. H. (1989). Habituation and maternal encouragement of attention in infancy as predictors of toddler language, play, and representational competence. *Child Development, 60,* 738–751.

Tamis-LeMonda, C. S., Bornstein, M. H., and Baumwell, L. (2001). Maternal responsiveness and children's achievement of language milestones. *Child Development, 72,* 748–767.

Tarabulsy, G. M., Tessier, R., and Kappas, A. (1996). Contingency detection and the contingent organization of behavior in interactions: Implications for socioemotional development in infancy. *Psychological Bulletin, 120,* 25–41.

Teo, T. (1997). Developmental psychology and the relevance of a critical metatheoretical reflection. *Human Development, 40,* 195–210.

Tizard, B., and Rees, J. (1974). A comparison of the effects of adoption, restoration, to the natural mother, and continued institutionalization of the cognitive development of four-year-old children. *Child Development, 45,* 92–99.

Tomasello, M. (1995). Joint attention as social cognition. In C. Moore and P. Dunham (eds.), *Joint attention: Its origins and role in development* (pp. 103–130). Hillsdale, NJ: Erlbaum.

(1996). Do apes ape? In C. M. Heyes and B. G. Galef (eds.), *Social learning in animals: The roots of culture* (pp. 319–346). New York: Academic Press.

(1999). *The cultural origins of human cognition.* Cambridge, MA: Harvard University Press.

(2000). Culture and cognitive development. *Current Directions in Psychological Science*, 9, 37–40.

(January, 2003), personal communication.

Tomasello, M., and Call, J. (1997). *Primate cognition*. London: Oxford University Press.

Tomasello, M., and Camaioni, L. (1997). A comparison of the gestural communication of apes and human infants. *Human Development*, 40, 7–24.

Tomasello, M., and Farrar, M. J. (1986). Joint attention and early language. *Child Development*, 57, 1454–1463.

Tomasello, M., Kruger, A. C., and Ratner, H. H. (1993). Cultural learning. *Behavioral and Brain Sciences*, 16, 495–552.

Trehub, S. (1976). The discrimination of foreign speech contrasts by infants and adults. *Child Development*, 47, 466–472.

Trevarthen, C. (1979). Communication and cooperation in early infancy. A description of primary intersubjectivity. In M. Bullowa (ed.), *Before speech: The beginning of human communication* (pp. 321–347). Cambridge: Cambridge University Press.

(1991). The self born in intersubjectivity: The psychology of an infant communicating. In U. Neisser (ed.), *The perceived self: Ecological and interpersonal sources of self-knowledge*. Cambridge: Cambridge University Press.

Trevarthen, C., and Hubley, P. (1978). Secondary intersubjectivity: Confidence, confiding and acts of meaning in the second year. In A. Lock (ed.), *Action, gesture and symbol: The emergence of language* (pp. 183–229). New York: Academic Press.

Tronick, E. Z. (1989). Emotions and emotional communication in infants. *American Psychologist*, 44, 112–119.

(2002). A model of infant mood states: Long lasting organizing affective states and emotional representational processes without language or symbols. *Psychoanalytic Dialogues*, 12, 73–99.

(2003). Things still to be done on the still-face effect. *Infancy*, 4, 475–482.

(2004). Selective coherence and dyadic states of consciousness. In J. Nadel and D. Muir (eds.), *Developmental studies of emotions* (pp. 293–315). Oxford: Oxford University Press.

Valsiner, J. (1997). *Culture and the development of children's action*. New York: Wiley.

van den Boom, D. C. (1994). The influence of temperament and mothering on attachment and exploration: An experimental manipulation of sensitive responsiveness among lower-class mothers with irritable infants. *Child Development*, 65, 1457–1477.

Vecera, S. P., and Johnson, M. H. (1995). Gaze detection and the cortical processing of faces: Evidence from infants and adults. *Visual Cognition*, 2, 59–87.

Vedeler, D. (1994). Infant intentionality as object-directedness: A method for observation. *Scandinavian Journal of Psychology*, 35, 343–366.

Verschueren, K., Marcoen, A., and Schoef, V. (1996). The internal working model of the self, attachment, and competence in five year olds. *Child Development*, 67, 2493–2511.

Von Hofsten, C. (1982). Eye–hand coordination in newborns. *Developmental Psychology*, *18*, 450–461.

Vygotsky, L. S. (1962). *Thought and language*. (Edited and translated by Eugenia Haufmann and Gertrude Vakar.) Cambridge, MA: MIT Press.

(1978). *Mind in society: The development of higher psychological processes*. In M. Cole, V. John-Steiner, S. Criner, and E. Souberman (eds.), Cambridge, MA: Harvard University Press.

Walden, T. A., and Ogan, T. A. (1988). The development of social referencing. *Child Development*, *59*, 1230–1240.

Walker-Andrews, A. S. (1997). Infants' perception of expressive behaviors: Differentiation of multimodal information. *Psychological Bulletin*, *121*, 437–456.

Watson, J. B. (1928). *Psychological care of infant and child*. New York: Norton.

Watson, J. S. (1972). Smiling, cooing, and "the game." *Merrill-Palmer Quarterly*, *18*, 323–339.

(1979). Perception of contingency as a determinant of social responsiveness. In E. B. Thoman (ed.), *The origins of the infant's social responsiveness* (pp. 33–64). Hillsdale, NJ: Erlbaum.

(1985). Contingency perception in early social development. In T. M. Field and N. A. Fox (eds.), *Social perception* (pp. 157–176). Norwood, NJ: Ablex Publishing.

Watson, J. S., and Ramey, C. T. (1972). Reactions to response-contingent stimulation in early infancy. *Merrill Palmer Quarterly*, *18*, 219–227.

Wellman, H. M. (1990). *The child's theory of mind*. Cambridge, MA: MIT Press.

(1993). Early understanding of mind: The normal case. In S. Baron-Cohen, H. Tager-Flusberg, and D. J. Cohen (eds.), *Understanding other minds: Perspectives from autism* (pp. 10–39). Oxford, England: Oxford University Press.

Wellman, H. M., and Banerjee, M. (1991). Mind and emotion: Children's understanding of the emotional consequences of beliefs and desires. *British Journal of Developmental Psychology*, *9*, 191–224.

Wellman, H. M., and Estes, D. (1986). Early understanding of mental entities: A reexamination of childhood realism. *Child Development*, *57*, 910–923.

Wellman, H. M., Harris, P. L., Banerjee, M., and Sinclair, A. (1995). Early understanding of emotion. Evidence from natural language. *Cognition and Emotion*, *9*, 117–149.

Wellman, H. M., and Woolley, J. P. (1990). From simple desires to ordinary beliefs: The early development of everyday psychology. *Cognition*, *35*, 245–275.

Werker, J. F., and McLeod, P. J. (1989). Infant preference for both male and female infant-directed talk: A developmental study of attentional and affective responsiveness. *Canadian Journal of Psychology*, *43*, 230–246.

Wimmer, H., and Perner, J. (1983). Beliefs about beliefs: Representation and constraining function of wrong beliefs in young children's understanding of deception. *Cognition*, *13*, 103–128.

Wolff, P. H. (1966). The causes, controls, and organization of behavior in the neonate. *Psychological Issue*, *5* (Monograph 17).

(1987). *The development of behavioral states and the expression of emotions in early infancy: New proposals for investigation*. Chicago: University of Chicago Press.

Woodward, A. (1998). Infants selectively encode the goal object of an actor's reach. *Cognition*, *69*, 1–34.

Yonas, A., Petterson, L, and Lockman, J. J. (1979). Young infants' sensitivity to optical information for collision. *Canadian Journal of Psychology*, *33*, 268–276.

Zeedyk, S. M. (1996). Developmental accounts of intentionality: Toward integration. *Developmental Review*, *16*, 416–461.

Index

Note: Page numbers in *italic type* refer to figures and tables.